Understanding and Managing the Credit Rating Agencies

A Guide for Fixed Income Issuers

Understanding and Managing the Credit Rating Agencies

A Guide for Fixed Income Issuers

Roger P Nye

Published by
Euromoney Institutional Investor PLC
Nestor House, Playhouse Yard
London EC4V 5EX
United Kingdom

Tel: +44 (0)20 7779 8999 or USA 11 800 437 9997
Fax: +44 (0)20 7779 8300
www.euromoneybooks.com
E-mail: hotline@euromoneyplc.com

Typeset by Phoenix Photosetting, Chatham, Kent
Printed and bound by CPI Group (UK) Ltd, Croydon, CR0 4YY

To Brian Keegan who planted the seed

To Arturo Porzecanksi who provided the launch pad

To John Chambers who shared his wit and wisdom

Contents

Contents

Part 2 – Managing the rating agencies

Part 3 – Appendices

Preface

The three major international rating agencies, Moody's Investors Service, Standard & Poor's Ratings Services and Fitch Ratings, dominate the credit ratings business around the world. Given their many decades of experience, the agencies believe their set of rating procedures and methodologies are the best way to assess credit risk. They hold a number of beliefs about how companies, banks and governments should operate so that the interests of investors are protected.

Their rating practices, while previously cloaked in mystery, more recently have seen public light and scrutiny. Their methodologies for assessing the credit risk of all types of issuers can be found in detail on their websites. They are well-constructed and exhaustively data-laden and will not be repeated here.

However, there is still a great deal to learn about how the agencies think and operate. What cannot be found in the public domain are their business principles, internal procedures and fundamental beliefs. Fixed-income issuers at all levels need to understand these elements if they are to achieve an optimal rating and/or defend themselves against possible arbitrary action on the part of the agencies. They need a more level playing field – one that has always been titled in favour of the agencies.

Aside from issuers, the author's intention is to bring other interested parties up the learning curve as well. For example, investors should be able to better appreciate what factors went into the ratings they depend on. Government regulators and legislators, who have shown repeatedly that they do not understand the rating agencies, might be in a better position to develop rational rules and laws. Academics may be able to appreciate that their mathematical models on ratings methodology are far from accurate and relevant. Misunderstandings and confusion at all levels can be reduced.

This volume is based on the author's own experiences at Moody's Investors Service and his 20-plus years of publishing a monthly newsletter on ratings and consulting to issuers around the world. It is hoped that the insights and advice here will instil greater confidence on the part of all fixed-income issuers, and particularly for those undergoing the rating process for the first time.

Praemonitus, praemunitus.

Roger P Nye
March 2014

Glossary

CRA	Credit rating agency; the generic term for any organisation that issues credit ratings.
ESMA	European Securities and Markets Authority, the EU agency that oversees CRA practices.
EU	European Union.
FCIC	Financial Crisis Inquiry Commission, a US government organisation that investigated the causes of the financial crisis of 2007–2010.
FSB	Financial Stability Board, an international institution that drew up principles and road maps to reduce European reliance on CRA ratings in standards, laws and regulations.
GDP	Gross domestic product, a measure of a country's overall economic output.
IFRS	International Financial Reporting Standards, a set of accounting rules that make business accounts comparable globally.
IMF	International Monetary Fund.
IOSCO	The International Organisation of Securities Commissions, a global body that published a code of conduct for CRAs in 2004 and sets standards for financial markets.
Issuer	Any public or private sector entity that borrows in the fixed-income market.
NRSRO	Nationally Recognised Statistical Rating Organisation. The official name for a SEC-regulated credit rating agency. Currently, there are 10 NRSROs.
OCR	Office of Credit Ratings within the Securities and Exchange Commission.
OECD	Organisation for Economic Co-operation and Development, a forum of 34 countries founded in 1961 to stimulate economic progress and world trade. The OECD is committed to democracy and the market economy.
Optimal rating	The best possible and sustainable rating for an issuer given its resources and financial goals.
RC	Rating committee at the CRAs.
SEC	Securities and Exchange Commission, the US government regulator of NRSROs.
SPP	Strategy, performance, persistence – a formula for achieving an optimal rating.

List of exhibits

Acknowledgements

I want to express my gratitude to a number of former rating agency analysts and officers who thoroughly read through the manuscript and offered helpful recommendations, additional insights, historical perspective and spot-on criticism. They are Scott Bugie, Guido Cipriani, Hans van den Houten and Ken Weinstein. Tom Harker, Mike McMullen, Nina Ramondelli and Thomas Rus kindly reviewed sections of the text relevant to their expertise and added key points. Several reviewers caught errors in the draft. Any errors remaining are those they missed or added. (All right, some are assuredly mine.) For any opinions that offend, the author asserts his rights under the First Amendment of the US Constitution, as the rating agencies have done for decades.

Aside from those mentioned above, I also wish to convey my appreciation to the following rating agency officials who over the years gave freely of their time and thoughts: Susan Abbott; Chris Baldwin; Philip Bates; David Beers; Eric Bigelsen; Uwe Bott; Jim Bray; Richard Cantor; Ray Carty; Marie Cavanaugh; John Chambers; Claire Cohen; Joe Connolly; Rosemary Conforte; Paul Coughlin; Sam Crawford; Guillermo Estebanez; Jerome S Fons; Lacey Gallagher; Harold Goldberg; Clifford M Griep; Helena Hessel; Mara Hilderman; W Bruce Jones; Mahesh Kotecha; Hendrik J Kranenburg; David Larson; Scott Latham; Yves LeMay; David H Levey; John Lonski; Anne McDermott; Andrea Merenyi; Fareed Mohammedi; Beth Morrow; Loretta Neuhaus; Donald Noe; Leo O'Neill; Paul Pannkuk; Fred Pastore; Kristel Richard; Marilyn Ricker; S Melvin Rines; Katie Rossow; Roderick Rumreich; Jonathan R Schiffer; Pam Stubing; Tulio Vera; Doug Watson; Roy Weinberger; Suzanne Wolkenfeld and Theodore Young.

In preparation for this book and other publications, I spoke with 55 rating agency analysts and officers, current and retired. In return for frank talk, most requested and received anonymity. They provided a solid research base and good anecdotes, and I thank them.

My enthusiastic and understanding editor at Euromoney was Melissa Oshungbure. Project manager Sarah Abel ably guided the enterprise forward. Justine Bottani was in charge of marketing the book. I offer my gratitude to all three.

About the author

Roger P Nye has spent more than 30 years investigating the political, economic and financial factors that affect the growth, stability and creditworthiness of countries, corporations and banks around the world. He has enjoyed an extensive career as a consultant to ministries of finance and central banks, and to the private sector regarding credit ratings, country risk, emerging markets, foreign investment and the capital markets.

Mr Nye is the founder and president of Global Investment Advisors, Inc. (GIA), a consulting firm that specialises in assisting borrowers in the capital markets with their credit ratings, guiding start-up rating agencies in methodology and marketing, and advising central banks on establishing or privatising credit bureaus. See www.gia-inc.com.

Prior to establishing GIA in 1991, Mr Nye worked at Moody's Investors Service in New York as a Senior Analyst in the Financial Institutions Department, which was responsible for assigning credit ratings and assessing the creditworthiness of government and bank borrowers in the global capital markets. Prior to that, he served as country risk manager for Atlantic Richfield Company in Los Angeles.

Mr Nye has a PhD in international relations from Washington University and a BA in political science from Williams College. He has published more than three dozen articles and books on investment-related topics encompassing Africa, Asia and the Middle East. He has addressed numerous forums on issues of direct and fixed-income investment and has taught classes at several universities. He served overseas as an English teacher in the US Peace Corps. His hobbies include historical fiction, Sudoku, golf and classical music.

Part 1

Understanding the rating agencies

Chapter 1

Getting started

Précis

This chapter covers the initial steps that issuers, especially new ones, should take to become familiar with credit ratings and the rating agencies as a precursor to seeking access to the international fixed income markets.

Issuers should seek an optimal rating, defined as 'the best possible rating given their resources and goals'. The first step toward that end would be to get familiar with the layout of the pitch, how the agencies think and operate, how their business principles guide their processes, and the role of information asymmetry and secrecy.

Next an issuer should choose one or more appropriate agencies to rate the contemplated debt instrument. Choosing the right agency involves some homework and an interview with two or three of the major agencies. New issuers need to choose one that will meet their needs. The agencies differ in several respects, such as their fees and their experience in your industry or your part of the world. A ratings adviser or investment banker can assist in the choice.

Once these steps are taken, the issuer should be comfortable with the rating process, although going through the actual rating exercise will add another and much deeper level of learning that will be very useful in years to come.

The main point is that without understanding the agencies' goals, assumptions and processes, an issuer's rating will not be optimal, and cost-effective funding may not be achievable.

Caveat emptor.

1.1 The basics

The function of credit ratings is to provide a guide to credit risk for investors. Credit ratings, or opinions on default risk of debt securities, are produced by credit rating agencies (CRAs) in both local and international markets. In a liquid bond market, those bonds with higher credit risk (lower ratings) trade differentially from those with lower credit risk (higher ratings). If the market works, there should be spreads (measured in basis points) among the various categories of ratings to reflect differential credit quality. These spreads in themselves help make bond markets more liquid and efficient. Investors benefit from a wider choice of investment risks, and borrowers benefit from access to the credit markets at a reasonable price.

The three largest CRAs in the world are Moody's Investors Service, Standard & Poor's Ratings Group, and Fitch Ratings, hereafter referred to as Moody's, S&P and Fitch. As at the end of 2011, Moody's and S&P were the two largest CRAs based on the number of credit ratings, with approximately 1 million and 1.2 million ratings, respectively. Fitch was the third largest with approximately 350,000 ratings. Moody's and S&P accounted for approximately 83% of all credit ratings. Moody's, Fitch and S&P account for approximately 96% of all bond ratings in the world. According to the 2012 report by the Securities and Exchange Commission (SEC),[1] the total revenue of all Nationally Recognised Statistical Rating Organisations (NRSROs) was approximately US$4.2 billion.

Aside from these Big Three, there are seven other NRSROs currently permitted to do business in the US market, but they are mainly niche players who cannot compete in the broader ratings market dominated by the oligopoly. The CRAs' job is to assist investors in the essential task of determining the 'creditworthiness' of fixed income instruments that are issued in the capital markets, most commonly bonds. The issuers are in large measure industrial and service companies, governments (both national and subnational), banks, and non-bank financial institutions such as insurance companies and securities companies.[2]

Definitions and benefits

This term creditworthiness is defined as 'the capacity and willingness to service debt in full and on time, without recourse to involuntary exchanges or other forms of debt relief'. Estimating capacity and willingness of issuers to meet their debt obligations is more art than science, as we will see in much that follows. Missing a payment on a financial obligation amounts to a default, the risk of which ratings try to measure.

Default is defined as a missed or delayed payment of an interest or principal payment that is obligated by contract. The rating agencies also consider as a default any 'distressed exchange' whereby an obligor: (i) renegotiates original contract terms so as to avoid a payment default in the future; and/or (ii) changes the payment terms, such as the maturity, interest rate or currency involved. Different rating agencies may have different opinions about the default risk inherent in a debt instrument, just as there is a variety of opinions in the market about the direction of interest rates or where the stock market may head.

Let us start with the agencies' official definitions of what a rating is and what a rating is not. A credit rating is:

- a professional opinion on the risk of non-fulfilment of a financial promise;
- a measure of the likelihood of default on a debt instrument, an evaluation of credit risk;
- an informed judgment about an issuer's ability to make timely payment of principal and interest in the future; and
- a subjective assessment of the potential for credit loss.

More important from a legal standpoint is what a credit rating is not:

- a guarantee or protection against default;
- a recommendation to purchase, sell or hold a security;
- a comment on market price, market supply, or suitability for the investor;
- an evaluation of other forms of investment risk, such as interest rate risk, prepayment risk, liquidity risk or currency risk;
- an audit of accounts; or
- a testament to authenticity of information supplied by the issuer.

These public definitions have protected all the rating agencies from lawsuits by disgruntled investors, issuers and regulators for decades, permitting them to build their businesses quite profitably into global enterprises. The CRAs have never been successfully sued in court by investors or issuers alleging damages or financial loss caused by CRA actions. Their view, upheld by the courts, has been that their rating judgments are 'opinions' protected by the freedom of speech guarantee in the First Amendment to the US Constitution.[3] However, the lack of First Amendment rights outside the US has exposed the agencies to greater regulatory scrutiny in recent years by non-US regulators.

There are major benefits of a rating for all parties involved. Aside from the agencies themselves, the most important beneficiaries are the investor and the issuer.

For *investors* a rating provides an easily understandable and reliable guide about the likelihood of issuer default on a particular fixed-income instrument. It provides the basis for an informed investment decision. Ratings do not protect investors from mistakes, but ratings can reduce uncertainty, giving investors greater confidence. Ratings provide a benchmark or reference point for investors.

A rating helps long-term investors, such as pension funds and insurance companies, to judge the suitability of the various long-term investment options through a common rating scale. The ratings agency is presumed to be impartial, not a salesman for the debt issue, as the investment bankers are. The rating and the rationale supporting it allow the investor to compare the issuer's credit fundamentals against its industry peer group. It helps the investor to consider the credibility of management's goals and expectations for the future.

A credit rating is a key factor in helping the investor make a more informed investment decision and in facilitating sound portfolio management.[4] 'Ratings also reduce investors' costs of gathering, analysing and monitoring the financial positions of borrowers because rating agencies provide scale economies and specialisation in performing these functions.'[5] Ratings permit the investor to focus more attention on other technical factors, such as suitable portfolio allocation, terms and conditions of yield, maturity, issue structure and call provisions, if any.

Because many investors will not buy an unrated bond, a significant bond issuance almost always has at least one rating from a respected CRA – generally two – to avoid being under-subscribed or being offered a price too low for the issuer's purposes.

Banks that invest in corporate debt issues benefit from a CRA's opinion, one that supplements that of the bank's own risk evaluation team. Banks also check a corporate borrower's credit rating before making a loan. Finally, foreign direct investors can use ratings as a benchmark when deciding whether or not to place funds in various countries' debt issues.

For *debt issuers*, those that acquire ratings, the benefits include:

1 a passport to a wider audience of investors, lenders, customers and business partners;
2 alternative financing options, often more cost-effective, dependable and longer term than bank loans;
3 a standard to measure how creditworthy you are compared with others in your industry or in your country;
4 lower financing costs and a more dependable access to liquidity;
5 a more accurate estimate of borrowing costs, which facilitates budgetary planning; and
6 a useful discipline on senior management, because the process creates an awareness of global credit standards.

To encourage companies, banks and governments to acquire an initial rating, these entities are sometimes 'warned' by their investment bankers that having no rating at all implies to investors that you cannot get a rating or must have defaulted in the past or are afraid to open your books. No rating is a signal to investors to be cautious. Investors often have investment guidelines which require one or more ratings to be minimally acceptable for consideration. Moreover, requesting a rating avoids an imposed unsolicited rating and allows you to be in control of the process. These arguments can be convincing if an issuer's peers are acquiring ratings.

If the issuer is a *corporate enterprise*, there are additional benefits.

1 A rating usually brings lower financing costs, always important in a highly competitive business environment. A successful rating will pay for itself many times over in lower financing costs.
2 With a rating in hand, the company can approach its bankers and negotiate better rates.
3 A rating gives the corporate issuer the basis for offering and promoting its debt issue in the market.
4 Having a rating brings higher visibility and credibility, and it sets the company apart from its competitors.
5 A rating is a useful tool for corporate executives because it shows how their company compares with other similar borrowers or peers worldwide.
6 A rating constitutes an independent check on a company's own SWOT analysis.
7 Rating allows the company to review its own operations and rethink its business assumptions and governance procedures; it is an aid to self-examination.

If the issuer is a *commercial bank*, then in addition to the above, a rating will give confidence to depositors, regulators, those seeking credits from the bank and perhaps attract equity investors.

If the issuer is a *sovereign government*:

1 a rating helps attract the international capital that a country needs for its development;
2 a rating helps support the development of local capital markets, giving the private sector potential access to global capital markets;
3 a rating brings a country further into the global financial community and helps meet international standards of transparency and co-operation;
4 a rating helps achieve greater funding stability through expanded relationships with a core group of institutional investors worldwide;
5 it prompts foreign investors to take notice of a country, since an independent assessment from a respected outside source has been done; and
6 a rating exercise provides a taste of the kind of international scrutiny a government must expect in today's interdependent world. It forces a certain awareness and discipline on government officials.

If there is any doubt remaining about the benefits of a rating, Exhibit 1.1 is the ultimate persuader, illustrating that ratings and the cost of debt vary inversely. The higher the rating the lower the cost of borrowings as measured here by the spread between rated issues and the US Treasury bill rate.

Exhibit 1.1

Ratings and the cost of debt (estimated spreads as at January 2003)

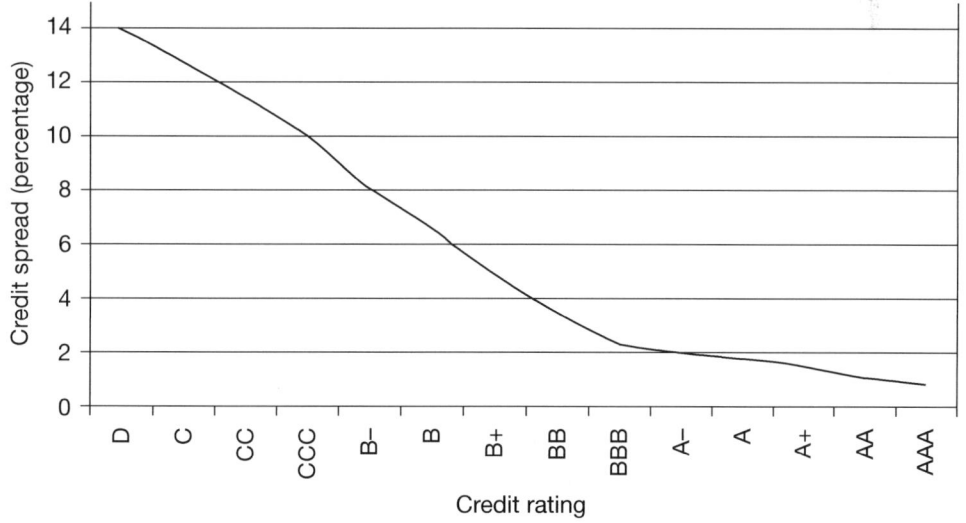

Chart of credit rating versus the associated cost of debt (spread above the US Treasury bill rate).

Source: INSEAD, based upon US companies

Regulators find value in ratings because they help assure the health and stability of the financial system and promote efficiency by reducing market volatility and arbitrage based on rumour. Ratings can indicate to supervisory authorities where new rules may be needed or where additional scrutiny is required of regulated institutions, and whether the liquidity and capital adequacy requirements of banks need to be tightened or loosened. Banking sector supervisors can use ratings to establish credit risk weights for a bank's risk assets.

Intermediaries or *investment bankers* use ratings to help in the planning, pricing and placement of securities. A rating can suggest to the underwriters where credit enhancements to the issue may be needed. Because of the widely shared benefits, ratings have become an inescapable component of the international capital markets. Attempts by critics in Europe and the US to find alternative means of producing rankings of credit quality have failed.

Rating symbols and meanings

Exhibit 1.2 shows the familiar symbols the rating agencies use. Moody's scale is different from those of Fitch and S&P. Moody's attaches to its letter ratings the modifiers of 1, 2, 3, while the other two agencies use the more familiar plus and minus signs to differentiate within categories. Here are the official definitions of what each rating symbol means. The rating in parenthesis is Moody's variant of the more common designations.[6]

AAA (Aaa) means *extremely* strong capacity to meet financial obligations – the top rating category.

AA (Aa) means *very* strong capacity to meet financial obligations.

A (A2) means *strong* capacity to meet financial commitments.

BBB (Baa2) means obligations with moderate credit risks and possible speculative characteristics; there is currently *adequate* capacity to meet financial obligations but the issuer is subject to adverse economic conditions.

BB (Ba2) means the company or bank or country is facing major ongoing uncertainties in economic or business conditions, so its obligations are subject to substantial credit risk.

B (B2) means speculative obligations vulnerable to adverse business, financial or economic conditions resulting in high credit risk.

CCC (Caa) means vulnerable and dependent on favourable conditions going forward in order to meet commitments.

CC (Ca) means currently highly vulnerable and default to be a virtual certainty.

C (C) means on verge of bankruptcy but continuing to meet debt payments or under regulatory supervision; highly vulnerable to non-payment.

D (D) means default in payment of one or more of the issuer's financial obligations.

According to Fitch's website, the terms 'investment grade' and 'speculative grade' (or 'non-investment grade') have established themselves over time as shorthand to describe the ratings categories shown above or below a certain point on the scale. The terms are market conventions and should not imply any recommendation or endorsement of a specific security for investment purposes. 'Investment grade' categories indicate relatively low to moderate credit

Exhibit 1.2

The agencies' rating scales

Moody's long-term ratings		S&P/Fitch long-term ratings

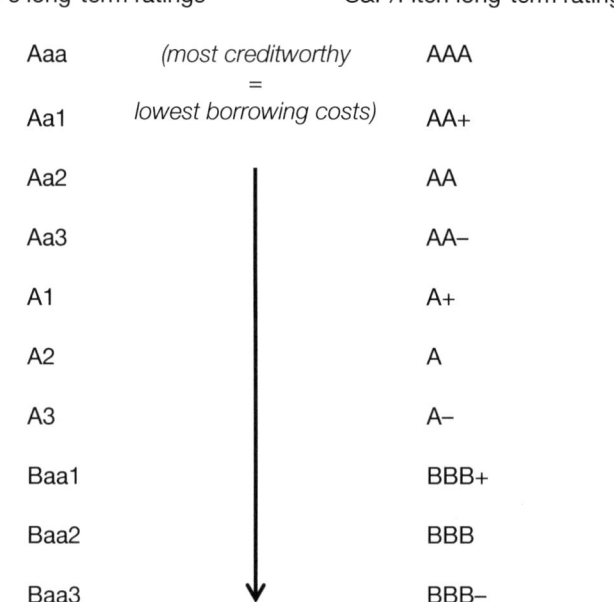

Aaa	*(most creditworthy*	AAA
	=	
Aa1	*lowest borrowing costs)*	AA+
Aa2		AA
Aa3		AA–
A1		A+
A2		A
A3		A–
Baa1		BBB+
Baa2		BBB
Baa3		BBB–

Investment grade *above* this point … speculative grade *below* this point

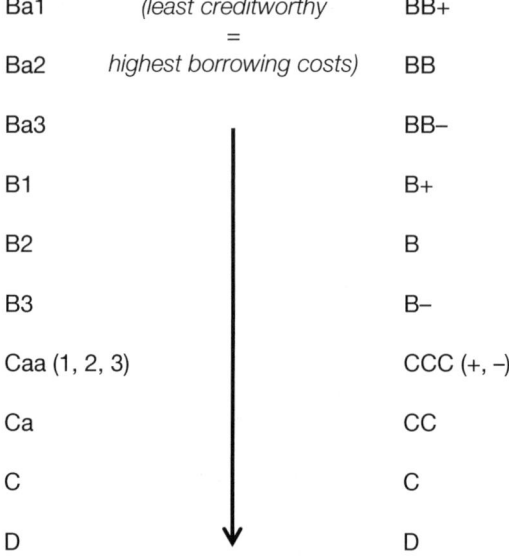

Ba1	*(least creditworthy*	BB+
	=	
Ba2	*highest borrowing costs)*	BB
Ba3		BB–
B1		B+
B2		B
B3		B–
Caa (1, 2, 3)		CCC (+, –)
Ca		CC
C		C
D		D

Source: Author's own

risk, while ratings in the 'speculative' categories either signal a higher level of credit risk or that a default has already occurred, as shown in Exhibit 1.2.

Ratings originally measured the risk of default on a fixed-income instrument. Ratings were assigned to the issue itself. Now, debt ratings can also apply to the issuer or obligor directly, that is, the borrower, guarantor, insurer or other provider of credit enhancement. The distinction is necessary since debt issues from the same issuer can vary by levels of seniority and support, implied or direct.

More recently, ratings at Moody's have taken on an added dimension – incorporating the severity of loss in the event of default, or the likely percentage recovery of the principal owed. 'Severity' can only be an estimate, of course, as no one can predict the dollar amount an investor might lose under certain circumstances. However, the agencies can develop a good estimate of possible loss by paying attention to the seniority of the debt instrument and any effective security underlying it, such as a government or holding company guarantee. In addition, the agencies have decades of default and recovery data on securities they have rated augmented by academic research on the topic of defaults and recoveries.

Ratings are meant to be valid across countries, across industries and across sectors. In other words, the bonds of a BBB– Chinese bank and a BBB– Saudi Arabian corporate and a Baa3 Croatian utility and a BBB– sovereign should all ideally have the same risk of default no matter in what market they are issued. It is obvious this is no easy task. The rating agencies make sincere efforts to create this cross-border and cross-industry validity, but success in this effort is difficult to measure.[7]

As seen above, the rating scale has many categories and distinctions within categories, either numbers or pluses and minuses. One might ask, what is the purpose of all these distinctions? The answer is that ratings are opinions about a wide range of possible outcomes in a bond's life, about many degrees of uncertainty. Here is how Moody's President, Raymond W McDaniel, Jr expressed it in testimony before the SEC.[8]

> In the most basic sense, all bonds perform in a binary manner: they either pay on time, or they default. If the future could be known, there would only be two ratings for bonds: good or bad. Because the future cannot be known, credit analysis resides in the realm of opinion. Thus, ratings are, by nature, opinions about the future with degrees of uncertainty.

---

[1] www.sec.gov/.../nrsroannrep1212.pdf. CRAs officially recognised by the SEC are given the designation of Nationally Recognised Statistical Rating Organisation (NRSRO). We will commonly refer to them here as CRAs.

[2] This book applies to the basic ratings market, that is, ratings on financial institutions, corporate issuers, and government securities but not the class of assets called structured finance. For those interested in collateralised debt obligations and other structured transactions that expanded rapidly in the early part of this century, there are many reports and books on the topic. The major CRAs played a large role in their acceptance in the US market and share the blame for the crisis in the global financial markets that ensued in 2007. See the 2011 report of the Financial Services Inquiry Commission (FSIC).

[3] Plaintiffs have been unable to prove that ratings were issued with 'reckless disregard' for the truth. Carelessness or negligence on the part of CRAs has not been a sufficient basis for plaintiffs to win a lawsuit.

4 CRA ratings and rationales are designed to help steer investors away from the type of borrower, such as Richard Brinsley Sheridan, who asserts 'it is not my interest to pay the principal, nor my principle to pay the interest'.

5 Fons, JS, 'Understanding Moody's corporate bond ratings and rating process', special comment, May 2002, p. 5. CRA specialisation and the savings that investors derive from outsourcing the credit ratings function are key reasons why US regulators are reluctant to set too many constraining boundaries on CRA activities, as we will see in Chapter 3.

6 Except for Moody's, virtually all NRSROs in the US and the dozens of local CRAs around the world use the more common AAA, AA, A nomenclature to signify creditworthiness. The definitions provided here are an amalgam of the words used by Moody's, Fitch and S&P, which largely overlap. The agency websites provide the specific wording for each category.

7 As early as 1996 and prior to the imposition of further regulatory requirements, Moody's realised that ratings consistency across the globe and across industries and sectors needed improvement. So, Moody's established eight standing committees to facilitate creative dialogue within the company, all reporting to the Chief Credit Officer. There are even Global Co-ordinators for each sector rated. See Cantor, R, 'Promoting global consistency for Moody's ratings,' May 2000.

8 Written statement, 21 November 2002, p. 5.

1.2 Information asymmetry

Asymmetric information is a common occurrence where one party to a transaction has more or better information than the other party. This often happens in deals where the seller knows more than the buyer, for example, the used car market, putting the former in a position to take advantage of the buyer's relative lack of knowledge. As long as there is no way to 'equalise' the imbalance, there will be the potential for abuse, deception and swindles.

Carrying this concept a step further, in the financial markets the predominant paradigm has been the 'efficient market' hypothesis, namely that everyone has perfect information and therefore all prices reflect the real value of goods and services for sale. But this assumption flies in the face of reality, since we all know that finance professionals (including rating agency analysts) know more than others in the market about the value of a product they are selling or the creditworthiness of a customer.

> The outstanding fact is the extreme precariousness of the basis of knowledge on which our estimates of prospective yield have to be made.
>
> *John Maynard Keynes, 1936*
> *General Theory of Employment, Interest and Money*

No one is fully informed. We are all dealing with different degrees of no information.

Given that no one can foretell the future value of financial assets, we are obliged to place our bets on differences in degrees of known information. All this applies to credit ratings, and there are two aspects to consider.

1. The difference in the quantity and quality of information between sellers and buyers of financial assets.
2. The difference in the quantity and quality of information between the rating agencies and issuers of securities.

Sellers, buyers and intermediaries

As to the first point above, look no further than the recent turmoil in the markets. The sellers of the securities (the investment banks) that were backed by sub-prime mortgages and the intermediaries who judged their credit quality (the rating agencies) presumably knew more about the securities than those who purchased them (institutional investors and traders) – an asymmetric condition that ended in disaster. The latter put their faith in the reputable knowledge of the CRA without doing their own due diligence on the products for sale.

When the CRAs' computer models about the US housing market proved flawed, the whole façade crumbled. By certifying the transformation of sub-prime mortgages into triple-A rated securities, the rating agencies contributed to the infection that spread throughout the global financial system.

The fallout has not ended, but the remedy should be clear – a return to fundamental credit analysis and due diligence on the part of all parties to a transaction. That is easy to say, but as we know, greed and hubris run as rampant as a bull on Wall Street and are not likely to be curtailed short of human re-engineering.

Similarly, as intermediaries in the chain, the rating agencies (sellers), based on their access to confidential issuer information that no one else in the market had, were deemed by investors (buyers) to have an information advantage such that the seller's opinions on credit quality were considered 'inside', accurate and trustworthy.

Transparency and the agencies

For the past 100 years there has been a persistent gap between the rating agencies and those they rate. Issuers have had little concrete knowledge about the one institution that largely determines their borrowing costs – the rating agency. Issuers have not been certain how best to present their case in the due diligence meetings, or what their rights are with regard to appeals, or who might comprise the rating committee that determines the outcome.

Because of the rating agencies' power in the financial markets and the minimal amount of time most issuers spend on managing the ratings process, corporations, banks and other issuers tend to be at a natural disadvantage vis-à-vis the agencies. Issuers did not know the methods by which the agencies were going to evaluate their credit quality. What criteria were important and which variables have more weight in the decision? Was a credit rating arrived at by quantitative or qualitative methods?

The rating agencies have always demanded that issuers open their books completely and disclose strategies and policies, yet they are reluctant to reciprocate by explaining their methods and procedures fully. This 'information imbalance' favours the agencies and makes the whole rating process asymmetric and more mysterious than it should be. At a minimum, this imbalance heightens issuer anxiety and can affect management performance in due diligence meetings. At a maximum, it can increase the chances that the agencies can proceed cavalierly and in the end, due to non-accountability, produce an inaccurate credit analysis.

Until recently, the agencies have felt they could assign any rating without having to explain themselves beyond an often vague press release. They published some generic statements, methodologies and opinions. Issuers in turn have been passive and willing to pay the agencies rating fees in order to fund themselves in the financial markets.

For example, here is a list of '10 things the rating agencies will not tell you'.

1 How the rating committee really operates.
2 That you are not legally obligated to pay for a rating you do not ask for.
3 The degree to which guesswork and subjectivity play a role in ratings.
4 The extent to which an analyst's personal and ideological biases affect ratings.
5 That investors do not really 'demand' opinions on new cross-border issues or issuers, despite the agencies' use of that word.
6 That the agencies do not really make meticulous, let alone global, peer comparisons.
7 That their forecasting tools are no better (and sometimes worse) than others in the market.
8 The weight placed on social and political factors as opposed to the numbers.
9 That their press releases do not always give the real reasons for a rating change.
10 Why analyst turnover is so high at the rating agencies.

Recent changes

Why has this situation persisted for so long? First, Moody's and S&P comprise an effective duopoly, and it suits their business purposes to retain an aura of mystery about their workings and to be seen as the 'experts'. The agencies were not likely to change their secretive procedures or internal workings without some assertive, persistent demands on the part of issuers and/or investors, pressures due to competition, or, as we see now, pressure from the US and European regulators.

The information advantage enjoyed by the rating agencies has diminished in recent years due to the advent of the internet and pressure from regulators for more disclosure (see Chapter 3). Investors and issuers have moved up the knowledge curve, and the information asymmetry has moderated. All major rating agencies have exhaustive data and details on their websites compared with 10 years ago, including the definitions of all their ratings and public access to many ratings in all categories. Thus, the worst abuses in this regard are behind us as the CRAs are now overcompensating with fulsome websites.

In the 1980s, Moody's and S&P had headquarters in New York City and a hundred analysts at most covering a narrow range of fixed income issuers. As the Eurobond market grew, they opened offices in London, Frankfurt and Paris. As the Asian market beckoned, they opened offices in Hong Kong, Tokyo and Sydney. As their franchises continued to expand due to rising issuance and demand for ratings plus the free hand provided by government regulators, the agencies became true worldwide businesses. According to their websites, S&P now has more than 1,400 analysts spread out over 23 countries and some 6,000 employees. S&P has published more than one million credit ratings that cover some US$45 trillion in rated debt. Moody's employs 7,000 people worldwide and has a presence in 29 countries. Fitch has 50 offices in 30 countries and some 2,000 employees.

Not only are these numbers astounding (they have risen exponentially in the past 25 years) but also they tell issuers that ratings are an inevitable fact of financial life and that business success and survival depend on playing the game by agency standards. Many of these standards are displayed systematically on the agency websites; others are less visible and subtle and can be found in this book. The global reach of the agencies and the ubiquity of the internet should also in some sense assure issuers that they are not as likely as before to be misunderstood and short-changed by parochial US analysts and murky methodologies.

The information gap persists to some extent (and thus the power imbalance), but it is not as pernicious as in the past. The agencies are less arrogant and a bit chastened following their recent failures in the sub-prime securitisation scandal. Nonetheless, issuers need to continue to press the agencies for clarity, a process that this book was designed to aid. This book will offer tools to reduce the information asymmetry and will alert issuers to their rights vis-à-vis the agencies. We turn first to how the agencies think and function and then to the business principles that drive their operations as commercial enterprises.

1.3 Rating agency principles and practices

Who knows better how the agencies really think and operate than one who has spent a decade or more in one of them? The author spoke with more than 50 agency analysts, some former, some current, in order to collect inside facts about agency procedures and to uncover strategies that will help issuers in their pursuit of better ratings. In some cases those interviewed confirmed what we already knew, and in other cases they added substantive information and anecdotes. To ensure candid responses, we guaranteed anonymity.

It is hoped that one of the benefits of this book will be to 'de-mystify' the rating agencies, to explore the terra incognita, and to illuminate how they operate. What follows applies to banks, corporates and governments that issue cross-border debt and who are obliged to obtain credit ratings. The intention is to lift the smoke and fog enough that issuers can understand better this agent or partner they must rely upon. More information should improve their management of and relationship with the agencies.

Moody's bank analyst and Vice President, Lynn Exton gave the agency's standard 'mission speech' to a group of investors and intermediaries in Melbourne on 4 April 1996.

> Moody's mission [she said] is to increase capital market efficiency by assigning ratings to fixed income obligations. In order for us to accomplish this mission, we need to not only get our ratings right but make every effort to ensure that investors understand the credit issues each set of Moody's ratings is designed to address, so they can use the ratings with confidence.

These words could have come just as easily from any analyst or executive at S&P, and indeed they have, in all the set speeches given by the agencies. The Big Two agree on this much: the capital markets depend on them for accurate, reliable and unbiased assessments of credit quality, and the agencies depend for their livelihood on the continued confidence of the markets in them.

Underlying principles… and the impact on issuers

The framework that defines the agencies' global business strategies as well as the structure of their daily work of assigning ratings has two pillars: their operating principles and their standard practices. Here are four main principles that guide and sustain the agencies' work.

Principle 1: the substance and appearance of credibility

To maintain their lucrative franchise, it is absolutely critical that Moody's, S&P and Fitch be perceived as professional and credible in the market's eyes. Without credibility, their franchises would be eroded quickly by competitors whose ratings would be trusted more. The agencies maintain the *substance* of their credibility by producing ratings on a wide variety of fixed income products that are seen by the market as timely and accurate. Since it is essential that they show a competent face to the markets, they look to hire skilled and experienced analysts. When not available, the CRAs hire young candidates just out of business school and train them.

They maintain the *appearance* of their credibility by erecting a semi-permeable wall of secrecy around their operations, methods and earnings. They also publish reams of turgid reports to buttress their authoritativeness. They repeatedly demonstrate the value of their work by showing the historical performance of ratings. Survival for the CRAs depends on their preserving a pristine and competent reputation, which in turn depends on the market's perceptions of them.

They believe that the larger the share of the market they rate for each instrument (bonds, commercial paper, medium-term euro notes, money market funds, counterparty obligations), the more accepted and therefore indispensable ratings become for both issuers and investors. The more indispensable ratings become, the stronger the foundations of agency credibility. In new markets, new ratings themselves eventually create incremental investor demand for more ratings. And the process keeps rolling along.

For all the agencies, survival depends on maintaining a pristine reputation. Their reputations have suffered 'hits' in recent years, from the Asian financial crisis (1997 to 1998), to Enron (2001) to Worldcom (2002), to collateralised mortgage securities (2007), but they have recovered, given the lack of credible alternatives for investors and somewhat-enhanced regulatory oversight.

Why do investors not do their own credit research instead of relying on the rating agencies? The answer is: (i) investors do not want to incur the time and cost of having additional staff for that purpose; and (ii) investors want a common set of benchmarks that they can use to assess the risk of securities, and these agencies provide it at a reasonable cost. For investors stability and continuity are better than rapid or severe changes in the current rating system.

Impact on issuers

It follows that issuers cannot avoid dealing with the existing rating agencies. Only Moody's, Fitch and S&P have instant credibility with institutional investors, and only they offer access to the larger, deeper markets. However, this does not mean that the aura of the CRAs cannot be tarnished or their market share eroded by competitors. Nor does it mean issuers need to accept all their rules, procedures and methods. If need be, as in a potential upgrade situation, these methods and procedures can be successfully challenged with the proper preparation and insight into their operations.

Principle 2: the need for secrecy

One of the principal ways that the Big Two maintain the credibility so critical to their survival as business entities is to operate as much below the radar as possible. Despite their importance in the markets, very little has been published about the rating agencies. Until the recent sub-prime financial crisis, you seldom if ever saw their senior executives interviewed on television or commenting on the financial trend du jour. Their public speeches stated only the obvious or the non-controversial. Retired executives do not publish their memoirs. The agencies have historically assumed that the less known about them, the less there is to challenge, criticise or regulate.

Few know how they really operate relative to issuers and intermediaries, the subjective criteria they use for ratings, how their methodology differs from what they publish, and how their fee structures amount to turning on a cash tap. This book hopes to redress the balance.

The agencies say the reason for their low profile is that they handle sensitive information from issuers, which they often know before others in the market do and which they have to hold closely. This is true, but secrecy also helps the agencies from a business standpoint. By having inside information from issuers, they allege they can produce more accurate and credible ratings, which reinforces their franchise. There is still an air of mystery and power that suits the agencies' image and marketing purposes.[1]

Impact on issuers

Issuers need to assess the degree of openness in their relations with the agencies and decide if they are comfortable with it. If not, issuers should ask the agencies to be more candid about their methods and criteria so that the relationship becomes less one-sided. By not fully disclosing their decision criteria, the agencies can generate images of arbitrariness and unfairness. Information sharing should be a two-way street. But, to mix metaphors, the road has been and will continue to be uphill. Maybe it is a 45 degree incline now instead of a 60 degree incline.

Principle 3: better too low than too high

One of the most important principles guiding rating deliberations is that the agencies cannot be embarrassed by low ratings; they can only be embarrassed by ratings that are too high. Another way of viewing this 'given' is the fact that if the agency rates an issue too high and then has to downgrade it, an investor loses money and that makes the agency look bad.

If the CRA rates an issue too low because of inferior information or undue caution, then, on the one hand, from the investor's standpoint this may disqualify a given investment because it does not conform to investment policy. Therefore, the investor suffers an opportunity cost. On the other hand, when the agencies rate an issue too low, the investor earns a slightly higher return as compensation for the CRA's over-estimation of default risk.

There is nothing worse for the franchise and the agencies' reputation (and the analyst's career) than getting a rating wrong on the high side. When a P-1/A-1+ rated issuer of commercial paper barely escapes from a liquidity crisis, the natural question investors ask is, why did the agencies not see this vulnerability? An incorrect rating tells investors the agency did not do its homework and must have overlooked key credit factors. If they got this one wrong, investors will say, how do we know their other ratings are right?

There is a 'balancing dynamic' involved in the rating process that avoids extremes and produces market-related outcomes. On the one hand, the agencies have an incentive to assign high ratings in order to capture business, but on the other hand, they have an incentive to assign low ratings to avoid reputation loss. These conflicting incentives result in a balanced outcome, especially as rating determinations are made through debate by a diverse rating committee.[2]

Impact on issuers

Issuers must expect the agencies to be cautious and conservative. If they err, it will almost always be on the downside. This principle explains why it is easier to suffer a downgrade based on trivial news than it is to win an upgrade based on solid progress. If there are any lingering doubts on a credit, the rating committee will take at least one notch off a rating just to be safe. There is an inherent conservative bias at the agencies.

Principle 4: incomplete, insufficient or suspect data

Where the data in the public domain or the data supplied by the issuer are incomplete, opaque or insufficient for a clear rating decision, the rating committee will either decline to assign a rating or will assign a rating lower than otherwise might be merited. The reason given is to capture the uncertainty caused by insufficient information. Lower ratings may also result if the agency believes the issuer's data are tainted or 'doctored'. If this situation continues, the agency will simply withdraw its rating. They do not want a questionable rating outstanding. Basing a rating on public information only, such as a company's annual reports, does not add value to the market and does not capture the nuances behind the numbers or a sense of the company's competitive strategies.

Impact on issuers

In today's capital markets, the vast majority of issuers co-operate when the agencies request material. Nonetheless, a few issuers maintain that certain data are secret or proprietary, and thus they do not want to comply fully with agency requests for full disclosure. Ministries of finance and CFOs only harm themselves if they do not disclose their information and share their plans and future policies.[3]

Issuers need not worry about their confidential information being leaked or disclosed by the agencies inadvertently.

- The CRAs will not publish everything the issuer gives them; they just need the information to reach their rating conclusion.
- The more information provided to the rating agencies, the more favourably the issuer is perceived, because it implies that the issuer has nothing to hide. The CRAs appreciate openness and co-operation because it makes their task easier and the resulting rating more accurate.
- Making the effort to gather this information will not be wasted – it will have later payoffs when used with other external audiences, such as counterparties and creditors.

Whatever information the issuer supplies is indeed secure in agency files. To the author's knowledge, there has never been a leak or untimely disclosure of issuer information by the agencies. If there were, it would be an immediate firing offence and more importantly a major blow to the agency's reputation for confidentiality.

Underlying practices... and the impact on issuers

There are a number of basic practices followed by the rating agencies that are inherent in their way of doing business. Some of these practices follow naturally from the operating principles explained above. Here are four of them.

Practice 1: obscure operations and mysterious processes

The agencies try to keep their internal practices relatively inaccessible to issuers and to the public. They give out little information about themselves and their operations. They do not routinely give speeches or write papers on how they determine ratings. Except for Moody's, which is a publicly traded company, they publish no financial records or separate annual reports. Their revenues, costs and net profits are buried in the accounts of their parent companies. Until recently, they have been virtually unregulated. (See Chapter 3, 'Regulating the raters'.)

The agencies have created the impression that the credit rating process is mysterious, complex and not susceptible to mortal comprehension. Ratings were often deemed a 'black box', even on Wall Street, where the CRAs seem to have some proprietary interest in preserving the element of surprise. (S&P was less guilty than Moody's in this regard.) The agencies have seldom been subjected to serious scrutiny by the US or foreign media. From 1975 to 2008, the author was unable to find a single penetrating article on the major CRAs in the *New York Times*, *The Financial Times*, the *Wall Street Journal* or any other publication. The mystery was maintained. Since the financial crisis and the S&P downgrade of the debt rating of the US, however, the media have opened the door a bit. Now virtually all coverage of the CRAs is negative. It is hoped this book will add further perspective on their world.

The old Wall Street saying that 'Moody's is mystical and S&P is statistical' no longer holds. Both agencies have evolved over the past 20 years into more transparent organisations where the notion of a 'black box' method of rating determination is outdated and untenable. There are no fixed weightings of variables at either agency, and both readily admit to the large role of non-quantitative factors in rating decisions. They both make an effort to explain their rating rationales, to focus on fundamentals, and to produce timely and concise updates on rated credits. The publication and updating of their methodologies systematises the process and assigns explicit or implicit weights to the rating process.

Impact on issuers

There are several impacts on issuers from this state of affairs:

1 Issuers have a world of information about their investment bankers, their commercial bank lenders and even their investors. But they have little concrete knowledge about the

one institution that will largely determine their borrowing costs. Proactive issuers must remedy this information gap if they are to optimise their ratings.

2 Because of the vagueness attending agency procedures, issuers are not certain how best to present their case in the annual rating meetings, or what their rights are with regard to appeals, or who might comprise the rating committee that determines the outcome.

3 Borrowers tend to passively acquiesce in what the agencies say and do because of some unspoken fear of the power of Wall Street or some misplaced worry about ratings 'retaliation' by the agencies. At a minimum, this imbalance heightens issuer anxiety and can affect performance in the due diligence meetings. At a maximum, it raises the risk that the agencies will act arbitrarily. This impact has been reduced recently under tighter government regulation that holds the agencies accountable for their practices.

Practice 2: rule-maker, agenda-controller

The agencies undertake their business of rating issuers based on procedures they have developed over decades – ones they feel meet their needs for information and for maintenance of their market power. Whenever they contact potential fee-paying clients,[4] the agencies naturally provide the context in which the business proceeds from that point on.

It is their framework, their contracts and their criteria that set the tone and substance of the rating relationship from the beginning. The rules are made by them and imposed on issuers with hardly a protest. There is an arrogance of power or *maître du monde* mentality at work at the agencies.[5] Issuers very seldom consider the idea of negotiating a business relationship with the agencies from the outset. When due diligence meetings take place, it is the agency agenda that is followed. Although the timing of visits can be negotiated, the topics to be covered are generally provided by the agencies based on their own list of standard issues plus some issuer-specific concerns.

Why are the US rating agencies such powerful actors in the capital markets? Their influence derives from their size, credibility and government-supported mandate, but more fundamentally, they have the ability to alter investor perceptions and behaviour and to influence the decisions of all market participants.[6] Their power is also related to the central position of the US capital markets and the long-abandoned practice of 'name lending' by banks.

There are really only two limits to this power. One is the agencies' need to stay credible with investors so that they will continue to use CRA products and services, and the other is action by governments in the US and Europe to rein in CRA authority. Rating agency power could be reduced, of course, if investors starting doing their own homework, that is, determining what assets to invest in based on their own credit assessments. It will become evident as we proceed that this option is most unlikely.

Impact on issuers

Issuers are at the mercy of the rating agencies throughout the rating process. Many issuers report they do not feel in control of the proceedings. They believe they have few rights vis-à-vis the agencies. As a result, the rating process becomes distasteful and intimidating, if not frightening.[7] It is almost as if the CRAs, Moody's in particular, had embraced Caligula's malicious message: '*Oderunt dum Metuant*' (Let them hate, so long as they fear.)

A detractor at one of the agencies told the author off site one day, 'Have you ever heard of a business that succeeds despite treating its paying customers with disdain?' The agencies can do that, of course, because both issuers and investors have no other alternative guide to creditworthiness in the capital markets. A protected duopoly does not have to spend effort building customer satisfaction or meeting customer expectations. How clients are greeted and treated is not on the analysts' agenda, except perhaps by the CRAs' marketing teams. If an analyst is too sociable with an issuer, he risks a 'discussion' with his supervisor for appearing too gullible and lighthearted and not serious and aloof enough – the image CRA management (at least at Moody's) wants to portray.[8] S&P always prided itself as more accessible to issuers than Moody's as the means to garner better co-operation with issuers.

Issuers believe they cannot influence the outcome very much. This unbalanced situation results in a more adversarial relationship with the agencies than is necessary, a less respectful relationship than should be obtained, and a rating result that may not have benefited from the issuer's best input.

Practice 3: rating committee membership

Rating committees include agency analysts not otherwise associated with your credit situation in order to enhance objectivity in reaching a rating decision. The committees usually comprise five to nine analysts and officers, some of whom have never visited the country or client whose debt they are rating.

Impact on issuers

Issuers do not know the identities and proclivities of rating committee members. The membership of the committee varies depending on the importance of the decision and who is available to attend. Committee proceedings are never published or discussed with issuers. As a result, issuers are unable to engage the agency at the point where it counts most or check to see if due process was followed or if all the relevant information was presented. They must rely on their assigned analyst to state their case before the committee. For issuers, this is the most crucial link in the chain leading to a rating but one over which they have the least control.

Practice 4: in line with market realities

Ideally, ratings are not supposed to mirror the market or follow its contours. To merely echo market views would cause the agency's credibility to suffer. Thus, while the agencies do not follow (or have time to follow) the periodic gyrations of a client's stock or foreign exchange holdings, they become alert when the financial markets move in sudden or unexpected directions.

At that point, they are likely to get on the phone and ask their contact at the company or ministry, what is behind the sudden shift in these markets? They want to know, is the event ephemeral or fundamental? The agencies need to stay *au courant* with market developments in order not to get caught off guard. This is assuredly not to say the agencies change their ratings based on any single day's or week's events. Ratings are meant to take the long-term view.

In addition, while the agencies do not base their rating decisions on any other agency's rating, each is aware of the other's ratings and treats them as one more element in the market's prevailing view. As one former agency analyst told the author, '[in doing ratings] we didn't follow the market to see how it viewed a credit. This was not a formal tool, but it was a reality check. We looked at the secondary bond market to see that we weren't too far off. If we just tried to mirror the market, then there's no incremental value to ratings.'

Impact on issuers

Issuers may not be satisfied with their current ratings from the Big Three, but they can be assured that these ratings are generally within the boundaries of market perceptions of their creditworthiness. If their ratings are not in line with market expectations, they eventually will be in line, especially if the rating rationale the agency offers is weak. Gaps between an agency's opinion and that of the market tend to close over time for most credits.

Relative bond yields and spreads do not determine ratings or the timing for upgrades, but they do play a role at the margin. Market participants must remember also that default risk, symbolised by ratings, and in the market by spreads from risk-free benchmarks, is only one factor in the price of a bond. Two other perceptions are factored in by the market: how much a bondholder will get back in event of a default, and how long it would take to resolve any dispute.

Ratings and the prices of bonds

The prices of bonds reflect a variety of factors in addition to non-payment risk, including supply and demand, maturity, coupon, tax status, and liquidity. Over time, prices of regularly traded issues *will* reflect all available information. Ratings, on the other hand, primarily reflect the agency's perception of relative risk of non-payment and not these other factors with which the market is concerned.

Market pricing may reflect any number of factors other than ratings, such as general sentiment about the health of the economy, the scarcity of new financings, and regulatory changes that impact the supply and demand for a specific security. At times, the market places less emphasis on credit quality and more emphasis on liquidity or yield.

Other perceptions can play a role: how much a bondholder will get back in the event of a default, and how long it would take to resolve any dispute. A widely-recognised name in the market may benefit a borrower despite its rating. However, the expectation remains that like-rated issues of similar maturity and coupon should trade at like prices, and higher rated issues should sell at higher prices (provide lower yields). When they do not, issuers would be wise to investigate and take action.

When the price of a regularly traded bond is 'out of sync' with its rating, it can be assumed that either the market knows more than the agencies, or the agencies know something the market does not. The market reacts to news more quickly than the agencies, but that does not mean the market better reflects the underlying *default* risk. Markets can move quickly and sometimes disproportionately on rumours, while the agencies try to look at underlying economic strength and verifiable facts.

Lesson for issuers

What is an issuer to do when the bond market says something different from the agencies when it clearly is not a result of timing differences or market imperfections? The first thing should be to note the degree of difference between the two and the trend of the discrepancy. *The greater the discrepancy, the greater the call for action with the agencies, and this applies on both the upside and the downside.* How to respond can vary widely based on any number of factors, including:

- the current rating and the outlook associated with it;
- whether the market perception is better or worse than the agency perception of risk;
- plans for bond issuance;
- the frequency of trading of outstanding securities and the visibility of your name; and
- existing rating agency relations.

Relative bond yields and spreads do not determine ratings or the timing for rating changes, but they do play a role at the margin. Astute issuers looking to get an upgrade or avoid a downgrade can subtly use these market data to build their case.

---

[1] That aura of power was reinforced in an article in the *New York Times* on 22 February 1995 by Thomas Friedman titled 'Don't Mess with Moody's'. He says that Moody's is 'one powerful agency. In fact, you could almost say that we live again in a two-superpower world. There is the US and there is Moody's. The US can destroy a country by levelling it with bombs; Moody's can destroy a country by downgrading its bonds.'

[2] It was not uncommon that rating committees at one CRA would check to see what rating the other CRAs had on an issuer or issue before their final decision, just to be sure their own rating was not too extreme or out of line. The agencies also want to ensure they are offsetting the inherent optimism of client management and their bankers.

[3] The US government rating is unsolicited and uncompensated.

[4] The CRAs do not use the term 'client' because it implies a duty to them rather than to investors. Nonetheless, we will use that term here.

[5] Part of the perception of arrogance derives from the fact that agency analysts are typically younger than the management of companies they are assessing and they have to ask critical questions that are resented as rude.

[6] A former Moody's officer told the author that he witnessed a rating committee chairman in the 1980s turning to an analyst with a clenched fist and remarking, 'Just think of the power you have in your hands'.

[7] The July–August 1994 issue of *Treasury & Risk Management* magazine carried an article 'Rating the rating agencies', which claimed that 'the rating agency industry has created a franchise of fear', p. 2.

[8] 'Ingrained in Moody's corporate culture is a conviction that too close a relationship with issuers is damaging to the integrity of the rating process.' Ibid, p. 31. Moody's neither confirms nor denies this allegation, saying simply that their focus is on their primary constituency – the investor.

1.4 The business of ratings

There are 16 business practices the rating agencies adhere to as commercial enterprises. These business protocols underlie agency strategies and daily operations, and they overlap the principles and operations listed earlier. We state each one and follow with an explanation of what the practical result is in the marketplace and for issuers.

Reputation and trust

Business practice 1: a rating agency must evaluate fixed-income instruments in a totally unbiased fashion, committing itself fully to the interests of investors. Ratings cannot be 'bought' or negotiated. Any hint or perception about outside influence over a rating will ruin the agency's reputation with investors and with the financial markets. The foundation of any credit rating business is the reputation of the company, the credibility of its ratings, and its independence. Without these characteristics, the business will fail from lack of investor and issuer support.[1]

Practical result: the ownership of the agency should be widely held by retail and wholesale participants in the market. Government ownership of a rating agency, whole or partial, introduces politics into the mix, or at worst coercion, which immediately undermines an agency's objectivity and independence. Therefore, governments should restrict their involvement only to an oversight and regulatory role. In some emerging markets the private financial sector may not be mature enough yet to assume this intermediary role, in which case initial government sponsorship may occur, and local investors take this influence into account.

Business practice 2: the rating agency's whole business must be ratings analysis and publications. It must not be doing other market-oriented activities at the same time, such as consulting, where the potential for real or perceived conflicts of interest could arise. S&P and Moody's recognised the need to segregate non-rating activities from rating activities and created ancillary services outside the regulated ring-fence, such as Moody's Analytics Inc and other risk management advisory services. Fitch Ratings created Fitch Solutions Inc and Fitch Training Inc to avoid the appearance of conflicts of interests with its primary rating business.

Practical result: rating agencies are commercial enterprises. They need to make a profit to stay in business. For Moody's and S&P, issuer fees comprise about 80% of revenues, while subscription fees account for about 20%. The agency must decide how to price each type of issue it rates (commercial paper versus bonds) and on what grounds (the complexity of the security and time required to analyse it, the size of the issue or the number of issues done per year). Moody's and S&P are running very successful businesses – their gross margins average around 50%.

An agency's published credit reports have multiple purposes: to earn revenue, to enhance the agency's reputation, and to disseminate information about issuers. These reports and the rating rationale in them cannot be based on historical exposition because ratings are meant to be predictive and prospective. Prose must be concise and convincing, giving reasons why a particular rating was chosen.

At the same time, the agency must be totally removed from the direct influence of its parent, especially if the parent is a major participant in the financial markets as a dealer or corporate adviser. Otherwise there could be perceptions of outside influence that compromise the agency's independence. Allegations about possible agency abuses under these circumstances have arisen in recent years as part of legislative pressure for reform of the agencies. We look at these charges in Chapter 3, 'Charges against the agencies'.

Business practice 3: the ratings business must be built on trust and built for the long term. It cannot be built on fear or on quick profits.

Practical result: of all the business principles listed here, this one – the ratings business cannot be built and sustained on the basis of fear – may have been honoured the least. Since the mid-1980s the CRAs have built their businesses rapidly on the basis of fear and intimidation, the unwitting target of which has been the issuer. The tactic the agencies used to expand their franchises was (and to some extent still is) the 'unsolicited rating,' announcing a rating on an issuer without its consent or participation. We devote a section in Chapter 2, 'Unsolicited ratings', to this topic.

Conversely, the matter of trust has been an enduring and honoured principle. Trust between agency and issuer can be built only if the issuer trusts the agency to hold its finances and business projections confidential and to give the company a fair assessment. The agency must trust the issuer to be open and honest with its data and its plans. Without adequate and timely information from the issuer, a rating cannot be issued.

Therefore, to acquire a rating useful in the market, issuers must co-operate and be willing to share even their inner secrets (for example, hidden reserves, strategic plans). Issuers must be confident in the agency's assurances of confidentiality and discretion. If the issuer does not disclose full information, the agencies will assign a rating lower than optimal to reflect the uncertainty caused by the insufficiency of data or its quality. If the agency perceives that the data are purposely deceptive or continually incomplete, then it will cancel any existing ratings of that issuer, for example, Mali, Moldova and Turkmenistan. Other reasons for withdrawing ratings might be inability to comply due to revolution (Libya) or US sanctions that prohibited US companies from doing business with the country (Iran).

Of course, issuers may always ask the CRA to withdraw their ratings, as S&P did when the governments of Benin and Tunisia requested it in late 2013. The reasons are usually that the issuer is expecting lower ratings quite soon and wants to avoid that negative publicity, or they do not have the time or resources to manage multiple agency requests and visits.

Confidentiality and ethics

Business practice 4: absolute discretion and confidentiality of information must be promised and assured by the agency.

Practical result: strict safeguards to confidentiality have been put in place at every agency. Leaks of proprietary information constitute an offence punishable by firing. Trading securities based on material non-public information gained in the rating process is a federal securities law violation. Without this assurance, companies will not share their financials and strategic plans with the agency analysts.

Business practice 5: the appearance of proper and ethical behaviour within the agency is critical.

Practical result: it is best that the analytical department at the rating agency be separated from the billing department so that the analysts are not influenced by the payment status of the client. The two departments should have different senior managers and different reporting lines. Government regulations today ensure that separation. The SEC rules currently require that analysts not participate in or know the rating fees associated with the work they do. The SEC has proposed rules to more thoroughly separate marketing from analytics.

Business practice 6: to minimise the chance of a 'leaked' rating to the market, the agency must announce its rating decisions immediately after a rating committee decision so that all capital markets participants are informed at the same time. A rating decision until released is considered material non-public information with the attendant safeguards required.

Practical result: the agency needs to have the technological capability to link up electronically with the markets. It is the agency's obligation to the markets and to its shareholders that it impresses upon its analysts and others within the agency the need for absolute secrecy.

Business practice 7: rating assessments and rating changes must be produced and disseminated in a timely fashion to reduce rumours and arbitrage in the market.

Practical result: once the rated issuer has had the opportunity to check for errors in agency rationale, then ratings must be announced as soon as possible after the committee decision. The accompanying written or electronic reports must be published and disseminated quickly and widely.

Business practice 8: ratings are not supposed to mirror the market or follow its contours on a daily or monthly basis. Ratings are designed to take the long view.

Practical result: to reflect this long view, ratings must not change frequently. They must be accurate for several years or through a business cycle, especially for corporates. (Event risk is an exception, that is, the chance that some rapid change in a company's prospects or financial condition results in a sudden, often dramatic, shift in credit quality, the precise timing and nature of which could not have been predicted by the normal tools of fundamental credit analysis, for example, a merger or acquisition.) Ratings that persist gain credibility.

Wanted: experienced analysts

Business practice 9: ratings must be based on clear and solid analysis so that investors trust the judgment behind them. The rationale for a rating must be straightforward, logical and clear. It must be solid, not shallow, and it must be based on fundamental research, not a quick pass at the numbers.

Practical result: only highly trained and qualified analysts should be hired by the agency. They should have advanced academic credentials in finance, economics and government. They should have career backgrounds in the industries they rate. They should be carefully chosen and trained before any ratings are released into the market. However, the reality is that given the high analyst turnover at the agencies, younger and less experienced analysts are often hired.

Lesson for issuers

Be aware of the level of experience of the lead analyst assigned to you and work to educate him to your way of thinking. This will require patience and persistence; qualities we strongly recommend for issuers (see Chapter 6.)

Ratings are fundamentally judgments or opinions, so the analysts must not be wedded to any academic or automatic modelling technique. The value of a rating lies in the cogency of argument and reasoned inferences and forecasts behind it, not on strict formulas or quantitative models. As ratings are a view of the future capacity of an issuer to meet its obligations, the analysis must place the issuer's finances in a forward-looking context. A simple recitation of last year's results will not answer the question issuers need to know: what factors will influence the debtor's future capacity to repay me?

Business practice 10: the real competition among credit rating companies is for experienced analysts. Their analytical qualities, their speaking and writing abilities are what give credibility to the ratings.

Practical result: an agency must hire the best fixed income credit analysts in the market and pay them well. The analysts require special skills and attitudes. Rating analysis can get very complex, especially with structured transactions, increased event risk and hybrid instruments, so they require the best minds and work ethics available. Their training may be reflected in the sample curriculum shown in Box 1.1.

Box 1.1
Educational background for rating agency analysts

Psychology 101: 'The best predictor of future behaviour is past behaviour.'
Finance 101: 'The higher the debt, the more likely the borrower will miss a payment.'
Economics 101: 'A product that adds value in the market (for example, new information) has value.'
Decision making 101: 'More information is always better.'

Only an experienced analyst can take into account the subtle interplay amongst causal factors, such as deciding how likely it is that a company's strategic plan can be implemented and will eventually contribute to its financial health, given all the internal and external forces acting on the company.

Business practice 11: since much of the financial market's interface with the rating agency will be through the analysts themselves (their reports, their press releases or their public remarks), the analysts play both an expert's role and a marketing role. Their performance in both roles reflects on the agency directly.

Practical result: analysts must be accessible to the financial press and to interested investors who want to question their reasoning or get more insight. In doing this, the analysts help 'sell' the agency as an important and competent institution whose intermediary role is essential to the smooth functioning of the markets.

Business practice 12: ratings must be comparable across industries and even across borders. That is, a rating of single A on the debt of a paper and pulp company must mean the same risk of default as a single A rating on the debt of a steel company or a bank or a municipality.

Practical result: a senior committee of rating experts at the agency should oversee all ratings to ensure comparability. Ratings should be reviewed regularly for accuracy and consistency.

Business practice 13: the rating agency is a provider of credit information and opinion, one of many in the financial markets,[2] for example, Dun & Bradstreet, TRW Credit Services. A rating from a CRA does not protect investors from losses. Ratings as opinions are just a guide to default risk.

Practical result: the agency must make it clear that its views are only an opinion, albeit highly informed, and a part of the puzzle that investors need to make their own decisions. There are no guarantees regarding market gains and losses and no assurance that events and trends might not alter the agency's perspective over time.

Business practice 14: it is not unusual for a new rating agency to be a financial drain on its owners for several years. It takes that long for the new agency to find its niche and get accepted by the financial community and for revenues to flow in sufficient volume to offset early losses. The lack of funds was among the reasons for the early demise of the first EuroRatings effort which began operating in 1987.

Practical result: shareholders must be willing to underwrite financial losses for several years. Start-up costs remain high in terms of analyst salaries, computer equipment, building rental and travel expenses. Shareholders must take the long view. The rating business is not for short-term traders or opportunists. That said, many governments in emerging markets have encouraged the establishment of local CRAs as a way to develop the local financial market and to inculcate a credit mentality in its citizens. The major CRAs frequently sign 'technical service agreements' with budding local CRAs, for example, CRISIL in India, Korea Investors Service, Pefindo in Indonesia, to boost their success rate and position them for acquisition.

Emerging market CRAs

Business practice 15: in emerging markets, there is often initial resistance to ratings. Ratings are seen by participants in the local market as a new and threatening element. Issuers sometimes resist having a 'report card' made on their practices. The time and cost involved can be prohibitive. The commercial banks sense their role as financial intermediaries will be threatened by the access of their corporate loan clients to financing through the capital markets. Issuers do not like the public scrutiny and fear their confidential information, once divulged to the agency, will be leaked to competitors.[3]

Practical result: extensive marketing of ratings concepts (what they are, how they work and the benefits to the market) must be an integral part of the early stages of creating an agency. A credit culture must be created in the capital markets. Credit bureaus and rating agencies have perhaps the most important role in fostering this culture.

Issuers need to realise that in order to gain access to the world pool of savings, they must abide by world standards of disclosure and creditworthiness. Ratings are not a measure of currency risk, prepayment risk, market risk or interest rate risk. They do not predict the value of securities, and they are not recommendations to buy or sell a security. These distinctions need to be reiterated so that the market does not misunderstand or misuse ratings.

Some central banks in emerging markets have required that in opening their capital markets the first round of issuance may only be done by rated companies, often the highest rated enterprises such as telecom, electric power, water, or toll roads.

Business practice 16: investors in fixed-income instruments are concerned about the default risk of the paper they hold or plan to buy, but at the same time few investors want to take the time to do their own credit analysis or even know how to do it.

Practical result: therefore, for a century investors have relied on outside professional organisations to define and assess credit risk – the rating agencies. Investors have supported the development, growth and profitability of the agencies. The rating opinion expressed in letter symbols is a shorthand assessment of credit quality, one easily understood and used by investors. The written and electronic products emanating from the rating agency are concise, easy to understand, and overwhelmingly accurate and timely. Over the years ratings have added value since investors use them for their purchase decisions and issuers have seen that their investor base has grown.

---

[1] Building on its reputation and independence, Moody's Executive Vice President, Thomas J McGuire stated in an internal meeting in 1986 that 'our goal is to become an independent variable in the marketplace, making the market move because of our evaluations'. A lofty goal and one that has been realised by S&P as well.

[2] Rating agencies are not to be confused with credit information bureaus (CIB), such as Experian, TransUnion and Equifax. See Appendix 1 for a comparison of CRAs and CIBs.

[3] Countries intending to develop their local bond market by creating a CRA should not look to the Argentine example. The government in Buenos Aires in April 1992 issued a decree requiring that each security issued in the domestic bond market must have ratings from two different agencies. The ratings regime was imposed by the government, not created by investor demand for credit opinions. Regulators over-managed the private agencies with an expected result – confusion in the market, inflated ratings, no trust in ratings and excessive costs of compliance. The author undertook a World Bank sponsored study in 1999 and made recommendations to the government for improving the situation.

1.5 Rules and secrecy

To maintain their lucrative franchises, it is absolutely critical that the major CRAs are seen by the market as professional, trustworthy and credible. Without both the substance and appearance of credibility, their business model would be eroded.

The agencies say the reason for their low profile with the media is that they handle proprietary information from issuers which they often know before others in the market and which they have to hold closely. This is true, and the agencies have indeed been exemplary in this regard. Leaks of insider information, such as telegraphing a rating change before it happens, have been rare.

What the agencies do not admit publicly, however, is that there are at least two results to playing their secrecy game. One is that if issuers did not trust the agencies enough to share their data and plans, then the agencies would not have the information they need to make credible assessments. Thus, the secrecy they tout is not just to protect issuers; it is good business for the agencies as well.

Secrecy and trust are selling points for the agencies. The CRAs' public and private dicta have ranged from the abstruse to the apodictic. The cloak of secrecy also provides just the right air of mystery and power that suits the agencies' marketing purposes. It remains to be seen if new SEC rules related to methodologies and internal processes will make a difference in disclosure and transparency.

Myths and misunderstandings

The other consequence is that secrecy has begotten an array of myths and misunderstandings about the rating agencies. The persistence of these misunderstandings has reinforced their seeming accuracy. Fortunately, as agency disclosure has grown over the internet, some of these myths are less prevalent than 20 years ago.

1 The rating process is mysterious; there is some 'black box' involved. It is like the Wizard of Oz pontificating behind a curtain. *Reality:* the process is relatively straightforward, and ratings result from a mix of qualitative and quantitative factors.
2 Ratings are done by mechanical formula; numbers drive everything. *Reality:* numbers give only an early approximation of where in the rating range a rating might reside. Ratings reflect the future for which there are no data.
3 The ratings affect your personal consumer credit, like those of the credit bureaus TransUnion and Experian. *Reality:* the credit bureaus are an entirely separate business.
4 The agencies are a tool of the US government; the Secretary of the Treasury calls the agencies and politely suggests what a rating should be. *Reality:* this has never happened.
5 The agencies are under pressure from issuers to give a good rating, because the vast majority of agency revenues derive from fees paid by issuers. *Reality:* the issuer-pay model appears to be a clear conflict of interest, but this has not yet been proven, even when the US Federal Reserve Board examined the issue several years ago. The ratings and commercial sides of the business are supposed to be separated within the agencies, but the failure of the whole asset-backed securities market raised serious questions about the commingling of the two sides.

6 The agencies are vast collectors of data (a veritable private sector CIA) and they have unique advantages in knowledge. *Reality:* analysts are not always able to get all the information they need to do a rating but must decide based on what is available. Data are always limited and always time constrained.

7 Ratings are based on projections and future behaviour. *Reality:* ratings are based on historical performance with an educated guess about trends going forward. Any forecast covers only two to three years, not the life of a 10 or 30-year bond.

8 Just meet with the senior people at the CRA, and you can convince them to give an upgrade. *Reality:* this tactic is a serious misreading of how ratings are determined. Attempting this approach will never succeed. In fact, the CRA will wonder how naïve the issuer must be to think that it could succeed.

9 The analytical work done by the agencies is super sagacious. *Reality:* it is not as fine-tuned as they indicate it is in their literature.

10 The whole rating business is tainted and unreliable. *Reality:* the media have castigated the CRAs en masse, whereas it was only the structured finance part of the business, for example, packaged mortgage bonds, that merited criticism due to its poor performance during the latest financial crisis. Ratings of banks, companies and governments continue to be quite accurate, with some exceptions to be discussed later, as shown in data that strongly correlate high ratings with very low default occurrences and low ratings with much higher default occurrences over a period of decades.

11 The agencies tend to discount a lot of what the issuer tells them, assuming it is biased or self-serving. *Reality:* issuers are the best source of information.

12 Market participants want the CRAs to change radically. *Reality:* this may be true for the regulators in the US and Europe, but the primary beneficiary of ratings – institutional and retail investors – believe that the steadiness of ordinal ratings over time is more important.

One-way street

Issuers trust the agencies to hold secret what they divulge in terms of strategies and plans. The CRAs do that, but the trust and information flow should work both ways. The agencies should reciprocate by informing issuers about their methods and procedures. The process has historically been open on only one end – the issuer's. The playing field was always tilted in favour of the CRAs. Now under government and competitive pressure, the agencies display their procedures and methodologies quite revealingly on the internet.[1] Nonetheless, there is more to the story than is publicly known.

---

[1] These methodologies and the terminology are complex and require much study to ascertain their applicability and relevance to any one issuer's case – another reason why issuers need to devote time and resources to the task of managing the agency relationship.

1.6 Rating agency fees

The question of rating agency fees receives no public attention. Issuers do not criticise the agencies for fees, and the agencies, with the exception of Moody's, do not fully reveal their financial results, so the whole matter has always been low key and private.

The agencies try to downplay the topic by arguing that their fees are really quite reasonable, amounting to 'rounding errors' on the bills of the lawyers and bankers that issuers pay large sums to. This is basically true, but it understates the importance of these fees to rating agency revenues. One recent estimate showed that fee income from issuers ranges from 80% (Moody's) to 85% (S&P) of total revenue for these Big Two. The remainder derives from paid subscriptions to their publications, both print and online.

Since issuers certainly appear to pay the agencies willingly for what they perceive as the benefits of a credit rating, one can draw the following conclusions.

- Issuers do not mind paying for the market access and credibility that ratings buy.
- The fees are low relative to other financing costs and relative to the perceived benefits. According to one former Moody's analyst, 'What is US$75,000 for a government or a corporation that wastes that much in a week or a month?' Moreover, a rated issuer will pay fewer basis points on a loan compared with a non-rated issuer, so the rating pays for itself.
- Issuers may simply not be aware of some issuers who have not paid the agency fees for one reason or another.

Fees vary and are negotiable

The secret is that agency fees are negotiable. Issuers can actually discuss fee options with the agencies, and the agencies are flexible in their pricing. Fitch, in particular, used this approach with new clients to increase their market share and succeeded especially in Africa.

Competition among CRAs keeps fees relatively modest, and modest fees encourage issuer payment. Given their legal mandate to rate securities and oligopolistic position, the agencies should be able to raise their fees whenever they want to, and they often do, but issuer objections have been known to stay an increase. In any case, the rising number of issuers worldwide and the growing volume of debt rated have kept the agencies' profits buoyant.

Agency fees vary depending on the entity being rated (bank, company or government), the geographical region, and the type of any prospective issuance (bond, commercial paper or medium-term notes). For example, in 2006, S&P charged between US$80,000 and US$100,000 for a sovereign debt rating in Asia. There are also annual surveillance or monitoring fees. Since these fees change over time, issuers or bankers should contact the CRAs directly for the latest schedule.

1.7 Choosing a rating agency

New issuers need to get comfortable with the rating process and they need to choose a rating agency (or two) that will meet their needs. A practical way to do this is for an issuer to interview the analysts and managing directors at the three international rating agencies and then decide on the one that best fits their needs. It is customary for a ratings adviser to accompany government authorities to the interviews to ensure the right questions are raised. Issuers need to understand market practice in their region, which may benefit from having two ratings on an issue.

Anxiety can be high for new issuers because the whole rating process is daunting; there are many unknowns and uncertainties for the novice. Exhibit 1.3 illustrates how vast the distance is between a first-time issuer and an experienced one. It will take the newcomer years of issuance and agency interaction to bridge the gap.

Exhibit 1.3

Experience level of issuers

First time issuer	Experienced issuer
• Uncertainty, anxiety about the agencies	• Confident, proactive relationship
• Unfamiliar with rating process and agency procedures	• Knows agency methods; helps guide the process
• Unaware of rating criteria	• Understands key rating criteria
• Unaware of role of subjective assessment	• Influences the subjective aspects
• How do we prepare for the meeting?	• Regular communication with agencies
• What data do the agencies want?	• Supplies data ahead of request
• Borrowers' rights? What is that?	• Exercises rights, gains leverage

Source: Author's own

Once the decision has been taken to acquire a rating, the next step for the issuer is to ensure they have chosen the 'correct' agency, that is, one that will help them achieve their financial goals.

Ask these questions

Here is a suggested list of questions an issuer should ask to determine an agency's qualifications and suitability.

1 What countries, companies and banks in the region have you rated?
2 Who will be the lead and backup analysts on this assignment? How many years of analytical experience do they have? How many years' experience in the region?

3 Which of our peers or competitors does the proposed lead analyst cover?

4 Whom do you see as our peers in the region?

5 How much weight do you assign to the qualitative and quantitative aspects in a credit evaluation?

6 What degree of weight do you place on governance factors in a rating decision?

7 How does your analysis differ among geographical regions?

8 Do you offer a confidential indication of a rating rather than a public one?

9 How long does that confidential indication last?

10 How much would such an indication cost?

11 Do you offer a quick rating assessment or 'indicative' rating for a lower price? With this less than full-scale rating exercise, will we learn how you view our strengths and weaknesses and what the obstacles to a higher rating are?

12 Do you offer a discount for multiple first-time ratings in a country?

13 What kinds of ratings are included in your package – long-term and short-term foreign and local currency ratings?

14 Do you allow a first-time rated entity to reject the rating assigned? What follows thereafter in terms of fees and agency follow-up?

15 Do you cover your own travel costs?

16 Do you have an annual monitoring fee and when does it start? How much is it?

17 Please show us the contract between yourselves and an entity such as us.

18 Who will comprise the rating committee?

19 When would you be able to start?

20 How long will the assignment take?

21 How many meetings will be needed?

22 Which of our management team will you need to meet?

23 What information do you need from us to get started?

24 What other documentation will you require as we proceed?

25 What will give us comfort that you will get our rating right?

Assuming their fees are more or less comparable and reasonable and that they have experience in your part of the world and industry, then the agency that answers your questions in the most straightforward, sincere and non-facile manner is the one you should choose.

Chapter 2

The nature of credit ratings

Précis

Credit ratings and all their variations are explained in detail on the rating agencies' websites. What is not divulged is presented in this chapter. We look behind and beyond the public information on the agencies. For example, ratings as forward-looking symbols are necessarily qualitative in nature and not the result of strict formulae. Ratings may lag behind what the markets already know about an issuer, but there are many reasons for that.

What makes a rating 'right' or 'wrong' is a matter of conjecture, depending on who is asked, the time horizon selected and the perspective of the bond markets. The answer is not as simple as agency critics and regulators assume.

Moody's, Fitch and S&P do, from time to time, differ on ratings assigned to a particular issuer, making for 'split' ratings. The reasons for these divergences are disclosed here.

Since 1985 the agencies have been practicing a market-penetration method called unsolicited ratings. The overriding objective is to expand business globally, but it is controversial and can be a none too subtle form of client coercion. We examine the reasons behind this tactic and its current somewhat more mellow status.

Finally, we examine a few agency practices and discover that ratings are not really globally comparable, stable outlooks on ratings are not really stable and the agencies do not have the time or manpower to constantly monitor all the issuers they have rated, despite their claims to do so.

For we know in part, and we prophesy in part.

2.1 Inherent subjectivity

Credit ratings encompass both quantitative and qualitative factors – channelled through the experience of the analyst. The result of this mix is a subjective judgment of an entity's credit quality. It is not a question of whether ratings are subjective or not – they certainly are. The agencies admit that credit ratings are just their opinions. The real issue is, how good is the judgment and analysis behind the ratings? How experienced and qualified are the people offering these opinions? In any profession, some opinions are worth more than others.

Informed guesswork behind ratings

Subjectivity is often cast as a pejorative element in ratings, when instead subjectivity is inherent and necessary in ratings. For example, there is a lot of room for interpretation in assessing: (i) the competence of senior management of a company and its competitive environment; (ii) the quality of political leadership and level of financial acumen among ministries of finance; and (iii) the credit quality of the assets and liabilities of banks in emerging markets. Informed guesswork is a natural part of the rating decision.

The only alternative is simply a quantitative model based on all the numbers available. The trouble here, of course, is that there is no such thing as a purely quantitative model of credit quality, since human interpretation needs to be applied to any model. How many variables are relevant and what weights should be assigned to them? Which financial ratios are more robust and for which type of borrower? How do you compare the cash flow of a private corporate borrower in Germany with the cash flow of a state-owned Australian utility or with the 'cash flow' of the Brazilian central government?

The famed economist, Ludwig von Mises called economic forecasting 'questionable conjectures'. The rating agencies might go so far as to adhere to the following statement in a similar guise: all economic models are useless because they fail to account for the coercive and distorting effect of government interventions, such as the tax code and the weight of federal bureaucracies. And many economic models fail to incorporate what is now termed the 'behavioural finance' of fear and greed.

> You cannot extrapolate any curves in which the human element appears.
>
> *Barbara Tuchman*

Statistics and ratings

It follows then that *ratings are not statistically driven*. Statistics are just a starting point to the analysis. Statistics are by nature historical and lack currency. Statistics are even subject to disagreement among professional data gatherers and are subject to revision periodically; hence, it is not even suitable to rely on the assumption that today's statistics are the last word. Checklists and ratios and formulas may be used for comparative purposes, but they do not generate an automatic rating conclusion. The danger in rating decisions would be to rely on statistics too much.

Even if ratings were based 90% on numbers and ratios, which they are not, the role of the rating analyst is to bring his or her expertise to the table and judge which factors are more important than others, given the issuer's operating environment and competitive context. Human analysts, not computers, make the rating decision based on all the qualitative and quantitative factors known. Ted Young, a Moody's analyst and executive for 20 years with expertise in financial institutions, said, 'We didn't upgrade or downgrade anyone based just on the numbers or ratios. We tried to get behind the numbers to see the strengths and weaknesses that generated them'.

Perhaps the most important qualitative factor in a rating decision is the 'quality' of the management team running the business, bank or government. You cannot assign a number to that. As an ex-Moody's financial institutions vice president stated it succinctly, 'The numbers are just a flash, a moment in time that can change in a hurry so you have to look beyond them to management style.'

In its publication 'Corporate finance criteria,' S&P forthrightly states: 'The [rating] judgment is qualitative in nature, and the role of the quantitative analysis is to help make the best possible overall qualitative judgment, because ultimately, a rating is an opinion.'

As a former Managing Director of Moody's once wrote, 'Ratings are projections or estimates of future reality based on a series of assumptions. Hence, they're essentially subjective'. Scott Bugie, a former bank analyst with 25 years' experience at S&P, opined that 'Bank and sovereign ratings are all about economics and politics, the soft social sciences' and are, therefore, inherently qualitative.

In sum, the subjective side of a rating decision is evident when one considers that:

- the rating scale is ordinal and issuers are judged relative to their peers;
- assessing an issuer's forecasts and assumptions requires personal input;
- analysts bring their prior experience, opinions, personalities, and degrees of common sense and scepticism to the exercise;
- statistics are historical, sometimes unreliable, and subject to revision and disagreement among experts;
- forecasting political developments is supremely qualitative; and
- evaluating future behaviour and forecasting trends and conditions is inherently expectational.

Bottom line for issuers: what is central to a rating decision is how the rating agencies perceive the suitability and credibility of your policies and how they perceive the capabilities of senior management to effect them. The use of subjective criteria by the international credit rating agencies (CRAs) permits them to conveniently weigh variables any way they want. This situation often results in split ratings (see 'What causes split ratings').

Issuers need to know which variables the agencies deem most crucial and which subjective criteria they tend to use, what the agencies are looking for when they make this assessment, and how to alter their perceptions in your favour.

2.2 Projected performance

All rating agencies are criticised to some degree for basing ratings on future financial performance. How is it possible for the agencies to accurately forecast a country's budgetary position one or two years out? How can they know a bank's future earnings or a company's future operating margins or market share? When no one can foresee the future, is it fair to rate an issuer based on projections rather than on current numbers?

The obvious answer is that making forecasts is an inherent part of the rating business. If you are measuring an issuer's capacity to repay a five-year bond, you have to make an effort to predict the issuer's future cash flow that can support repayment of that bond (*ability to repay*). Then you have to gauge whether the issuer would indeed use this anticipated cash flow to actually make a debt payment as opposed to directing payments to other needs (*willingness to repay*). Analysts need to use their judgment and manifest a healthy degree of scepticism. Ratings cannot be based on past repayment performance because then they would have low value to investors.

The basis of forecasts

Forecasts are a guessing game. When analysts forecast from past data, they are assuming that people's responses to past events will be repeated. Forecasting models rely on statistical relationships that held true in the past and may not hold true any longer, for example, the recent sub-prime mortgage debacle. It is easy to do a straight-line extrapolation from recent trends. The hard part is getting the inflection points right, that is, the sharp breaks with the past, such as the important turning points in recessions, fiscal balances and current account deficits. The Asian financial crisis of 1997 to 1998 showed how hard it is. There is no Quicken for creditworthiness.

In making future estimates of debt servicing and repayment, what do the agencies rely on? They look at the past (the issuer's track record) as one indicator of future behaviour, and they look at current management's projections and credibility. The past record is a given, but the future can only be expressed as an opinion. The result is a judgment call by the analyst and the rating committee. Willingness to pay debt on time in the future cannot be directly measured. How much weight do the agencies place on management's opinion of debt servicing disposition and capacity in reaching their own opinion? Do the agencies accept management's assurances and scenarios, or do they trim them with a 'haircut'?

It is common knowledge that forecasts are almost always wrong, especially those concerning the future, the weather and the economy. Hence, for the agencies it is not important whether an issuer's forecasts are accurate or not. What is important is *how* the forecast is structured (especially assumptions), because this tells the analyst how the company thinks and what the level of their technological sophistication is.

Lesson for issuers

Issuers should provide a range of forecasts (high, medium, low) with assumptions explicitly explained. Management should also provide probabilities as to the likelihood of the forecasts being reasonably accurate. Gaining credibility with the agencies is a process.

2.3 Ratings as lagging indicators

When the rating agencies downgrade an issuer's debt rating, they often find themselves the target of criticism by market players as being 'too late' in their rating actions. The critics maintain that the agencies are not telling them anything they did not already know. They say the downgrades 'lag' the market's knowledge. The agencies are just confirming what has already transpired and what the market has already priced in. In other words, ratings are often viewed as 'lagging indicators', not the predictive tool they are supposed to be.

Agency response

The agencies reply to the accusation this way: ratings reflect *the capacity to manage debt loads*, not reactions to current market swings, changes in bond or stock prices, shifts of ministers, or recent fluctuations in GDP and exchange rates. A rating is not a pricing or trading decision – 'we're not in business to provide market arbitrage opportunities'. Ratings are not to be viewed as a comment on investor preference and suitability and are not designed to reflect changes in the market value of a security in the secondary markets, which often swing on 'noise' and technical matters of liquidity. To call ratings 'lagging indicators' is a *common misreading of the intent* of a rating. Fundamentally, ratings measure the likelihood of default on a fixed income instrument; they do not measure current investor sentiment.[1]

We would add that the agencies can legitimately be accused of sometimes responding slowly and cautiously to macro-economic and financial developments in the countries and non-sovereign issuers they cover. The same as analysts everywhere, they can be deliberate in recognising trends. They may move only after the debt markets have already perceived and reflected important changes through the pricing of securities. An example might be the delay in downgrading Japan from Aaa in 1998, a deferral that lasted more than two years after the comparative data indicated a downgrade was warranted.

Why ratings are 'late'

There are several reasons for this perceived tardiness in rating changes. First and most broadly, the agencies are reluctant to change ratings for reasons that may be built on shifting grounds. They try to look at an issuer's long-term track record before they move the rating up or down. They attempt to see the broader picture and try to balance their long-term view with the market's current perspective. Rating committees will not agree to rating changes unless there is some concrete basis to support the decision.

Second, due to the nature of data gathering, there are inevitable delays before the evidence is on the analyst's desk. The data produced by issuers (for example, quarterly profit and loss (P&L) statements, balance of payments figures, budgetary results) take weeks, if not months, to assemble, be approved by local authorities and then disseminated, even with the speed of the internet.

Third, it takes time for the primary analyst to determine if the data comprise enough evidence to justify a rating change; anecdotal evidence does not suffice. Then it takes more time to prepare the case for a rating change and present it to a rating committee. The equity markets and secondary bond markets may move on the news of the day, but ratings do not and should not.

Thus, while markets can move quickly, and sometimes disproportionately, on rumours, the agencies spend time trying to understand the underlying financial strengths and verifiable facts. Just because the market reacts faster than the agencies to some news does not mean the market better reflects the underlying default risk. In any case, the result is the 'timing disconnect' between the agencies and the bond market.

To narrow this timing disconnect, the rating agencies have 'watch lists' that inform investors which ratings are under scrutiny for potential changes. In that way, investors have some sense that a rating may change in the near future, giving the agencies time to do a full examination.

Two more reasons why ratings are perceived as lagging, and these are not usually mentioned, are that:

1 the agencies would rather have stable ratings than volatile ones. They do not want to change ratings frequently, because oft-changing ratings seem capricious and imply the agencies cannot make up their minds or are reacting to transient phenomena; and
2 the agencies do not want to downgrade paying clients and make them unhappy.

Credibility is the agencies' lifeblood. The agencies would rather have ratings sit at a relatively lower level than risk embarrassment at a rating perceived by the market as too high. They want to avoid 'type 1' errors (rating something high that defaults), which is worse from a reputational standpoint than 'type 2' errors (rating something too low that never defaults.) Finally, from a career perspective, there is less incentive for an analyst to recommend an upgrade than a downgrade.

---

[1] S&P's former Chief Credit Officer, Clifford M Griep made this important distinction: 'The rating process must consider market sentiment to the extent that market sentiment indicates *a fundamental change in asset value or expectations for cash generation*. However, ratings that merely reflect prevailing market sentiment would add no value to the marketplace.' [Italics added.] Thus, S&P tracks market trends to determine if major swings in investor sentiment are happening but does not change ratings based just on that. S&P, *CreditWeek*, 6 March 2002, p. 34.

2.4 What makes a rating right?

Issuers often feel their credit rating from one of the international rating agencies is too low. Based on their peers' ratings, their rating would be 'right,' they argue, if it were a notch or two higher. The agency usually disagrees, believing: (i) that due process was followed in the assignment of the rating; and (ii) that a lower rating protects them from having to alienate investors by later downgrading the issuer's rating. The agencies will not verbalise the second, of course, focusing instead on issuer-specific risks.

So the question arises, when is a rating right and when is it wrong? Let us address both questions.

Since credit ratings are opinions, differences in ratings are natural and legitimate. As many as half of the sovereign ratings assigned by S&P and Moody's are different, and up to 25% of their corporate ratings differ by one or two notches. There is no consistent pattern to determine which agency is more conservative overall, that is, assigns lower ratings.

Right ratings

A rating is not 'right' just because the rating committee came to a decision, unanimous or otherwise. Such a decision may appear off base within months. Conversely, a rating decision that was internally controversial at the time may, with the passage of years, appear to have been an obvious call.

So when rating agencies disagree, investors and issuers may ask – which one is right? Unfortunately, there is no simple answer. In fact, the best answer is, 'neither one is wrong'. Ratings do not need to be consistent from one rating agency to another. The agencies can all be 'correct' insofar as their ratings reflect consistently applied criteria and peer comparisons.

> Ratings are 'right' if they are based on peer comparisons and have market acceptance.

What a rating agency needs to do in order to prove that its ratings are 'right' is to ensure that the ratings: (i) are consistently assigned within the particular class of issuer, for example, commercial banks; (ii) are consistent with their internal ratings methodology; and (iii) have market acceptance over time. To accomplish these ends, the rating agencies strive to apply a number of criteria.

1 The analysts must be experts in a particular discipline, such as banking or economics.
2 The factors and assumptions behind rating decisions must be explicitly stated.
3 Both the criteria used and the peer comparisons made should be provided so that investors can understand the factors supporting a rating and can anticipate to some extent what circumstances might lead to rating changes.
4 The rating process needs to have a large measure of input from experienced local analysts and not rely solely on the headquarters analytical team. The global perspective is crucial in major issuer categories, such as cars, petroleum, telecommunications and sovereigns, so that the relative ranking is correct.

5 Ratings should be determined by a broadly-based committee with experience across sectors so that no single country or individual perspective carries undue influence on the outcome. A diversity of perspectives in the rating committee produces a higher quality rating.

6 The rating rationale should disclose whether or not the rating process has involved the full co-operation of the management team of the rated entity. This information helps investors to weigh the quality of the information on which the rating is based.

7 The larger the pool of rated entities and the longer the history of the rating agency, the more credible the ratings are. Default statistics and transition studies illustrate the validity of ratings, and the agencies 'live off' these correlations. Ratings have historically proven to be accurate since numerous studies show a high correlation between ratings and actual default experience.[1]

It is easier to determine when a rating is 'right' from the standpoint of an issuer. First of all, it is not necessarily the highest rating. For an issuer, the right rating is the highest sustainable rating that allows the issuer to implement its business and financial strategy (including debt leverage) over the long term without unreasonable financial constraints, that is, to retain access to outside funds, to keep funding costs appropriate to the risk, and to generate an adequate return to shareholders. That is the optimal rating – the highest one possible and sustainable given the debtor's current internal and external circumstances, goals and prospects. Issuers should strive for optimal ratings.

The bond market's view

If history has shown that ratings accurately measure default risk, and if the agencies follow risk-averse policies internally, then it looks like the agencies' ratings are 'right' after all. But there needs to be one final reality check – acceptance in the market place.

If a rating is in tune with market perception, that is, the underlying security trades at a level roughly commensurate with its rating in a given interest rate context, then investors and traders in the bond market do not question whether the rating is right or wrong. If the market 'buys' the rating as reasonable, then it is validated. Data on spreads in basis points between variously rated corporate bonds and US Treasuries show a rising spread the lower the rating, as it should be.

However, investors, dealers and traders begin to question the rating when it fluctuates over a brief period, or when the new or changed rating is out of sync with market perceptions and bond pricing. Of course, views change as events evolve. Unforeseen happenings prompt a recalculation of probabilities. As famed economist, John Maynard Keynes aptly phrased it, 'When I get more evidence, I sometimes change my mind'.

This market check is not completely 'clean' since the agencies influence market perception and vice versa. Moreover, bond pricing, and in particular spreads from the risk free rate benchmark, are influenced by the supply of and demand for issues, not just by ratings. But this reality check – market discipline – is a good proxy for whether or not a rating is 'right'.

---

[1] There have been many academic and quantitative studies showing how closely credit ratings predict default risk (ex post), even controlling for type of issuer, type of debt and time period covered. For example, S&P gathered the records on all sovereign defaults from 1975 through to 2012 and published the results online on 29 March 2013. They showed that no AAA or AA credits had defaulted over any 10-year period and that only 4.2% of entities rated single A, only 4.8% of BBBs, 10.2% of those rated BB, and 28.7% of those rated single B have defaulted over 10 years. The trend validates the agencies' contention that ratings are very good predictors of the risk of default. Exhaustive data on this topic can be found on the CRA websites.

2.5 What makes a rating wrong?

As we have seen, what makes a credit rating 'right' depends on one's perspective:

- For the *rating agencies*, a rating is right if it does not embarrass them in the market, that is, neither too high nor too low but within market expectations and one that stands up with the passage of time. Right ratings are much more likely when the agencies apply their internal methodologies consistently, using peer comparisons to deduce relative creditworthiness.
- For an *issuer*, the right rating is one that is optimal, that is, the best achievable given the issuer's circumstances.
- For *investors*, a rating is right if it is broadly consistent with pricing in the secondary market. However, investors focusing only on this aspect may be making a mistake, since rating agencies often identify risks or strengths that the market has not properly appreciated.

Wrong ratings

> It is almost impossible to prove that someone in the rating business is wrong.
> *Robin Munro-Davies, Managing Director, IBCA, Financial Times, 29 January 1992*

In certain respects, it is easier to determine when a rating is 'wrong'. Despite Mr Munro-Davies' assertion, a rating is clearly wrong in two circumstances:

1 If a credit with investment-grade ratings defaults, such as, the defaults of more than US$2 billion worth of securities of the Washington Public Power Supply System in the 1980s which were initially rated Aaa/AAA and A1/A+. We also have the examples of WorldCom and Enron, but in these cases accounting fraud played a large role.[1]

2 If the credit has to be upgraded or downgraded by several notches within a short period of time, such as three downgrades within one year or a three-notch rating change all at once. An extreme example would be the 14 downgrades of Greece by Fitch and S&P in the period 2009 to 2012 as the global financial crisis swept southern Europe. Such large rating changes commonly mean the rating was not assigned correctly at the outset. Exceptions would include large rating changes driven by events such as a major debt-financed acquisition or product liability litigation.

Another example of this type of wrong rating was the Asian financial crash of 1997 to 1998 when the agencies missed several key indicators. They were asleep at the helm and should have noted:

- lack of disclosure by banks and public sector;
- poor bank supervision and regulation;
- poor bank asset quality; 'policy loans';
- distorted private sector investment decisions;
- high level of short-term borrowing and unbalanced maturity structure of debt; and
- enormous flows of 'hot money' moving into small, emerging market countries.

... and assigned lower ratings to begin with.

One cannot omit the recent financial crisis when ratings downgrades for sub-prime residential mortgage-backed securities dramatically exceeded those of corporate bonds carrying the same initial ratings. One survey showed that well over 50% of the sub-prime backed securities that started with single A ratings were subsequently downgraded, compared with well under 10% of the corporate bonds that started with the same ratings. Nearly all the corporates were downgraded just one notch to the next lowest category, for example, A to BBB, while more than four-fifths of the sub-prime securities dropped by three *categories*.

Most experts agree that far too many mortgage-backed securities received investment-grade ratings they did not deserve. The CRAs primarily blame the unprecedented nationwide housing downturn compounded by the underlying loans' short track record, which led to flaws in their computer models of risk. But others say common business practices at the agencies prodded them to act with bias and blinders.[2] This debate may never be resolved, but regulatory patches in agency operations have been inserted.

Negligent but infrequent

The rating agencies like to think there are no 'bad' ratings. All ratings offer information and credit perspective for the investor beyond the particular letter symbol. So a rating can act as a 'screen' for investors. If ratings are perceived by the market as 'wrong', it may be more appropriate to label them 'negligent'. Ratings are not done with malice aforethought and cannot be construed as the result of criminal behaviour. Therefore, we cannot expect legal penalties imposed on the agencies for their lax self-oversight or imperfect models.[3] However, after financial crises, politicians need scapegoats so politics enters the picture and one must then forecast with trepidation.

Neither of these two types of circumstances occurs very often. The fact that the agencies are still in business and relied upon by the investor community shows that the agencies simply do not make such obvious mistakes frequently. It would be catastrophic for the agencies if such errors became systematic.

Given the 'soft' and future-oriented nature of the rating process, it is clear that an issuer can do a lot to influence his debt ratings, that is, to nudge them in an optimal direction. Because subjective factors are central to the process, an issuer can help shape how the various elements of his business and credit condition are perceived and evaluated by the agencies. This is where learning to manage the rating agencies enters the picture.

If you think your rating should be higher, you have two choices: First, you can accept the fact that the agencies have a right to an opinion. Then you can get to work on meeting the agency's stated and unstated credit concerns so that next year you can argue for an upgrade.

> If issuers think we are wrong [in our rating], they are going to have to prove that we are missing something.
>
> *Don Noe, Head of international ratings at Moody's, March 1990*

Second, you can challenge the rating by going to the agencies with *new* and *compelling* information that convinces them to reconsider the existing rating. You need to show the agency that they missed some factors or there is important evidence they were unable to consider. And this has to be done quietly since agencies will not publicly admit that they got the rating wrong or that they changed the rating due to issuer pressure (see the 'Appeal process' in the Chapter 5). An appeal or challenge is best done between the time the rating committee reaches a decision and the result is published.

Ratings are a group activity. The rating process, including the rating committee and an internally consistent methodology, protects the agency by keeping rating judgments *relatively* consistent on an internal basis. The most important thing to expect from a rating agency is internal consistency. Ratings are likely 'wrong' when they are not consistent within the industry group or asset class. We will see in Chapter 3 that recent government regulatory moves are helping to improve consistency. Remember though that ratings do not need to be consistent from one rating agency to another, and there is no discernible way to forecast which agency will be lower on any class of rating.

Conscientious rating committee members often leave the meeting room wondering – did we make the right decision? Have we got the rating right? The answer to that question is simply – only time and the market will tell. A rating is just the professional opinion based on information known at the time and subjected to the agencies' criteria.

> The agencies do not strive to be right; they try not to be wrong.

Or as economist Keynes phrased it, 'It is better to be roughly right than precisely wrong'.

---

[1] CRA analysts do not search for pathological accounting practices. That is not part of their training or methodologies. They simply presume compliance by issuers with Generally Accepted Accounting Principles (GAAP) or International Financial Reporting Standards (IFRS) as attested by the auditor's report. In more recent years the CRAs have hired 'accounting specialists' who are conversant in the details of GAAP and IFRS to assist the rating teams.

[2] A former rating adviser to issuers and now rating analyst at one of the major rating agencies suggests that hubris also entered the picture – relying on models that had at their heart correlations among factors that were either not understood or were assumed to be correct. For example, a pool of home mortgages from New York, Florida and California were presumed to be diverse; yet when home prices fell, they affected all markets (presumed to be uncorrelated) driving more borrowers with 'option ARM' (adjustable rate mortgage) loans into bankruptcy and foreclosure as they could not refinance.

[3] Note that the Dodd–Frank Act of 2010 (see Chapter 3) does allow for the withdrawal of Nationally Recognised Statistical Rating Organisation (NRSRO) registration for classes of securities when fraud is determined by the Department of Justice.

2.6 What causes split ratings?

Why do the major agencies seem to disagree on the ratings of banks, companies and sovereigns more often than they agree? At one point the agencies differed by one notch or more on as many as two-thirds of international bank ratings and on more than half of sovereign ratings. Let us examine what causes so many 'split' ratings.

Sovereign foreign currency ratings separated by at least one notch have occurred between 45% and 55% of the time on issuers rated by both Moody's and S&P. In January 2000, for example, fully 60% of the 80 sovereigns that Moody's and S&P jointly rated had different foreign currency ratings; one-eighth of those were by two notches or more. The difference was even more striking in the domestic currency ratings of the Big Two, where 66% of their jointly rated sovereigns had different ratings, and 55% of these were by two notches or more.

Fast forward to September 2013. S&P rated 127 sovereigns and Moody's 124, of which 111 were rated by both. Of these 111 common ratings, 51 (or 46%) were split, 13 of them by two notches or more. Four or five notch differences in sovereign ratings are rare, but in this latest comparison, Greece and Slovenia showed such a gap. Moody's was the lower in both cases, indicating that these agencies hold vastly different outlooks on the politics and prospects for these two countries in the European debt crisis.

As at the end of 2012, Moody's and S&P differed even more on large bank ratings. Of the top 100 banks globally, the Big Two both rated 95 of them. Only 30 of the 95 ratings were the same, meaning split ratings amounted to 68%. Of the 65 different ratings, 25 were by two notches or more. This high rate of divergent bank ratings is most likely due to two factors: the CRAs' different sovereign ratings on the countries where the banks are domiciled, and differing levels of imputed or assumed support by the governments or shareholders in times of stress.[1]

When ratings are split by two or more notches, there is no evident pattern of closure of the gap. Sometimes the gap persists for years (for example, Cyprus, Sweden, Taiwan, Venezuela), and sometimes it lasts only months (for example, Lithuania, Qatar, Singapore, Turkey). Either agency could move first to bring convergence in the ratings gap, and that move might be up or down.

Fundamental discrepancies

The reasons behind split ratings are inherent in the rating process.

- Evaluations of creditworthiness are complex to begin with, more so in sovereign ratings than in bank or corporate ratings.
- Given the breadth of inferences possible on any set of facts or statistics, rating differences are due more to interpretation than to methodology.
- One agency may base its ratings more on past performance, statistical results, and historical trends, while the other may look more at expectations of future performance.
- One agency may place more weight analytically or subjectively on certain variables than the other does.

Frequently asked question

'To what extent are the rating agencies influenced by each other's ratings?'

Answer:

Analysts and rating committees do not have the time or inclination to rigorously follow the ups and downs of any other agencies' actions. They do not waste effort trying to match the others' ratings. It would be a serious skewing of their priorities and, if discovered, a serious blow to their credibility. They are aware that such activity would compromise their integrity and their independent voices.

However, analysts are certainly aware of the other agencies' ratings, but this knowledge does not drive their own rating decisions. Rating committees are interested when the other agency announces a new rating or initiates a rating *change*, but they are not necessarily persuaded by what the other agency did. If one agency lowers a rating first, the other agency may take a closer look at the credit to see if they have overlooked something, but this does not mean the second agency will follow suit. And even if the second agency does change the issuer's rating, it may not be for the same reasons. The agencies certainly do not coordinate rating reviews and rating announcements.

There are instances where both Moody's and S&P do appear to move in tandem with rating changes. But the explanations are simple. Both agencies:

1 evaluate the same information with similar methodologies and understand when the fundamentals and circumstances change;
2 tend to meet with issuers around the same time of the year, post-budget or post-annual report;
3 tend to move ratings as soon as they can justify it to show they are on top of matters; and
4 react similarly to occurrences they deem to be 'event-driven', such as corporate acquisitions funded by debt.

- The CRAs are independent of one another, and similarly analysts across Wall Street have been known to differ in their perceptions of companies and countries.
- With split bank ratings there can be differences in how the CRAs view sovereign risk as well as the rating benefit or 'uplift' from potential future government support of domestic banks.
- The agencies' own definitions of their ratings are quite similar but not identical, so one cannot expect a given set of facts to produce identical ratings. There are nuances and gradations in the language of what a certain rating means.
- Agency internal and procedural criteria differ as well.
- Unsolicited ratings, by their nature, which are based solely on publicly available information, are subject to wider variation in perceived creditworthiness.

Turning this around, one could say, since rating definitions vary slightly among the agencies, and since statistical data are always incomplete and historical by nature, and since individuals do the ratings (notwithstanding a rating committee), perhaps the question should be, why is it that so many ratings are the same? This is more than a rhetorical question but also more than we can adequately deal with in this space.

Investment grade or not?

If the rating agencies differ in their opinions by only one notch, the market does not see this as significant. The exception to this general rule is when there is a split with one rating above and the other below investment grade, for example, BBB–/Ba1 or Baa3/BB+. As at November 2013, the sovereign ratings of Indonesia, Morocco, Romania and Turkey are in this position, reflecting a basic inter-agency disagreement on what constitutes 'investment grade' for these particular issuers. An extreme example of a difference in agency perception was the four-notch difference in December 2013 between Moody's Ba1 and S&P's A minus ratings on Slovenia. Such a gap may be a record and is certain to narrow in coming months.

Two-notch differences, however, usually mean the agencies are making different assumptions, have different perceptions of the same data, or see the country's economy playing out differently going forward. These differences are based on subjective factors, such as weighting some variables more or less heavily. In such situations, cautious investors tend to base their portfolio decisions more on the lower rating since it is more likely to capture the 'worst case scenario.' Moody's knew this investor preference years ago and was sometimes more conservative in its ratings compared with S&P, hoping to ensure greater investor reliance on Moody's ratings.

Three takeaways

1 Because ratings of companies, banks and sovereigns frequently differ and because market convention is to seek two ratings, investors often seek a second rating. Its value is that it is independent of the first rating.
2 Split ratings are proof of the subjective and complex nature of ratings. Since there is no strict quantitative formula for determining ratings, issuers should be cognisant of the importance of 'managing' their ratings and the agencies.
3 Issuers have the ability to shape agency perceptions by taking a more proactive stance vis-à-vis the agencies and by preparing properly for due diligence meetings. Proper preparation means knowing what the agencies deem important and what they do *not* want to see or need to see. We deal with these matters in Chapter 4.

---

[1] Will someone volunteer to calculate how many of the thousands of municipal and company ratings are split by the Big Two as at 2013?

2.7 Unsolicited ratings

EuroRatings, a new European rating agency, opened its doors in London in 1987. Sponsored by Fitch of New York and credit insurer Cobac of Belgium, EuroRatings needed to make an impact at its London launch, so it announced 48 unsolicited ratings based only on publicly available information. This initiative provided a platform open to criticism but also laid the groundwork for EuroRating's own credibility in the fixed-income market.

However, it soon became clear that issuers in the Eurobond market did not need or want a rating. EuroRatings attempted to educate issuers about the importance of using a rating to obtain a more favourable reception from investors, but many Eurobond issuers were issuing relatively small bond issues and did not see major benefits in going through the rating process.

Only a few large corporations were issuing debt or commercial paper in Europe where ratings were neither in demand nor required for issuance in the Eurobond market. They saw no reason to get a rating, especially if it meant having to share their corporate secrets with a rating agency. Nor did most sovereign entities in Europe wish to enter the market without ensuring they would get a AAA. EuroRatings lasted only 18 months due to the management mistakes of its main shareholder (Fitch) and issuer reluctance to undergo the rating process. No true successor to EuroRatings has emerged (although a German company Feri EuroRatings is using the name).

Starting with sovereigns and euro yen issues in the late 1980s and moving on to corporations in the early 1990s, Moody's began to rate selected issues and issuers in new debt markets. Many of these ratings were done without the request of the issuer. Euphemistically called 'investor initiated ratings' (IIR), these unsolicited ratings were aimed at establishing a bridgehead overseas before Moody's main competitor S&P did. It was a clever but provocative way to open up markets for future ratings.[1] The idea was to extend the rating range down into the single A and Baa categories worldwide where there were few ratings at the time. Those assigned an unsolicited rating did not have to pay the agency a fee for the rating; it was Moody's gratis entrée or loss leader with expectations of future gains.

Moody's justification

Moody's thinking was that by assigning an IIR to a sovereign outside the US, other participants in that country (banks, corporations, provinces) would eventually see the benefits of a rating and would actually request a rating. These borrowers would have one of two motivations: fear that they may lose control of the rating process if they do not accede, or a competitive desire to join the race and try to achieve an equivalent or even higher rating than their peers who were already rated.

Moody's justified its IIRs in several ways.

1 Heavy investor pressure to expand our rating coverage has forced us to express an opinion on your credit. We are being told by investors that some information is better than no information.[2]
2 We want to raise market consciousness about ratings in new markets.

3 We want to correct what we see as misperceptions in the market of credit quality.

4 We want to provide a larger sample of ratings for broader comparative purposes.

Underlying these rationales is an implied threat: either co-operate with us by sharing all your data and holding a management briefing for us, or we will issue a rating anyway based on whatever information is publicly available. In other words, wake up and begin to examine the option of applying for a rating – which they will then have to pay for. Moody's was placing pressure on a particular unrated entity and in the process putting other issuers under pressure to get a rating. Recipients of unsolicited ratings called the practice 'blackmail,' but maybe they just didn't like the involuntary disclosure of their competitive information.

Justification number 4 – to provide a larger sample of ratings – is actually a valid reason for the practice of IIR, since the larger the pool of rated entities, the more robust the ordinal scale becomes. Of course, large samples up and down the rating scale should eventually generate large revenues, too. To put this into perspective, fewer than 5% of Moody's ratings are unrequested.[3]

Ratings are much more than an assessment of an issuer's public financial statements; they are about what a company's strategy is, what its plans are, and what its projections are. They are about the credibility of issuer management and their willingness and ability to address the risks facing the enterprise. An agency cannot get this information with an 'unsolicited' rating, that is, one that is imposed by an agency on an issuer without the issuer's consent, co-operation or participation in the rating process.

Therefore, while building this greater pool of rated entities over a period of years, the risk for Moody's (and for other CRAs that engaged in this practice) was that without a face to face assessment of management, the rating stands a good chance of being wrong, that is, not accepted by investors. But Moody's would say sotto voce as long as we have a good reputation in the market and as long as our IIR is unique, investors will acquiesce and buy into the opinion. The agency also calculated that it will not hurt if the capital markets perceive them as aggressive, fearless and innovative.

The US Department of Justice (DOJ) opened an investigation in March 1996 of Moody's much maligned method of rating public debt securities without the permission of the issuer. The question was whether implied 'threats' by Moody's to rate an issue or issuer without their full co-operation constitutes an attempt to generate fees through coercive tactics. Is it using improper leverage? When does such arm-twisting become uncompetitive behaviour and thus illegal? The DOJ subsequently urged the Securities and Exchange Commission (SEC) to require all the agencies to disclose when they assign these unsolicited ratings, the reason being that investors need to know when a rating is based on less than full information and co-operation from the issuer. The SEC now requires that disclosure by CRAs, in part also to permit smaller CRAs to use unsolicited ratings to gain market share and to enliven competition in the ratings industry.

Experience in several countries indicates that once ratings have penetrated a new market, regulators in that country are apt to require credit ratings as a precondition to borrowing in the capital markets (but not from banks) or to issuing shares of stock. The regulators readily see the benefits to the overall financial system of more thorough, independent 'audits' of the creditworthiness of key banks, corporates and municipalities. They favour the higher standards of disclosure and transparency required in today's globalised investment environment. Hence in the process, these regulators are actually assisting the CRAs to penetrate the market further.

Most issuers now realise they will eventually need a credit rating in order to access the public debt market and to maintain relations with key counterparties. Thus, the CRAs' policy of unsolicited ratings has paid off. The initial 'baptism by fire' may not be comfortable for issuers, but ratings do raise an issuer's profile and open important financing options.

Current practice

Given its antagonistic and controversial nature, do the CRAs still undertake unsolicited ratings? Given the success of this tactic in opening up new markets to rate and given that there is no regulatory prohibition, they certainly do continue to assign unrequested ratings. These ratings are done only infrequently, but they do cover all classes of issuer: banks, corporates, municipalities, provinces, and sovereigns anywhere in the world.

Today, *Moody's* website declares, 'As a publisher of opinions about credit, Moody's reserves the right to issue unsolicited Credit Ratings.' These ratings are limited to ones that Moody's initiates (not the rated entity) and to a first time rating for the entity. Unsolicited ratings are designated as such in the initial rating press release and on the website. Moody's determines the need for an unsolicited rating by assessing its 'usefulness to the capital markets and our determination that sufficient information is available to allow Moody's to assign and maintain the rating.' As recently as November 2012, Moody's rated Kenya, Nigeria and Zambia in this fashion.

A potential client for this service is contacted and invited to participate and told that Moody's will not seek or accept from the issuer remuneration for the rating for at least one year after publication of the credit rating. One wonders how many recipients of unsolicited ratings revert to the CRAs after one year and say, 'Ok, let's establish a full paying relationship.'

As for *S&P*, they initially opposed the practice of unsolicited ratings, calling them 'high handed and not a very good strategic move'.[4] Yet in the mid-1990s S&P tinkered at the edges with some unrequested 'assessments' and 'implied debt ratings' of non-rated issuers. Then in November 1996, acknowledging a loss of market share to Moody's, S&P announced it would begin assigning unsolicited ratings to emerging market banks, using a 'pi' notation to indicate that the local currency rating was based only on 'public information', not management assistance.

Today, S&P has relented and states in various online publications that they do unsolicited ratings when they think they 'have access to sufficient public information of reliable quality to support our analysis and ongoing surveillance, and we believe there is significant market interest in these government ratings'. Their rationale is twofold:[5]

1 to help investors be well informed on any and all of the financial instruments they may purchase; and
2 to provide ratings across an entity's capital structure in order to reduce instances of second-guessing or inferring what unrated debt obligations might be rated in any segment of the capital structure.

Similarly to Moody's, S&P reserves the right to do unsolicited ratings anywhere in the world and in any rating category (banks, corporates, local governments, and so on) for previously unrated issuers. However, this is reportedly a very infrequent practice.

Fitch's rationale for unsolicited ratings is:

1 unsolicited ratings are a fundamental element in the independence of rating opinions;
2 omission of [the public disclosure] of unsolicited ratings distorts rating portfolios, with a bias that will likely understate credit risk; and
3 exclusion of unsolicited ratings will also have a systemically negative impact on the number of rating opinions in the marketplace.

Fitch denies that their unsolicited ratings are predatory; per their website, these ratings are designed to build up market coverage and give investors alternatives in the rating market. The analytical and committee processes are identical for both solicited and unsolicited ratings, they say. Issuers are given the opportunity to participate directly in the rating process.

The CRAs' unsolicited sovereign ratings in Europe include Austria, Belgium, France, Germany, Italy, the Netherlands, Switzerland and the UK, as well as the cities of Oslo and Vienna and most cities and regions of Italy. S&P lists other sovereign ratings where they do not have a rating agreement with the government: Australia, Cambodia, India, Japan, Singapore and Taiwan. The full list of these ratings is found on the CRAs' websites, and they do span the globe, including such diverse countries as Argentina, Mauritius and the US.

Issuer options

An issuer receiving notification of a pending unsolicited rating by one of the CRAs has several options. The choice of option will depend on the issuer's current financing options and future borrowing plans. It will depend on the financing needs of domestic banks and corporations and their need or willingness to face international standards of disclosure. Initial advice is as follows.

1 Do not commit to any path before you have examined all your options and created a strategy. An element to factor in: the CRAs do not change ratings frequently, so if your first-time rating is lower than optimal, it will be difficult to raise it for several years.
2 Ignore the notification, refuse to meet with the CRA and abide by whatever the rating outcome is, which will most likely be a rating lower than a full exercise would generate.
3 Be responsive but non-committal, gaining time to make a well-considered decision.
4 Accede to the CRA's notice and confirm that you will not have to pay for the rating.
5 Tell the CRA that you prefer to acquire a 'real' rating and are willing to pay for it. That way you can control the timing and the presentation more.
6 Initiate delays in working with the agency. Request an information package and say you are considering engaging in a full relationship with the CRA, including meetings and full documentation, which you will pay for. Ask the CRA a series of questions and try to delay the due diligence meeting so that you can prepare better. For example, you could say you have serious reservations about the whole process, and ask, 'How can we have

confidence that a foreign CRA can fully understand our economic and financial dynamics while spending a few days in research prior to a visit and a few days on the ground here?'
7 Keep a record of all written and oral communication with the CRA to protect yourself and to have leverage with other CRAs.

Backing up one step, an issuer can pre-empt an unrequested rating by taking the initiative before receiving the unwelcome IIR notification. Simply call the nearest CRA office and ask for ratings information and a fee schedule. You could say, 'You know, we were thinking about getting a rating, but we need to know more about it first: the process, the criteria, and so on. Please send us some information, we'll look it over and get back to you.' Let the CRA think they may have a paying customer in the waiting room. This proactive approach is non-committal on your part while forcing the CRA to delay its unsolicited call.

---

[1] Australian Ratings, another small CRA in the early 1980s, used unsolicited ratings from the beginning in order to establish credibility in the market place. It was reported that Tom McGuire of Moody's travelled to London and saw the potential for opening up new markets this way, as EuroRatings was doing, and returned to New York to put Moody's on that path as well.

[2] The term 'IIR' was a misstatement in that investors did not beg Moody's for these ratings. IIR was a hard-nosed business decision to expand the Moody's franchise, couched in vague and misleading terms to justify the action.

[3] After all, it is costly for a rating agency to devote manpower and time to issuers who do not pay fees.

[4] Hendrik Kranenburg, Executive Vice President, Global Ratings Development at S&P, quoted in Monroe, A, 'When ratings are unsolicited', *Global Finance*, May 1990, p. 75.

[5] Paul Coughlin, Executive Managing Director, Global Analytics, S&P, 19 June 2012, S&P website.

2.8 Are ratings really globally comparable?

The rating agencies claim that they provide meaningful and accurate ordinal rankings on issuer creditworthiness no matter where in the world, no matter what type of issuer, and no matter what type of issue. How are the agencies able to produce ratings that have the same meaning around the world? The short answer to the question is: they try very hard but often fall short.

With the globalisation of information, the proliferation of the internet, and the abundance of data, the job of agency analysts has shifted from attempting to acquire information to attempting to effectively select and interpret it. In this task, they face the daunting job of comparing differing accounting systems as well as varying levels of disclosure around the world.

Easier said than done

The agencies say they make an explicit effort to 'look through' these different tax and accounting systems and produce a comparable framework for analysis. They say they have developed 'certain analytical tools' to make financial statements roughly comparable.

In fact, Moody's admitted in a letter to the International Accounting Standards Committee in April 1999: 'It is clear that differing accounting systems and methods across borders make comparisons of financial data very challenging, if not impossible... [It] is at least very time-consuming for the analyst, if not impossible within an economic effort [that is, very costly for the time and effort required].' For Moody's or any rating agency, this is quite a frank statement. Its implications are several.

1 To protect their reputations, the agencies need to say they adjust for differing tax and accounting systems in order to arrive at comparable ratings. However, agency analysts who cover banks, corporates and sovereigns are not generally trained as accountants or lawyers. Therefore, to save time and effort they are forced to make some broad assumptions, which should be disclosed. That is what 'adjusting' really means. As mentioned earlier the agencies now have on staff international accounting specialists to assist in rating assessments.
2 These adjustments and assumptions are usually not favourable to the issuer. In cases of doubt, the analyst always errs on the side of caution, that is, not favourable to the issuer. If the rating committee is not comfortable with these assumptions or with the transparency and accuracy of the financial data they are examining, the safest approach is to assign a rating that is one or two notches lower than it would otherwise be if the data were clearer and more comparable.
3 Given the lack of standardisation of accounting systems worldwide and the large element of subjective 'adjustment' the agencies need to make, issuers may pay higher risk premiums, which investors usually require in the face of uncertainty.

2.9 Stable outlooks are not stable

One expects upgrades to follow from positive outlooks and downgrades to follow from negative outlooks, and they usually do – between 65% to 80% of the time. What investors and issuers do not expect is for rating changes to occur from a *stable* outlook. Yet, this happens more often than one might suppose.

Exhibit 2.1 shows how frequently the three international rating agencies have changed sovereign ratings when the outlook was stable on the country's debt. The time periods covered are different because each agency started assigning outlooks at different times. Nonetheless, the data points are sufficient and time periods overlap enough for us to draw some conclusions.

S&P and Fitch keep a running public record on their websites of their sovereign rating changes, while Moody's still lags behind in updating its historical rating information. S&P wins the prize for the longest and least ambiguous record of sovereign rating changes.

Exhibit 2.1

Rating changes from stable

	Moody's	*S&P*	*Fitch*
Period covered	March 1997 to February 2004	June 1989 to December 2005	September 2000 to December 2005
Number of upgrades	85	163	96
Number from stable outlook	25	59	39
Percent from stable outlook	29.4%	36.2%	40.6%
Number of downgrades	64	127	44
Number from stable outlook	19	21	7
Percent from stable outlook	29.7%	16.5%	15.9%

Source: Author's own

The evidence shows that a country is most likely to be upgraded from stable by Fitch and most likely to be downgraded from stable by Moody's.[1]

Here are some possible explanations for this phenomenon of rating changes from 'stable'.

1 Events move too fast in some countries for the agencies to keep up.
2 An agency may be forced to play 'catch up' with the market after having missed a key trend or development in the country.
3 Economic and political change are more volatile in countries below investment grade, and rating changes, even from stable, reflect that accurate and up-to-date information for assessing creditworthiness is less available in those countries that had the most frequent 'unexpected' upgrades or downgrades.

4 To upgrade from stable is emblematic of the agencies' caution and their preference to move one step at a time, whereas to downgrade from stable seems to be more of an analytical error on the agencies' part, for example, insufficient weight given to a key variable. Or the 'error' could be on the issuer's part by not keeping the agency apprised of the latest negative developments.

Lesson for issuers

Whatever the explanation, the lesson is – you cannot be complacent with a stable outlook. An issuer needs to keep the CRAs informed at all times to avoid a downgrade from stable.

Clearly, the odds for an upgrade are better if your outlook is positive, but the feat can be accomplished from a stable position as well. To be upgraded from a stable outlook position requires: (i) economic and debt performance exceeding expectations; (ii) a good case built and presented by the issuer; and (iii) the rating agency's ability to perceive these.

As a final note, one should understand that reaching a positive outlook in no way guarantees that an upgrade will follow. Exhibit 2.2 shows the number of sovereigns that have 'lost' their positive outlook when the agencies pulled them back to stable. The time periods covered are the same as in Exhibit 2.1.

Exhibit 2.2

From positive to stable outlook

	Number of positive outlooks withdrawn	*Examples among rated sovereigns*
Moody's	12	Korea and Costa Rica 2003; India and Indonesia 2001; Romania 1998
S&P	33	Turkey 4 times; Suriname 2003; Mongolia 2002; Iceland 2001
Fitch	7	Croatia 2005; Poland 2004; Ecuador 2003; Malaysia 2001

Source: Author's own

Lesson for issuers

The agencies can change their minds and outlooks swiftly when new information becomes available, so it pays for issuers to supply the CRAs with the right information on a timely basis. That helps insure against mistakes in outlooks (or worse) and enhances the odds for an upgrade.

---

[1] Data for periods later than those shown here can be found throughout Gaillard, N, *A Century of Sovereign Ratings*, 2011, Springer.

2.10 The myth of monitoring

One myth the rating agencies propagate is that ratings are 'monitored continuously'. The key word is 'continuously'. The reality is that following outstanding credits is really a case of 'catch-up', meaning the analyst tries to keep up with developments as best he/she can, given their heavy workload. For example, one analyst can be responsible for covering 30 to 40 rated companies or 15+ sovereign issuers. Even with access to the internet every day, no analyst can stay on top of meaningful information at a company, a bank or a country.[1]

There was one sovereign analyst at Moody's who was responsible for covering 19 different sovereigns and supranationals with a report due on each one annually. The analyst was unable to conscientiously monitor them all, let alone visit each one as part of mandatory due diligence.[2]

Equity analysts on Wall Street are more likely to stay up to date on the companies they follow compared with the bond analysts at the rating agencies. In part, this is due to the number of supporting junior analysts assigned to the equity research team. Rating agency credit analysts are just not plugged into daily developments as well as equity analysts are. Then again, the agencies take a time perspective longer than the next quarter's results. The equity analyst is attempting to recommend buy-sell orders in the short-term, while the bond analyst attempts to look deeper into trends relative to peers over the longer term.

Monitoring existing ratings is the weak link in the rating process. It is not a priority for them to follow developments in the market that might affect outstanding rated securities. Rated entities are required to regularly send their latest financial data to the agencies, but it is only when the credit metrics at the CRAs flag something unusual or out of an expected normal range that an analyst will undertake a more thorough review.

Evidence of the agencies' approach to credit surveillance was provided by a former Moody's official who was head of compliance at the agency. He testified before Congress in September 2009 that 'Moody's does not adequately monitor credit ratings it assigned to tens of thousands of municipal bonds'. The agencies' practice of non-surveillance is not limited to municipal bonds.

Instead, the incentive is to put effort into *new* ratings, to build the agency's portfolio relative to competitors, rather than look after already-acquired clients. In sum, 'continuously monitored' means more like 'periodically reviewed' or 'occasionally assessed'... if time permits.

The important counterbalance to this lack of full-time attention is that the analysts are actually held responsible for following their credits closely, and they could lose their job if surprises appear that make the agency look like it was asleep on the job.

The long-standing 'issuer-pays' framework indirectly reinforces the tendency for the agencies *not* to pay more attention to outstanding ratings. The reason is that the issuer pays the agency an annual 'maintenance fee' in advance to monitor the credit. All issuers have is the agencies' word that they are actually monitoring their credit. The author is not aware of any issuer who has asked an agency for proof of this continual surveillance.[3]

Lesson for issuers

If the agencies are not following your credit condition carefully, what does this mean for you as an issuer? Agency negligence means they will not be aware in a timely way of positive and/or negative developments affecting your creditworthiness. This situation could postpone your getting an upgrade and it could even hasten a downgrade. The agencies are reactive to new information while issuers must be proactive.

---

[1] Just after the structured finance debacle, authors Joe Nocera and Bethany McLean wrote, 'The analysts in structured finance were working 12 to 15 hours a day. They made a fraction of the pay of even a junior investment banker. There were far more deals in the pipeline than they could possibly handle. They were overwhelmed. Moody's top brass... wouldn't add staff because they didn't want to be stuck with the cost of employees if the revenues slowed down.' See *All the Devils Are Here, the Hidden History of the Financial Crisis*, 2010, Penguin p. 123.

[2] Reacting to regulatory pressures and the fact that they realised they missed key trends in Europe, Moody's doubled its staff of sovereign analysts to more than 50 between 2008 and 2013.

[3] In its annual examination of the CRAs, the SEC, however, does require proof of a once a year review of rated credits.

Steps to take and questions to ask

Steps to take now:

1

2

3

4

5

Follow-up questions to ask:

1

2

3

4

5

Chapter 3

Convictions and regulations

Précis

Since the late 1990s, full disclosure and transparency of accounts have become a higher hurdle for issuers and rating agencies. Both are now subject to much closer scrutiny, and failure to comply has financial consequences.

Rating methodologies are available online, but the credit rating agencies' (CRAs) beliefs and assumptions behind them are not always clear. These standards and norms determine all ratings on banks, companies and governments. The agencies' conventions and deeply held tenets with respect to corporate and banking issuers underpin their whole approach to ratings. For example, they believe that ratings are an assessment of management. As to size of the issuer, bigger is better.

Topics covered here include the importance of a risk management culture within rated entities, the key statistical measures in corporate and bank rating analysis, how good governance affects ratings, corporates and banks in emerging markets, the critical due diligence meeting with the CRAs, and the determinants of upgrades and downgrades.

Finally, critics of the CRAs have levelled many charges of incompetence, conflicts of interest and worse against the agencies since the 1990s. We examine and opine on those allegations. Meanwhile, government regulators in Europe and the US have stepped up efforts to supervise and oversee the rating agencies, with mixed results.

Plus ça change, plus c'est la même chose.

3.1 Transparency – the higher hurdle

Since the Asian financial meltdown of 1997 to 1998, the rating agencies have become a potent force in demanding transparency in the accounts of issuers they rate. In order to ensure the accuracy of their analyses, not to mention their reputation, they have placed more emphasis on clearer data and more open accounting conforming to international standards.

Having been embarrassed by their belated and rapid downgrades in Asia at that time and then by several investment-grade corporates that went bankrupt, and then by the financial meltdown of 2008 to 2010, the agencies have since insisted on greater disclosure from all clients and have penalised those who do not comply.

The rating agencies, along with the International Monetary Fund (IMF) at the international level, are a potent force in demanding transparency. The CRAs monitor whether new systems of financial control are in place. Is management following their announced plans? Are the governance structures in place exerting sufficient control to prevent fraudulent financial statements? They are digging deeper to determine if lending decisions are based on commercial viability or political priorities.

Guide to agency thinking

From the broadest perspective on the subject of transparency, the agencies are guided by these beliefs:

- markets increasingly penalise those financial institutions who do not fully disclose key items, such as loan quality;
- transparency of financial accounts (meaning 'clear, open, complete') is very important to counterparties;
- without complete and credible information, investors assume the worst;
- transparency builds confidence; secrecy breeds caution; and
- capital flows to those financial institutions whose data conform to international standards.

It follows that:

- without transparent accounts, an issuer's real liabilities are unknown. For example, what obligations has the government undertaken outside the budget, such as, pensions, guarantees?
- without a willingness to disclose, an issuer is likely hiding evidence affecting its rating; and
- without good internal governance, the foundation of an institution will be shaky and hence its debt-repayment capacity unstable.

At the issuer level, the CRAs have responded with:

- more aggressive questioning of off balance sheet transactions, contingencies and obligations;
- less willingness to accept company borrowing plans based on their *projected* growth in cash flows, assessing risk instead on historical performance, liquidity and assets; and

- stronger focus on the relationship between a banking system's non-performing loans and how regulators might respond to the possibility of systemic shocks when a large domestic bank seems about to fail.

One could sum up this orientation by saying there is more pressure on the agencies to be rigorous and 'tough' and even more sceptical now when a CFO says, 'Trust me on this one'.

Main lessons

The many lessons for issuers should be apparent from the above.

1 Issuers should expect greater validation and confirmation of disclosure standards and practices.
2 Do not become a casualty to any of these examples of poor transparency:
   - delays in financial reporting or the absence of quarterly and semi-annual updates;
   - misleading treatment of expenses;
   - asset or liability exposures not reflected in the statements;
   - no consolidation of the financial results of related companies;
   - lax accounting practices, especially relating to loan losses or loan impairment;
   - lack of independent outside auditors;
   - lack of clear ownership interests and hidden related party lending;
   - undisclosed derivatives activity or missing footnotes to the accounts;
   - lack of timely information about material events when they occur; and
   - opaque footnotes to accounts.
3 The rating agencies will punish issuers that produce opaque budgets and balance sheets or who submit overly optimistic forecasts.
4 Issuer assumptions underlying projections of future revenues and costs will be scrutinised and generally given 'haircuts' to reduce typical management optimism.
5 The agencies will reward those issuers whose financial assumptions are realistic and whose data are complete and current.[1]
6 Issuers should explain how they determine acceptability of counterparty risk. They should volunteer information about this and other topics of concern to the agencies. Being proactive means not waiting for them to raise the matter. Giving the agencies a short, incomplete or dismissive response will hurt your rating.
7 It is in the interest of national governments everywhere to insist on transparency because it brings: (i) the right prices for debt issued and traded; (ii) more foreign direct investment; and (iii) more stability in the economy.

With all this pressure over the past 15 years from the rating agencies, regulators and multi-lateral financial institutions, such as the IMF, how have governments, corporations and banks responded? The compliance record appears mixed. Fixed income borrowers and regulators in the EU have moved the most rapidly to adopt market-based rules and practices with regard to financial accounting. However, most emerging markets appear to be only lethargically and grudgingly surrendering to the demand for more open accounts.[2]

The reason appears to be that vested interests in these markets actually favour less transparency. Bank managers complain that it costs money to institute accurate and detailed accounting systems and to pay for auditors. Their poor loan portfolios would be revealed. Transparency also restricts management's ability to engage in self-sustaining practices, such as loans to politicians, friends and family. Companies argue that fully transparent accounting might reveal their strategies or vulnerabilities to competitors. Governments do not want to show their subsidies to loss-making state-owned enterprises or projects.

There is widespread verbal agreement about the long-term benefits of open accounts, but it is those pesky short-term impacts that hinder progress. In the meantime, the rating agencies will continue to assign low(er) ratings to those who lag behind this inevitable trend.

In the light of the stronger emphasis on transparency, we now turn to how the agencies perceive the accounts and the management of rated companies and banks where good governance is an important factor in the rating.

---

[1] The agencies will also be rewarding themselves in a more transparent world. First, ratings would be less volatile with less risk to their reputations. Second, the agencies are able to get more of their data reliably from the internet and other public sources without the costs associated with onsite visits. Taking this a step further, fewer analysts could cover more issuers.

[2] Paul Coughlin, S&P's Managing Director in Hong Kong commented in July 1997 during the Asian financial crisis, when alluding to Chinese mainland firms that have listed in Hong Kong, 'there really is no culture of disclosure, especially with state-backed companies'.

3.2 Agency convictions on corporations

This section will cover a broad range of matters that corporates, rated or not, should ponder if they want to understand how the agencies view their financials and what variables are leveraging in the rating decision.

The agencies rate the debt of a multitude of issuers in industries ranging from aerospace and cars to telecom and transportation as well as electric, gas and water utilities. Methodologies differ somewhat by industry, but there is a single theme running throughout – a conservative predisposition toward those they rate, an analytic inclination to distrust. This predilection manifests itself in two ways.

- *First*, the agencies focus solely on credit risk. Because they are a service principally for fixed income investors, the agencies try to uncover trends or events that will have a negative impact on credit quality. Almost any occurrence, for example, sudden shifts in senior management or corporate strategy, an acquisition or divestiture, a missed budget target, could suffice as a proxy for heightened credit risk and an excuse or opportunity to lower a rating.
- *Second*, an analyst will be criticised within the agency for ratings in his portfolio of issuers that are deemed too high, either by the market or in relation to rated peers. However, an analyst will not be criticised for ratings perceived as too low. The reason is that higher ratings have a greater potential to embarrass the agencies if something goes wrong with the issuer. It is built-in protection to have ratings almost a notch or so lower than perhaps merited so there is a 'cushion' against potential bad news. That is like an agency's admitting that an issuer's actual rating is a notch or two higher than the one made public. Remember that a fixed income investor's only possible compensation against credit risk misestimating is a slightly higher interest rate on the securities. Corporate issuers can reduce or eliminate this gap using the recommendations provided here.

Fundamental conventions

The agencies bring to the task of rating companies a set of underlying assumptions. These views drive their evaluations and underpin the eventual rating. These norms are their dogma. What follows looks behind and beyond what their websites offer.

1 The free market is the best creator of wealth; the government's reach into the private economy acts as a constraint on capital creation.
2 Cash is king – debt is repaid from cash, not earnings. The ability to generate cash depends to a large extent on a corporation's management – its skill in using resources wisely, in taking advantage of growth opportunities, and in maintaining constructive relationships with key constituencies such as creditors, regulators and customers. The ability to generate cash also depends on industry characteristics and where the company is positioned in its growth cycle.
3 Size matters – the bigger the enterprise the more control it has over its market, its pricing and the competition.

4 Past performance is the best indicator of future performance.

5 Profitability is a major determinant of creditworthiness because it illustrates management prowess in running the organisation.

6 Management (not external conditions) drives performance, specifically:
  • management's attitudes towards risk;
  • their focus on business fundamentals;
  • the realism of long-term strategies and goals;
  • the importance placed on corporate governance;
  • the quality of their management information systems; and
  • their ability to adapt in periods of rapid change.

7 Every company needs 'financial flexibility', defined as the ability of a company to accomplish its financing program without damaging its creditworthiness. If a company is under commercial or market stress, it needs to have a number of financial options to smooth the way, such as the ability to:
  • access bank lines or the equity market;
  • issue short-term or long-term debt;
  • generate cash by disposing of assets;
  • revise plans for capital spending;
  • reduce discretionary spending; and
  • draw on financial reserves.

An issuer may be able to convince an analyst about a trend in his finances but will not be able to make the agency change its mind on these seven 'givens'.

General guidelines

With these basics in mind, let us add another layer to agency thinking. Here are four general guidelines the CRAs use in assessing the creditworthiness of industrial companies.

First, they emphasise *the qualitative*. Financial statistics are just a starting point.[1] No ratios can capture the full complexity of a company's financial position or provide a clue about the availability of cash to meet its future debt obligations, let alone the willingness of management to use the cash to pay principal to bondholders. Numbers indicate where a company is now, but they do not reveal its future risk profile. Financial data must be interpreted by the analyst, relative weights assigned and comparisons made with peers. These require interpretation, extrapolation and subjective assessment based on the analyst's experience and knowledge of the industry.

Second, the CRAs search for *long-term fundamentals*, concentrating on uncovering a company's credit strengths and weaknesses related to its ability to generate cash. Analysts try not to react to short-term events, like quarterly earnings reports. That is the job of the equity analyst. The CRAs try to take a three to five year outlook and see through the next business cycle. Ratings are not designed to capture an issuer's credit quality at the peak or trough of the cycle but somewhere in-between.

Third, they focus on default risk under a variety of *possible futures*. What are the plausible stress scenarios that could cause a disruption of interest or principal payments, such as a recession, industry-wide overcapacity, an unfavourable change in regulations, or a change of management? They are always asking, 'What could go wrong?' Analysts develop worst-case scenarios, and if the probabilities attached to them are sufficiently high, the credit rating will be lower.

Fourth, the CRAs evaluate the elements of *future cash flow*. Prospective generation of cash from operations is the primary source of debt payment, so the CRAs focus on this measure. A secondary source of cash for repayment is future stocks of assets and other potential sources of liquidity. Of course, a company will likely have other debts and liabilities that will have a competing claim on the cash flow, and these need to be estimated.

The task of a credit analyst, then, is to forecast the degree to which there is a sufficient cushion of cash or margin of safety that will ensure debt servicing and repayment. The larger the cushion of cash and liquid assets relative to debt, the higher the rating is likely to be, *ceteris paribus* (all things being equal). After predicting the cushion, the analyst asks the following questions.

- What events or trends can throw off the forecast?
- What could hinder the company's ability to generate cash?
- Are management's forecasts validated by mine?
- Will management react well to adverse situations?
- How 'safe' is credit support offered by third parties, such as a parent company or a bank line of credit?

Clearly, there are no easy answers to these questions. It is a matter of making judgments about what factors will impact the cushion of cash over time. There are a number of early warning signs that serve as a wake-up call to an analyst, signals that point to a possible deterioration in that cushion of cash: weak consumer demand, higher interest rates, rising cost of energy or other inputs, greater competition from imports, the loss of a key supplier, labour problems, a sudden rise in borrowings, substantial litigation and audit problems.

Management delivery

A key factor correlating with rating changes is how well management meets its stated objectives year by year. Did management 'deliver' on the goals and promises it made last year? If they establish a pattern of producing predicted results, then agency confidence in management rises and so do its chances of an optimal rating or an upgrade.

A second key factor is the credibility of the issuer's strategic plans or their medium-term outlook. A former corporate and utility analyst at Moody's gave this example. Phillip Morris was an A1 company by the numbers but was rated A3 by Moody's because management would not level with the analysts about the company's plans. The company would go out and buy another company without telling Moody's.

A third key factor is management's awareness of what conditions are within their control and what conditions are outside their control.

Within management's control are such factors as cash flow, dividend policy, acquisitions, capital expenditures, people, and products. Management sets priorities, controls costs, oversees balance sheet risks and decides on the timing of capital expenditures. The agencies will judge the company's credit risk according to management performance in these areas.

Outside management's control are general economic conditions, the health of one's industry, the business cycle, currency fluctuations, government regulations, and earthquakes and other *forces majeure*. However, the agencies expect well-managed and highly rated companies to have a mix of policies in place (for example, currency hedging, disaster insurance, lobbying activities, personnel and pricing flexibility) that will mitigate the impact of unforeseen events.

While management cannot foresee these events, they can be prepared for them. In fact, they will be held accountable by the agencies if they are not prepared to deal with them when they happen. Issuers cannot just use the excuse, 'We were blindsided by this unexpected event'. Issuers should know their vulnerabilities to shocks and will be asked why they were not ready.

Harold Goldberg, Chairman of Moody's Rating Committee in the 1980s, put it this way: 'A rating reflects our confidence in the company's management to achieve its goals.' That pithy statement still holds true decades later. Ratings are an assessment of management. The real reason a company gets into difficulty lies within itself, not with others such as rating agencies or bankers or government.

The analytical pyramid

With these general guidelines and key factors in the back of their minds, analysts then turn intuitively to the analytical pyramid shown in Exhibit 3.1. It illustrates the agencies' bottoms-up approach in corporate analysis.[2] One could say it is really top-down because it starts with the largest macro picture and works down to very company-specific details. Analysts begin with the sovereign rating, assess the industry in question, look at the regulations affecting the company, the company's competition and market position, and finally examine the company itself.

The sovereign environment

Government creditworthiness impacts a corporation's credit. A company's financial performance reflects the economic conditions in its marketplace. Unstable politics, as in the US in recent years, can lead to unfavourable laws or other constraints imposed on a company. On the more positive side, governments have the power to support a company directly or indirectly in normal times or in the event of financial stress. A company may be too vital an employer or exporter to be allowed to fail. A sovereign analyst at the CRA will usually sit on the rating committee (RC) when international companies are being rated in order to add the government and macroeconomic dimension.

The industry setting

The dynamics of the industry in which the issuer resides can be growing or in decline; it can be inherently risky, volatile or cyclical like forest products, mining or homebuilding or

Exhibit 3.1

The rating analysis pyramid

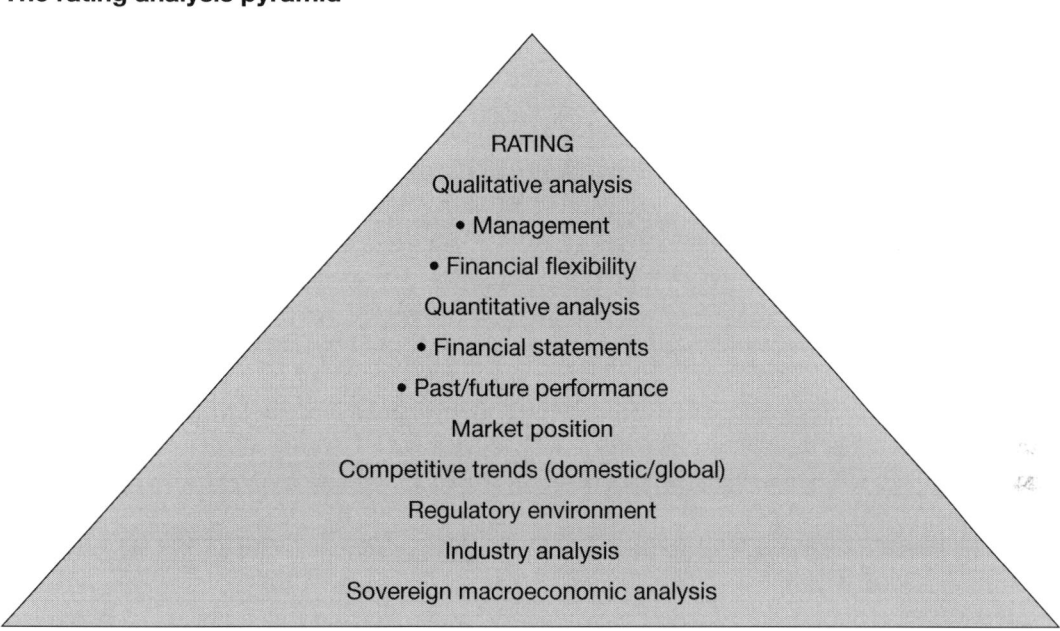

RATING
Qualitative analysis
• Management
• Financial flexibility
Quantitative analysis
• Financial statements
• Past/future performance
Market position
Competitive trends (domestic/global)
Regulatory environment
Industry analysis
Sovereign macroeconomic analysis

Source: Moody's special report, 'Moody's starts with the basics', August 1993, p. 3

steady like branded consumer products and publishing. Companies within the industry face risks and opportunities; are these companies leaders or laggards? Are they vulnerable to economic cycles, product cycles, or technological changes? Given the barriers to entry, what is the potential for new competitors?

The regulatory environment

Do the regulators of the industry, such as public utilities, allow sufficient rate increases to earn cash to repay debt holders? How much do regulatory interference and compliance burdens impact profitability? (The rating agencies themselves are asking this last question these days as we will see in 'Regulating the raters'.) Have regulators opened up or closed the way for increased competition, which could potentially reduce profit margins and thus debt holder protections.

The operating climate

Now we 'descend' in the analysis to the market position of the company being rated. Here is a sample of questions raised. How is the company's ability to generate cash flow under different economic conditions? What is its market share in the various product lines? Are revenue streams diversified or concentrated in certain products or services, which might increase vulnerability? The magnifying glass then focuses on a company's cost structure, operating efficiency and potential for labour unrest.

Organisational structure

Does the company have a parent or subsidiary that could drain its operating cash flow? Are financial statements consolidated or unconsolidated? Conversely, will a parent support an affiliate in the event of financial difficulty? Is management talent being grown internally or is there too much reliance on one individual? What constraints, if any, are placed on management by prominent shareholders?

Special event risk

Finally, the CRAs are alert to special one-time or infrequent events such as a merger or acquisition, a capital restructuring program or a leveraged buyout, all of which can have a major change in company management or a dramatic increase in debt leverage. Maybe there is major litigation pending against the company or an industrial accident that drains resources and acts as a drag on future cash flows. These events cannot always be predicted so there is an unavoidable element of surprise.

If the agency analyst suspects that such a 'special event' may take place, he will recommend 'event risk shading' to the rating committee, that is, adjusting the rating marginally lower in advance for a company susceptible to a takeover, such as where industry is consolidating or where management is making aggressive use of debt capacity, presumably to acquire another company.

Quality of management

Managerial expertise is difficult to quantify, but it can be estimated by evaluating management's past track record plus its intentions, plans, strategies, motivations and appetite for risk. The CRAs' central assumption about industrial ratings is the company's ability to generate cash ultimately depends on the skills and ability of management to make maximum use of existing resources and market opportunities, and to respond effectively to adverse conditions that might arise (for example, technological developments, regulatory changes, new competition), and to maintain constructive relationships with key constituencies, such as creditors, regulators and customers.

Risk management culture

How skilled is management in recognising and dealing with all the risks it faces in the economy, the industry, the regulatory environment, the operating climate and within the company? Is there a risk management 'culture'? Do line managers understand and manage risk? Does the company have a chief risk officer? Are operational as well as financial risks given attention? Favourable indicators of a thriving risk management culture would include:

- risk management policies and procedures are clearly stated and widely known;
- responsibility for risk management rests with a high-level officer;
- risk measurement and monitoring are independent from risk taking;
- risk tolerance is consistent with company's goals and board's expectations;
- the board of directors regularly receives and discusses reports on the company's risk positions; and
- incentive compensation supports the achievement of risk management objectives.

The following indicators show the opposite, that the risk management culture is lacking and an optimal rating is, therefore, not on the horizon.

- Management views risk management as a constraint imposed by external parties.
- Risk tolerance is unclear; management reacts on an ad hoc basis.
- Risk management responsibility is non-existent or dispersed among several middle-level managers.
- Risk management is purely an advisory role or solely a response to regulatory requirements.
- The board hears about risk only after a loss event.
- There is no risk management staff, or they are just learning.
- Procedures and policies are not fully documented.
- Only a few 'techies' understand the basis of risk measures and are not able to communicate this to management.

In sum, the overall objective of the CRA in this issuer category, the industrial corporation, is to determine a company's capacity to generate cash flow over the life of the debt instrument, which depends on a thorough assessment of the analytical pyramid with special attention given to the quality of management. Key financial statistics provide the analyst with guides to this question of capacity.

Statistical measures

The agencies are generous about publishing their various methodologies and key ratios on their websites, so there is no need to go into detail here.

There is no rigid formulaic approach to determining ratings, and a rating is not a matter simply of numbers or ratios. Nonetheless, there are certain financial measures that have proven important in the analysis of companies because they are indicators of capacity to meet obligations. The overwhelming focus is on cash – how it is generated and the sustainability of cash generation. Here are the four most important quantitative measures that the CRAs consider. These can vary by industry. See their websites for all the definitions and their permutations.

1 *Profitability.* The myriad profitability ratios used by the CRAs measure a company's ability to make efficient use of the assets and resources at its disposal. In the long run, profit potential is the critical determinant of credit protection. Higher returns on capital

means greater ability to generate equity capital internally, attract external capital, and withstand business adversity.

2 *Cash flow adequacy.* Cash flow can be measured a number of ways: earnings before interest and taxes, retained cash flow, and free cash flow. The analyst needs to determine which of these measures is the true *discretionary* cash flow, representing funds available to service and repay debt. Debt is paid out of cash, not out of 'earnings' (an accounting concept). Interest coverage (operating income / interest expense) reveals the safety cushion built in to repay the cost of debt, the level of protection in covering annual interest payments on the debt.

3 *Liquidity.* It is important to have pools of funds available to meet contingencies. These funds, such as short-term securities or bank lines, provide a degree of financial flexibility to meet contingencies, particularly under stress conditions.

4 *Leverage / capital adequacy.* A high level of debt relative to equity is risky because of the small level of equity to absorb losses and because of refinancing risk (it is harder to roll over obligations in a tight market). This ratio indicates the degree of risk that a company undertakes, and it captures the risk to creditors imbedded in a company's capital structure.

When these ratios move in one direction or another, the analyst will track them for several quarters and decide if the changes are structural, or temporary or cyclical, and then decide what rating action is necessary.

Most companies 'manage' their earnings annually to satisfy various stakeholders. This is no secret and in most cases not illegal. Companies should be open with the rating agencies about how and to what extent they do this. Nonetheless, there are some accounting gimmicks that either break the law or narrowly skirt the issue. The analysts keep their eyes open for them, for such artifices are used to hide a company's debt, boost reported earnings or otherwise distort performance in their favour. When discovered, the CRA will 'punish' the offender today and perhaps into the future because trust has been violated. Such tricks[3] include:

1 recording revenue too soon, that is, marking it 'sold' before actual payment;
2 recording bogus revenue, such as sending excess production to a distributor's warehouse and posting it as a 'sale';
3 shifting current expenses into other periods to enlarge net income;
4 capitalising what would otherwise be considered expenses; or
5 hiding liabilities by shifting them to outside partnerships.

Corporate governance

Corporate governance has to do with the management of a company in a way that respects the rights of shareholders, non-controlling shareholders, debt holders and the community. Governance means the way a company runs its business or the context in which officials make their decisions. Governance concepts used to apply only to corporations, but now they apply to banks and sovereigns as well. There is a clear link between governance practices and credit ratings.

If a company's finances are independently audited and disclosed regularly and transparently, and if the interests of shareholders are protected and if company management is held accountable for its actions, then we have 'good governance'. Good corporate management means improved accounting standards, better reliability of the audit function, and better information for better investment decisions. Investors and rating agencies search out these characteristics and respond according to their presence or absence.

Substandard corporate governance, on the other hand, will result in bad or incomplete information available to management for decision making and volatility in free cash flow to repay debt. The absence of appropriate governance principles in a company or bank will have a rating impact of at least one notch. Bad corporate governance is equated to bad management.

Bad corporate governance impacts a company's financials in several ways. Poor audit procedures and weak accounting standards allow for an overstatement of earnings and asset values totally apart from cash flow. Poor accountability and lack of transparency allow for weaker profits and the siphoning off of free cash flow away from the company, its shareholders and debt holders. If company finances are secret, if there is no regulatory authority to prevent abuses, if company management is not held accountable, and if there is no independent board of directors, then we have bad governance. The Enron bankruptcy in the US is a perfect example of bad governance.

An indication of the higher profile that one CRA is taking with respect to governance is S&P's new 'gamma' score (see www.governance.standardandpoors.com). GAMMA is the awkward acronym for 'governance, accountability, management metrics and analysis'. A GAMMA score reflects S&P's opinion of the relative strength of a company's corporate governance practices as an investor protection against potential governance-related losses of value or failure to create value. S&P maintains that GAMMA is a tool for investors in a company's stocks or bonds, and it serves companies as a road map for improvement.

In sum, good governance is important for all participants in the bond market.

- First of all, for *issuers*. A company's or sovereign's ability to gain access to capital from both domestic and foreign investors to finance growth depends on meeting the stronger requirements for transparency and more equitable treatment of shareholders. Companies, banks or governments that do not comply will find themselves at a competitive disadvantage in the search for capital and will be seen as riskier investments. Their ratings will ultimately reflect management's degree of compliance with practices that are increasingly common and accepted around the world.
- Second, *investors* want good management, good information and maintenance of asset values to safeguard their investments. They want to see their investments serviced and the debts repaid. Good governance raises the odds that a company will survive and therefore meet its financial obligations. Investors rely on CRA opinions to guide them.
- Third, the *rating agencies* care about good governance because it helps protect the integrity and longevity of their ratings. Good governance reduces operational risks and the possibility of shocks, which enhances a company's ability to meet debt obligations. That is what the agencies try to measure in the interest of informing bondholders about default risk.

- Finally, *regulators* everywhere want to reduce market volatility, bankruptcies and the possibility the government will have to bail out major players in the economy at great cost to taxpayers.

Corporates in emerging markets

When the agencies rate corporates in emerging markets, some of the emphases change. Unlike corporates in the OECD countries, there are larger concerns in developing countries about data reliability, transparency and timeliness, management skills, the still-evolving regulatory environment, and institutional underdevelopment, such as non-independent courts and legislatures, large gaps in the rule of law, a tradition of arbitrary decision making, and state ownership issues. All these uncertainties usually add up to non-investment grade credit ratings.

With regard to data reliability, there is a decidedly mixed record, for example, in countries of the former Soviet Union where the adoption of International Financial Reporting Standards (IFRS) is a work in progress. Moreover, management has a limited free market track record, having worked before in a command economy where the main issue was output, not efficiency and profits. A company that is or was state-owned tends to be slower to restructure and rationalise its operations, because this translates into layoffs or the fraying of political linkages. It may take two or three generations for management to be weaned from a central planning mentality that was formed and rewarded by the state.

In emerging markets, there is a still developing and inconsistent regulatory environment and less predictability in the legal system. Major issues such as property rights and the sanctity of contracts do not have a long history and cannot be relied on. How tight or loose is the regulatory framework? If local companies intend to compete internationally, how significant will the financing be to upgrade equipment sufficiently? Sometimes the ownership of a company is obscure and/or various shareholders are given special treatment. Sometimes the owners are the government and sometimes a strategic investor. Ownership issues can be murky at best and an Escher-like optical illusion at worst.

External support

There are two types of external support for a company: state ownership and strategic investors. The CRAs pay close attention to all the gradations of support available to an issuer.

State ownership can bolster a company's credit profile through explicit or implicit support. Such backing can take the form of a guarantee of the debt of a state-owned enterprise, or direct financial infusions, or preferences in wages, supplies, access to capital, pricing. The analyst considers the strategic importance of the company in the country of domicile. Does it provide a vital or strategic service, as in the energy, defence or telecom industries? Does it provide significant levels of employment or foreign exchange (FX) earnings? Will the state support the company in an emergency? How much non-commercial, that is, political, pressure is exerted on a company such that it resists international trends for greater transparency?

Strategic investors: when a company is privatised, wholly or partially, a foreign investor could take a large stake in the company. In some cases, if the strategic investor or parent company has a rating higher than that of the country in which the local company is based, then it is possible the local company could achieve a rating higher than that of the country, depending on the level and manner of explicit support from the investor. The agencies ask, how important to the strategic partner is the local operation, and what could go wrong in the relationship? Will the investor support the company in a financial emergency?

All these questions are complex and require seasoned analysts to address them and to understand the issuer's country and operating climate. If a potential corporate issuer in an emerging market cannot satisfy the CRA on these matters of governance and relative risk, then an optimal rating cannot be achieved. Absent the support of a strategic investor or of the government, the best advice would be to wait a few years before applying for a rating.

The due diligence meeting

When corporate issuers in any market meet with the rating agencies for the annual due diligence meeting, they need to keep in mind a key distinction: bond analysts differ from equity analysts. Presentations to each cannot be the same.

The CRA is looking for evidence that bondholder interests will be protected – a different set of calculations from what stockholders seek. For example, earnings per share may drive stock prices, but as we have seen cash flow is what is needed when it is time for a debt payment. Similarly, fast growth delights stockholders but worries bondholders since high-growth companies are usually consumers of cash. Finally, debt analysts take a longer view (two to four years) than do equity analysts.

When it comes to presentations to the CRAs, corporate issuers will need to adjust their agenda – the agencies will not – so that there is some common ground on which to proceed. Otherwise an optimal rating will absolutely not be in reach. Exhibit 3.2 shows how a rating agency and a company have differing agendas in meetings and can end up talking past each other.[4] The corporate issuer needs to ensure it is addressing the agency's needs.

Exhibit 3.2

Talking but not communicating

The CRA's agenda	The company's agenda
1 Cash flow predictability	1 Rapid growth
2 Evidence of contingency planning	2 Efforts to enhance shareholder value
3 Taking responsibility for performance	3 External influences on performance
4 Respecting the competition	4 Belittling the competition
5 Appropriateness of financial policies	5 Success of the last financial deal

Source: Weinberger, R; www.theratingexpert.com

We will discuss the rating meeting in detail in Chapter 4, but here are some points a corporate issuer needs to keep in mind.

- Describe your goals and how you intend to reach them.
- Do not repeat the annual report.
- Be clear, open and honest so an atmosphere of trust is developed.
- Do not exaggerate outcomes or forecasts.
- Comply with data requests and provide key documents.
- Show that you understand the needs of your prospective customers and how that translates into pricing decisions.
- Explain how the external environment affects your business and what you do about it.

In the crucial meeting with the CRA, written and oral presentations should focus on:

- a statement of business purpose and objectives, not just statistics;
- analyses of the company's various business segments, including strengths and weaknesses and key strategies;
- financial objectives and projections out three to five years with cash flow analysis, earnings statements, balance sheets, and segment data. These projections should clearly state key assumptions and show how the forward plan will build on past successes;
- proof of management depth so that others can succeed current senior people; and
- evidence of financial flexibility and contingency planning.

When discussing your planning assumptions, take care to avoid giving the impression that your plan is the product of wishful thinking. Make your assumptions conservative and realistic; that way you are more likely to meet and exceed your targets.

As to comparisons with others in your industry, the agency analysts like to see whom the issuer considers his peers and competitors. The analysts make their own comparative analyses but sometimes an issuer can convince the CRA that the companies you include in your studies are more representative of an appropriate peer class. Since operating data, which show relative cost efficiency, are often the single most telling basis for rating differences among manufacturing companies, it would make sense for the issuer or presenter to develop a series of ratios about competitors. The agency may not accept these comparisons, but they do show the analysts that the issuer knows his competition in the market.

Regarding what to say about the competition, issuers should not ridicule other companies because this tells the agency that the issuer does not view their presence as a risk and does not intend to learn from them and their role in the market. Showing a healthy respect for the competition shows the agency that you take them seriously and are, therefore, less vulnerable to competitive threats and more open to business opportunities that might emerge.

By this point, the analyst has a good picture of where the company is now both qualitatively and quantitatively. The analyst will then sit back and ponder on what could go wrong with this picture. What could happen to change the company's ability to generate cash or to pay down debt? What could happen to alter the value of the company's assets? What could alter the company's capital structure or other claims and liabilities?

These questions will arise in the rating committee so the analyst wants to be ready with some well thought out responses. Here is what issuers can do to minimise the risk that the analyst will find their financials, forecasts and contingency plans not credible.

Advice for issuers

1 Issuers should openly show the agencies the procedures they already have for oversight and accountability in all sectors affecting their rating.

2 The CRAs will assign lower ratings to a company if they see such red flags as inadequate disclosure or hiding of information, non-credible data based on poor accounting practices, cronyism instead of competence, and unaccountable management. Issuers cannot remove these danger signals just in the weeks before a due diligence meeting. It could take years of restructuring internal practices, so do not hurry for a rating if you are not ready.

3 The CRA concern is a company's ability to compete in the future, more so than its present performance. Leave the analysts with the impression that you have a well-conceived plan to adapt to the changing manufacturing (or retailing, natural resource) environment. They will ask, how do you intend to position yourself within the changing competitive arena?

4 Give the CRA access to the top level of management, including the CEO, the CFO, the Treasurer and key operating people – in person or by teleconference.

5 Show how your past performance lends credibility to what you say you intend to do. Show how future earnings and cash generated will maintain your competitive position. Past performance is the best indicator of future performance. The historic ability to stay in business indicates management's ability to cope with changing conditions.

6 If there has been financial deterioration, show how it has not impaired debt holder protection measures. Show how future strategic plans and actions will not increase the risk factor for debt holders, that is, have an impact on cash generation and capitalisation. Management remains fundamentally prudent. Explain motives for strategic moves.

7 Communicate clearly, completely and forthrightly regarding all the key factors mentioned here. That way you are minimising the risk that the agency will misunderstand your business and your story and assign an incorrect rating.

8 All the major credit issues important to the company should be placed on the table. There is no reason to have a lower rating only because important information never emerged in discussions.

9 Always show respect for the analyst even if you disagree about an important issue. Remember that an analyst cannot possibly know as much about your business as you do, so be patient and as helpful as you can.

10 Remember that your goal is an optimal rating, one that comfortably fits into your projected risk profile. Not often considered is the somewhat counter-intuitive notion that sometimes a lower rating is more desirable because it gives the latitude to incur more risk without incurring a rating downgrade.

1   Tom Harker, industrials analyst and executive at Fitch Ratings for 15 years put it this way: 'The numbers are done first and then the analyst is asked to *interpret* them, to adjust them based on his experience and qualitative knowledge. In the end, the agencies look at adjusted numbers.'

2   The pyramid is derived from a Moody's special report, 'Moody's starts with the basics', August 1993, p. 3.

3   This is just a sample list, drawn from Insana, R, 'Looking for weird', *Money Magazine*, April 2002, p. 60. There are many more accounting artifices that the CRA analysts uncover.

4   Exhibit 3.2 is copied with permission from a presentation made by ratings expert Roy Weinberger titled 'Techniques for effectively managing credit relationships'. See www.theratingexpert.com.

3.3 Agency beliefs on banks

We begin with some elementary beliefs that guide how the agency analysts approach the assessment of a bank's creditworthiness.[1] These standard assumptions or core tenets are conservative and include many 'haircuts' or discounts when constructing ratios and in final deliberations.

1 *Bigger banks* are deemed to be better banks because it is assumed they have pricing power, more experienced management, and a greater capacity to invest in computer systems, planning, product development, and advertising. Bigger banks benefit from economies of scale at the retail level and are deemed to be more likely to receive state aid in an emergency.

2 High *core profitability* is crucial both to support balance sheet growth and to be better able to fund emergencies such as loan losses without impairing capital. The basic standard measure of core profitability is pre-tax operating income before provisioning, net of abnormal items. The agencies look for core profitability to exceed 2% of assets and to reflect a stable or improving trend over time. If core earnings can absorb anticipated future loan losses, then the bank is sound. If they cannot, stress will result. Whether that stress will be damaging to a credit rating will depend on the strength of the business franchise and (as always) on managerial skills. Lack of product diversification or overdependence on one market limit franchise strength and will show up in the performance record.

3 Analysts look carefully at the trend in *net interest margins*. In their view a 7% spread between interest received and interest paid is quite healthy, while 1% to 2% is not. With consistently high core profits, a bank can earn its way out of loan problems. Bankers – attend to your core earnings. Your equity partners will be pleased too.

4 *Core deposits* from customers are the safest and surest form of liquidity. These deposits are deemed stable and normally low cost. Retail customers are less likely to flee in a crisis than wholesale lenders.

5 *Wholesale funds* are inherently unstable, risky and costly. Their use exacerbates liquidity management risk and requires incremental capital to offset potential volatility.

6 *Steady growth* is better than rapid growth because rapid growth tends to imply an over-reaching for assets.

7 *Opportunity* is market driven. It is therefore limited by the environment, that is, the legal, economic and regulatory conditions. A slow-growth environment constrains a bank in terms of asset growth, portfolio diversification and often profitability. Analysts start with the market.

8 *Regulators* tend to be reactive not proactive, whatever the system or country because they take action after problems manifest themselves.

9 *Deregulation and technology* worldwide have increased competition so banks must keep pace or lose market share with an attendant loss of creditworthiness.

10 *Loan portfolios* should be diversified by industry, by customer, by geography. Concentrated exposures are to be avoided, including inter-bank concentrations. The analysts take a long look at the trend in provisioning for loan losses and make extrapolations accordingly.

11 *Bank management* is assessed on its past financial performance, its current risk mitigation performance, and its strategic plan going forward. Senior managers cannot escape scrutiny by the CRAs over their performance.

12 *Existing reserves* are usually inadequate in the minds of agency analysts. They deduct existing specific reserves from capital and assume there will be additional loan-quality problems. Under their conservative approach they write off all non-performing assets, testing for a 'worst-case'.

13 *Core capital* consists of equity and credit reserves. The calculation of capital excludes intangibles, such as good will, and non-performing assets. The result is 'economic capital' which is different from accounting capital. The agencies believe that regulatory capital calculations are too generous in that they may not reflect the probable diminution in value of asset portfolios.

14 When evaluating *non-performing loans* (NPLs), the agencies give no credit for any 'guarantees' that ostensibly back up the loan. There are two reasons why third-party guarantees of loans are discounted by the agencies: first, it is too difficult to assess the true economic value of such guarantees, and second if there was a guarantee behind a loan, why was it not called upon to cure the problem to begin with, that is, before it became non-performing? A bank's heavy reliance on guarantees implies weak underwriting criteria.

Inherent fragility and red flags

Why is this approach to rating banks so conservative? Aside from the agencies' innate stance of caution, they also deem banking systems to be inherently fragile. For them fragility is found in the following risks that affect many banks. The CRAs seek out these fragility factors, and they play a role in rating committee discussions.

- Illiquidity, such as in balance sheets with short-term deposits and longer-term loans.
- Asymmetry of information where banks have imperfect knowledge regarding borrowers.
- The risk of 'moral hazard' where banks take excessive risks because they assume ownership or government support in a crisis.
- Management and organisational structures that do not evolve quickly enough as operating environment changes.
- Bank lending based on government priorities or on preferences of the industrial group or family owner.
- High leverage and inadequate capital.
- Macroeconomic imbalances and volatility.
- Deficient prudential regulation, supervision, and enforcement, combined with a weak legal system incapable of enforcing contract rights and facilitating rapid bankruptcy, foreclosure, and liquidation.

We add to the fragility factors a number of 'red flags' that the agencies look out for and which banks should as well. These are signals that warn of trouble ahead [with author comment following].

- Too aggressive growth in loans or assets [but how much is too aggressive?].
- Excessive concentrations by product or market [but what is excessive?].
- Heavy dependence on purchased funds [how much dependence becomes too heavy?].
- Rapid expansion internally or via acquisition [when does rapid become excessive?].

Combining all these assumptions and intangible factors on banks, it is easy to see that bank credit analysis has a major *qualitative* component. The agencies do not deny this, repeatedly stating that their analysis requires them to:

1 evaluate the quality of management and its appetite for risk and leverage;
2 choose relevant peers in the region and adjust the data to make them comparable;
3 evaluate the assumptions behind the bank's financial data;
4 compare bank transparency and banking system transparency with others in the region; and
5 weigh competitive conditions, and government regulatory and support levels.

The agencies do not want banks with investment-grade ratings to fail on their watch so they begin their assessments with all these assumptions that result in a conservative rating, that is, one that is low enough to protect them from embarrassment and high enough to have credibility in the market relative to the bank's peers. When banks do fail, the agencies hold that it is due to some failure of bank management to cope with the risks in their institution's inherent fragility.

Moody's self-servingly assures readers that 'our analytical concepts remain constant and are applicable to banking institutions worldwide'.[2] Yet the agency exhibits a slightly contradictory view on the use of ratios in bank ratings. On the one hand, 'Moody's strongly favours ratios that indicate a bank's earnings capacity because these measures clearly demonstrate the entity's ability to earn its way out of a problem'. On the other hand, 'We are sceptical of ratio-driven rating conclusions. We believe that the data that generate these ratios are subject to considerable limitations.'

A likely explanation for this seeming contradiction is that the ratios measure historical performance, whereas ratings themselves are intended to offer a projection of future default risk. The agencies use ratios as a first step to place the rating within a range of possibilities relative to peers but then have to discuss how these numbers might change once bank management needs to react to economic cycles and structural shifts within the banking industry.

Banks being rated can address some of the agency's assumptions and concerns by providing analysts with the data they need to do their job so that their assessment becomes less intangible. Plus, by being proactive in supplying relevant materials, both beforehand and during the due diligence meeting, agency concerns about bank management co-operation and naiveté will be alleviated.

Here is a brief list of information issuers should provide that will make the analyst's job easier. See Chapter 4 for more ideas on useful information.

- Definition of key markets; protecting and enlarging the franchise.
- Forecasts, strategies, assumptions, plans: the CEO's vision.
- Structural changes in the market, and how the bank plans to stay competitive.

- Breakdown of the business by different product areas.
- Breakdown of revenues and their vulnerabilities to fluctuation.
- How the bank is going to finance its growth.
- Loan portfolio schedules, problem loan schedules, reserve reconciliation.
- Breakdown of all liabilities by cost and maturity.

As we saw in Exhibit 3.2, it is easy for the issuer and agency agendas to differ, resulting in miscommunication. They can talk past each other. Similarly, banks have a number of stakeholders they must satisfy, and they all have different agendas. The lesson in Exhibit 3.3 is that banks must ensure they are sending the right message to the right stakeholder. Addressing the rating agencies as you might address owners or employees will not carry the day.

Supplying the CRAs with the information suggested above will much reduce the risk that you are focusing on the wrong stakeholder.

Exhibit 3.3

Bank stakeholders

Who they are	What they want
Owners	Return on investment
Customers	Loans and services
Employees	Employment
Regulators	Safety and soundness
Rating agencies	Evidence of credit quality

Source: Author's own

Context, character and controls

Given all this background, how will a rating agency analyst approach his assessment of an unrated bank whose application for a rating has landed on his desk? Here are the steps in order. They are like the reverse pyramid shown in Exhibit 3.1, working from the most general to the most specific. Check agency websites for more detail. Banks should be aware that the questions shown will be asked.

First, an analyst looks at the *context* in which the bank operates, the 'operating environment'. He or she asks, what is the stage of development of the banking system, what are the levels of intermediation and disintermediation, what is the competitive landscape, and what is the nature of government regulation and support? Will the state support the larger, public-sector banks whose fundamentals are weak or will the state liquidate them? Are financial regulators equipped, especially in newly created institutional frameworks, to deal with either accounting insolvencies or funding crises? The higher the degree of accounting forbearance, the greater the potential for bank failures. How independent are officials charged with monitoring bank problems?

Second, the analyst looks at the *character of the institution*, which is determined by the origins of the bank and the market. If the bank's deposits depend more on the wholesale market (repurchase, certificates of deposit and commercial paper) as opposed to the retail market (individual depositors), then the bank is likely heading for funding problems. The market could flee, tighten, or not roll over paper in a crisis. Retail customers do not flee as readily. Banks relying on wholesale funds also tend to do more trading and bond dealing, foreign exchange contracts, and more fee business via letters of credit, all of which produce a more volatile earnings stream.

Third, the analyst checks for the bank's *internal controls*, its management information systems, its strategy, and its ability to catch problem loans early. Does the management information system (MIS) readily capture and display the bank's key markets and product lines? How thorough and available to management is data on operations, hedging, credit review and monitoring processes? What are the approval authorities, and do the reporting systems allow management to know the bank's exposures? A good determinant of MIS is for the analyst to ask the bank how many of its problem loans become non-performers?

Fourth, he looks at the *loan book*. What are the types of customers and how diversified are they by industry and geography (dispersion helps provide counter-cyclicality)? What are the bank's policies regarding collateral? How is credit originated (the approval process)? What are the strategy and controls associated with the creation and management of the loan portfolio? Banks tend to get into deep trouble when they expand their loan portfolios too quickly or undermanage the credit approval and surveillance processes.

Mara Hilderman, a former Citibank analyst and Associate Director at Moody's said, when interviewed, 'Asset quality is still the most important thing we look at. It's always asset quality that gets a bank in trouble.' One way to measure that is to look at the percentage of non-performing loans against total loans or against equity. 'Banks fail because of bad loans,' she said, 'so the most basic trend to watch is rising non-performers.' Another predictor is the rate of loan growth. Double digit loan growth over three or four consecutive years is a danger signal because it implies that management may be desperate to grow the balance sheet or market share.

Finally, the analyst examines the bank's *liquidity policy*. Every bank needs a strategy for dealing with uncertainties and emergencies, such as loss of confidence by investors who are unwilling to roll over their short-term obligations or depositors who withdraw their money from the bank. Banks need some protection against such adversity, a defence against extreme pressures. Having ample liquidity or 'nearness to cash' assures both investors and depositors. Where can the bank obtain funds to pay off scared depositors so as to prevent a 'run'? Liquidity is the ability to raise funds either by selling assets or borrowing. However, when business conditions are bearish in the economy, analysts become concerned because the usual outlets for raising liquidity (sales of assets, borrowing) are less certain.

The agencies consider liquidity important because: (i) debt holders are paid out of liquidity; (ii) the present liquidity status of a bank is a good an indicator of the importance of liquidity to management; and (iii) the ease of a bank's ability to roll over old debt in the market and replace it with new debt is an indicator of the ease of future repayment of debt. Thus, the analysts will ask, how stable are funding sources (the more deposits the better), what alternative sources does the bank have access to, and how able are they to liquefy assets through maturation or sale? Can the bank revise its plans for capital spending, thus freeing up resources?

While agency analysts are not forensic accountants, they do recognise lax accounting practices in banks worldwide and will penalise them for such tricks as:

- reclassifying loans that are not performing in order to minimise loan-loss reserves;
- overvaluing collateral and presuming high collectability;
- transferring problem loans to unconsolidated subsidiaries; or
- continuing accrual of interest for problem loans or lending to a borrower to finance his interest payments.

Bankers everywhere need to understand what factors are within their control and which are not. Otherwise, they may promise something they cannot deliver. *Within their control* in the short term, banks can manage their liquidity, asset growth and provisioning policy so there is no excuse for their making excuses in this regard. In the long run, banks have the power to implement business strategies that result in consistent earnings, that maintain or grow market share amongst their products, and that improve asset quality.

As to factors *outside their control* to influence, banks cannot affect general economic conditions, the government's macroeconomic policies, and what their peers and regulators are doing. The agencies will not hold banks accountable for this state of affairs, but they will ask how management intends to adapt when changes in these conditions arise. The agencies believe that an astute and conservative management should be able to anticipate and prepare for external conditions and shocks. They will fault management for not having contingency plans and for not retaining the financial flexibility (for example, excess capital, liquid assets, access to various funding markets) to cushion against adverse events.

Banks can be downgraded for reasons outside their control, as when the real estate market bottoms out or when there are significant shifts in the economic environment. But banks can mitigate the downgrade by demonstrating they are aware of the risk and have a diverse income stream. 'Face up to the problem immediately and get into the agencies. The more aggressively you take the case to them, the more likely they will believe you know what you're doing.'[3]

Banks in emerging markets

All the norms and assumptions mentioned above hold true for banks in emerging markets as well, but the agencies have a number of other tough criteria for emerging market banks. Bankers in emerging markets need to take these criteria into account in order to understand how the agencies will evaluate them. While there has been some convergence in recent years with Western banking practices, the following six CRA assumptions remain hurdles on the path to an optimal rating.

1 The agencies believe that financial statistics and ratios are less valuable as a way of measuring bank strength in emerging markets, because disclosure is often less comprehensive and auditing standards less strict. The figures may not give an accurate or adequate picture of what is really happening at the bank, and by the time the data catch up, the bank may already be on the point of insolvency.

2 Credit quality and earnings can deteriorate suddenly in emerging markets, whereas in developed markets such declines are often a reflection of the business cycle, which gives banks time to provision adequately. Thus, in emerging markets a strong earnings base is the best way to safeguard financial strength. The size of equity assumes greater importance since banks in emerging markets may be forced to immediately cover bad loans. In this respect, the solvency ratio is important (equity as a percentage of net loans) which indicates the proportion of a bank's loans it can charge off while still retaining a positive net worth (the higher the better).

3 The economy and operating environment for emerging market banks are more fragile and less stable by definition, and the scale of change may be far greater when political and economic events take place.

4 One finds the presence of 'policy loans' dictated by the authorities that were not generated by free market demand and are thus apt to be kept on the books despite project failure.

5 The status of MIS and IT infrastructure are not state of the art and their absence means management decision making is hindered.

6 It is common to find government ownership of a bank, which implies wasteful subsidies, high expense ratios, and refusal to accept bank failure given the unemployment (and political) consequences.

Governments can weaken a bank's creditworthiness by influencing its business decisions in two ways. First, governments can direct banks to lend to particular borrowers or sectors for political purposes (point 4 above). This 'policy lending' is viewed negatively by the CRAs because lending based on the bank's assessment of the borrowers' ability to repay will generally lead to fewer credit losses than lending based on a government's directions. Second, governments through their state-owned banks can alter the nature of competition in the banking sector by forcing commercial banks to compete on uneconomic terms.

Whether or not banks are state-owned, all three agencies consider the link between banks and government to be inextricable. Their interaction in the rating nexus cannot be avoided. The health of a country's banking system affects the sovereign rating since banks are contingent liabilities of the government. S&P makes the connection clear.[4]

> We view banks and sovereigns as having a special relationship. They operate in a financial system where authorities regulate the process of channelling savings into investment. In our view, the size and embedded credit risks of the banking sector in a national economy play an important role in evaluating the contingent risk to a sovereign.

We turn now to the subject of upgrades and downgrades for commercial banks and for corporations (or industrials in agency parlance). We will not be directly covering other rated issuers such as insurance companies, securities companies, building societies, public utilities, and US municipalities, although some of the information and all of the advice will apply to them as well.

Determinants of upgrades

A bank or company needs to position itself to display the following positive character-istics over several years. Doing so will differentiate the company from competitors and rated peers and will capture the agencies' attention. Based on studies of the factors behind rating changes, here is a set of key reasons why banks and companies receive upgrades and downgrades.

- Improving asset quality, rising earnings, and improving market share over time, giving a trend line from which to project.
- Credible management philosophy, strategy, and track record.
- Capital injections, presence of 'excess' capital to cushion against shocks.
- Being part of a growing industry with improving credit quality.
- Favourable agency perception of 'management style' – how the bank is run and how decisions are made.
- Patient, persistent, proactive advocacy to the agencies by senior management.
- An upgrade of the sovereign and/or overall banking system improvement.

Everyone knows that strong profitability is important for a bank's survival. But it is also crucial for an optimal or high credit rating. Here is the agency perspective on its importance.

1 Steady profitability is regarded highly by financial markets, assuring the bank ongoing funding.
2 Debt holders are more likely to be repaid by a profitable bank (profits are an added cushion).
3 Continued profitability indicates a company's ability to sustain and develop itself on a long-term basis.
4 It gives opportunities to expand dividends on a sustainable basis, pleasing shareholders and attracting new investors and/or depositors.
5 It provides the capacity to undertake new programs with a cushion of earnings.
6 It indicates bank efficiency and the ability to compete.
7 Profits are an indicator of successful management strategy.

The odds for an upgrade for banks rise when they can show: (i) improving asset quality, rising earnings, and improving market share over time; and (ii) capital injections or 'excess' capital to cushion against shocks. The larger a commercial bank's share of a nation's deposit base, the more control it has over pricing and hence profitability.

Conversely, small banks are deemed to be vulnerable, unable to control their future and incapable in a reasonable time frame to grow their market share. Bank products (mortgage lending, checking and savings accounts, certificates of deposits) are commodity products so a small bank finds it difficult to differentiate itself from the competition residing one street over. Similarly, for companies a key factor is their business position within their market. The more widgets a company makes and sells, the more it can determine its capital spending and diversity its financial options.

Lesson for issuers

Issuers should plan to get greater control over their market, because market share helps protect profit margins.

Determinants of downgrades

On a general industry level, we have seen a long-term secular trend since the 1970s for banks to be downgraded, as banking systems have been deregulated and state-owned banks privatised. Creditworthiness has declined throughout the industry. That trend could continue as governments are evincing less financial backing for banks when a crisis happens, such as a real estate bubble. The rating agencies will then remove from the calculations the 'uplift' in a rating previously included because of the presumption of government support. Thus, merely being part of an industry that has been in decline for years is a likely precursor to additional downgrades.

The agencies believe that ultimately bank failures are due to three factors: mismanaged liquidity, mismanaged asset quality and inadequate real capital. Multiple downgrades of an entity can occur before the situation is resolved by bankruptcy or merger. More bank-specifically, downgrades are triggered by:

- deterioration in the quality of the asset base, primarily the loan portfolio;
- erosion in earnings resulting from large provisions and classification of non-accrual loans;
- decline relative to peers (since ratings are ordinal in nature); and
- the analyst's perception of deterioration, whether real or not.

Once a few of these factors accumulate, the primary analyst will determine if they are issuer-specific or inherent in the whole industry. Downgrades for banks and corporates can happen quickly and will happen when the agency determines:

1 the issuer has lost market share and sales prospects are poor for the company's various products;
2 the competition is strong and getting stronger [a decline relative to peers];
3 management is weak or indecisive or not being forthright [trust once lost may never be regained];
4 financial measures have weakened [it could take years to get back to target and the agency will not wait];
5 a major acquisition to be funded with extra debt is pending; or
6 the issuer is part of an industry subject to 'environmental' shocks, for example, technology breakthroughs, deregulation, or real estate bubbles.

A former vice president and analyst in the Financial Institutions Group at Moody's explained the causes of rating changes at his agency. Upgrades and downgrades are predominantly the result of how management runs an institution, whether it is a bank, a company or a city government. 'We want to know how those in charge make decisions and how their decisions influence financial results.'

Lessons for issuers

1 The quality of management is the key rating driver. 'Quality' is in the eye of the perceiver and can thus be influenced.
2 Rating agency analysts are human and make mistakes.
3 Issuers need to minimise such 'errors' by making a convincing case to the agency that emphasises the right factors, that is, those that are critical to a rating decision.

Finally, a 19-year veteran at S&P with experience in several categories of issuers offered this perspective on key factors in rating changes.

Downgrades: for corporates a red flag is always deteriorating cash flow and earnings. For banks the primary trigger is deterioration in the asset base, caused perhaps by a collapse in the real estate market. For sovereigns it is the agency's perception that the country's international competitiveness is eroding, resulting in a greater reliance on external funding.

Upgrades: for corporates it is the perception by the agency that they have an increased capacity to handle the debt load due to improved cash flow. For banks it is the ability to grow the business while managing risk appropriately. For sovereigns, upgrades happen when there are stronger external and internal financial conditions coincident with political stability, which implies less need for external debt.

Lesson for issuers

Note how often it is the agency's *perception* of trends and conditions that determine rating changes. Perceptions can be modified by proactive management, the subject of all of Chapter 6.

---

[1] The bank ratings referred to here are senior long-term deposit or debt ratings found on the standard rating scale. We are not referring to short-term debt or deposit ratings, financial strength ratings, or any of the other recently refined financial institution rating types. CRA websites have details on them.

[2] Bauer, G, 'Ratios and bank ratings – what's the connection?' Moody's special comment, August 1998, p. 3.

[3] Good advice from Katie Rossow, ex-Salomon Brothers and Moody's bank analyst, phone interview 4 June 1994.

[4] Devi Aurora, Senior Director, Financial Institutions, S&P, 'How Standard & Poor's incorporates sovereign risk into bank ratings', video on S&P website, 1 July 2013.

3.4 Charges against the agencies

Over the years critics have levelled a number of charges against the international rating agencies. Some of these criticisms are on the mark and others reveal a lack of understanding of how the agencies really function. Let us examine the accusations and determine how valid they are.

Nine accusations

1 *Moody's and S&P are a duopoly.* This charge is true, in that the Big Two control more than 90% of the credit-rating business. Fitch Ratings accounts for most of the remainder of the ratings market. The Big Two do not have any real competition, critics argue persuasively, so they are not subjected to the normal checks and balances of the market. It is said that S&P and Moody's do not compete against each other in a meaningful sense. Abuses of power can thereby arise. A number of other CRAs have received official recognition from the US SEC, but they are non-factors in the overall picture.[1]

The next section of this chapter ('Regulating the raters') provides detail on how the US Government via the SEC has brought the major rating agencies to their current duopolistic position.

2 *The agencies do 'rear-view mirror' analyses.* It is true that the agency analysts (and rating committees) look at an issuer's historical record to see how the company, bank or government has performed in past periods of stress. They adhere to the maxim that 'the best indicator of a debtor's future performance is his past performance'.

When the analysts make their projections, they do necessarily start from data in the historical base and from there they extrapolate. There is no 'front-view mirror' other than the analyst's judgment, which is based on his or her experience. There is nothing new, hidden or surprising here. At the end of the day, ratings are educated guesswork, but one must admit that they have stood the test of time by providing investors with useful default risk judgments for over a century.

3 *The agencies are quick to downgrade and slow to upgrade.* There is truth in this statement from both an issuer's and investors' standpoint. The evidence confirms the adage that 'the path to downgrades is slippery while the path to upgrades is sticky'.

On the downgrade side, the agencies like to be seen as acting proactively on behalf of bondholders. In reality, they do not want to risk the chance that facts and trends they have not perceived yet could get worse, leaving them in the position of having to explain why they 'got it wrong' again as a result of their inaction.

On the upgrade side, the agencies want to be more confident that their decision is justified by the data before they announce an upgrade, so they would rather wait a quarter or two to see if the positive trends continue. Issuers are naturally eager to see their status elevated, especially if they carry a positive outlook on their debt rating. The agencies need to feel a certain 'comfort' before permitting an upgrade, and that feeling comes slowly and only after enough evidence is amassed to convince the rating committee that the trend will not be reversed and thereby embarrass the agency.

Therefore, it would appear that 'premature' upgrades rarely happen. Recent data show this supposition with regard to sovereign ratings to be correct. However, there have been many cases over the past 15 years of what are called 'rating reversals', that is, when a downgrade is followed within a year by an upgrade. These could be called premature downgrades and would validate our argument that the CRAs are quick to downgrade on scant evidence or out of fear of being embarrassed by a late rating change. Examples include Fitch's down/up ratings of the Dominican Republic within only 10 weeks in 2005, Moody's down/up ratings of Peru within 16 days (!) in 2000, and S&P's down/up ratings of Jamaica within six weeks in 2010.[2]

4 *The agencies play 'one-upmanship' with ratings.* This allegation does not hold true if it means that the agencies race to see who can upgrade or downgrade faster or first. Nor does it mean that one copies the rating actions of the other. That said, the agencies do compete to see who can have the most ratings in various markets and who can rate the most exotic instruments. They do look for opportunities to demonstrate their power by 'moving the market'.

If one agency makes a rating change, the other agency might also move in that direction within a year or so, not because of any 'copycat' motive but because the fundamentals driving the rating change will eventually be seen by the other agency. This view may hold more for corporates or banks subject to the same cyclical conditions within a country and less for sovereigns subject to different competitive conditions and more subjective considerations.

Finally, the agencies do not waste time trying to match each other's rating changes, either up or down. They are aware that the market would pick up on this, and such behaviour would compromise the agencies' integrity and independent voices. They know it would be a serious skewing of their priorities and a disservice to the market.

Thus, while analysts are aware of what the other agency's ratings are, this knowledge absolutely does not drive their own rating decisions. Rating committees are interested when the other agency initiates a rating change, but they are not necessarily persuaded by what the other agency did.

5 *Analysts do not always understand the facts and figures an issuer presents.* It is frustrating to some issuers that relatively junior analysts at due diligence meetings raise seemingly inane or irrelevant questions and yet have the power to determine an issuer's borrowing costs. It can appear that a novice analyst is not dealing with the pertinent issues. It is true that many analysts are not familiar with politics and policy and that too many look backward at the numbers. Some are obsessed with data from the past and have difficulty in scenario building and prognosticating.

Fortunately, the reality is that a rating decision is the result of collaboration among junior analysts, senior analysts, quantitative experts, and generalists – all combined in a rating committee. This combination of knowledge and skills results in rating decisions that have retained credibility in the market 99% of the time.

Any naïveté or inexperience on the part of one analyst is, theoretically, offset by the combined insights and experience of the whole team responsible for the rating decision. The agencies think foremost of their reputations and their franchises and do not permit capricious or non-credible decisions to result from their deliberations.

6 *The rating agencies do not independently verify information.* The agencies do not have the mandate, the time, or the need as part of their due diligence to check every piece of information supplied by the issuer. They usually, however, confirm the existence of backup lines of credit for commercial paper programs, and they do check company and sovereign supplied data with other publicly available data. The agencies are not supposed to be auditors, and they are not empowered or able to unearth fraud. The agencies assume that the data presented to them are accurate. If found to be otherwise, rating consequences follow.

7 *Announcements of Credit Watches and positive and negative outlooks are self-fulfilling prophecies.* The Big Two both started the practice of issuing Credit Watch (CW) announcements in 1981. The reason was ostensibly to inform markets ahead of time that the agencies were taking a closer look at the issuer in the light of changing circumstances. As Moody's put it, 'the purpose is to bring the investor up the information chain as we see it internally'.

Another reason why the agencies make these CW and outlook announcements is to preserve relations with issuers (who do after all pay fees to the agencies) so that issuers do not feel caught off guard and embarrassed in the market by sudden rating shifts. Not all positive outlooks result in upgrades and not all negative outlooks result in downgrades. Maybe these CW and negative and positive outlook announcements represent the agencies' catching up to the market's perception of a credit.

These announcements are indeed self-fulfilling in the sense that the market adjusts pricing immediately to reflect the news of a potential upgrade or downgrade. Therefore, issuers are affected immediately, as if they have already experienced the rating change. Some would say that bond prices even lead the CW status.

8 *Issuers that disagree with a rating have little recourse.* It is true that disgruntled borrowers have little recourse in US courts. Lawsuits in the US generally have been unsuccessful because courts have upheld the agencies' argument that they are publishers of opinions, like newspapers, and that their views are protected by the free speech language of the First Amendment of the US Constitution. The agencies argue that their ratings are inherently subjective rather than intentionally fraudulent. Implicit in this defence is the notion that the decision to invest is ultimately the responsibility of the buyer. Since the 2007 to 2008 financial crisis, more than 40 legal actions targeting S&P have been dropped or dismissed.[3]

However, issuers who want to protest their rating do have recourse – appealing to the agencies directly. There is a tested appeal process in place at the agencies (see Chapter 5) that gives issuers ample opportunity to make their case for a higher rating before it is made public. There is no mechanism in place, or even proposed, to handle rating disputes on a global basis, such as an international court of appeals.

9 *There is an inherent conflict of interest in the way the major agencies operate in at least three areas.*

- *Fee arrangements.* The first conflict is that the agencies receive the great majority of their fees from the companies, banks and governments they rate. The agencies get only a small portion of their revenues from the investors that they serve, primarily through subscriptions to publications and web-based information. This revenue structure leaves the rating process potentially open to influence by the paying clients. Critics say that it is possible that the desire of a rating agency to hold on to a paying client – or to recruit a new one – can at times interfere with the objectivity of a rating (meaning the rating could be higher than merited in order for the CRA not to lose the client to another agency). The thinking is that the agencies don't want to alienate their revenue sources, so they are inclined to be lenient with ratings. This allegation arises periodically but has yet to be proven.

The agencies are adamant about this charge. Moody's former CEO, John Rutherfurd, Jr said, 'The level of ratings does not depend on the commercial relationship with the issuers. Our analysts cannot invest in the companies they analyse, and their salaries are independent of ratings-related revenue.' And as a Fitch spokesman said, 'Fitch goes to great efforts to assure that our receipt of fees from issuers does not affect our editorial independence.'

However, the mortgage securities crisis in 2007 to 2008 proved otherwise. The Financial Crisis Inquiry Commission (FCIC) produced a report that said the agencies were beholden to the investment banks that were responsible for most of their fees. There was also criticism about rating changes to sovereigns at the height of the financial crisis in Europe and threats of increased regulation there, where no First Amendment protections are available.

'Whistle blowers' confirm this conflict of interest. William J Harrington, a veteran senior analyst at Moody's, resigned in 2010 and gave public testimony about how Moody's is 'corrupted to the core'. He presented a scathing indictment of Moody's processes, conflicts of interests, and management with regard to the structured finance business. He said the primary conflict of interest at CRAs is well known: the company is paid by the same issuers whose securities the CRA is supposed to rate objectively. This conflict incentivises everyone at the company to give Moody's clients the ratings they want, lest the clients fire Moody's and take their business to other ratings agencies. Analysts who object to this approach are viewed as 'impeding deals' and, thus, harming Moody's business. These analysts are often transferred, disciplined, 'harassed' or fired.[4]

- *Consulting services.* The second charge is that the agencies sell their own consulting services to clients whom they rate. The services are wide-ranging, from credit risk models to implied ratings and from special research on corporate bonds to studies of rating migration along the scale. Selling these services raises concerns that clients may feel pressured to buy them in order to maintain their relationship with the agency. In this situation, 'trading off their name' may not be intrinsically unethical, but it can and does raise eyebrows. Most accounting practices have curtailed offering consulting services to their clients to avoid such conflicts. The CRAs in turn have created separate companies under the same holding company to provide these services and have ensured they are unrelated to regulated credit rating activity.

- *Boards of Directors.* The third perceived conflict of interest is that the boards of directors of the rating agencies contain officers or directors of companies that they rate. While hundreds of companies and institutions, such as the New York Stock Exchange, have eliminated such potential conflicts on their boards, Moody's directors, for example, continue to serve on the boards of companies that also are Moody's clients.

In addition, members of Moody's Board of Directors also serve on the boards of companies that Moody's rates. Critics ask, does this raise not the possibility that these outside directors could use their influence to pressure Moody's or their other companies in some fashion? Moody's president, Raymond W McDaniel Jr said: 'The board has nothing to do with our professional ratings practices. They are not involved in individual rating actions.'

Some current and former members of Moody's board concede the appearance of conflicts of interest but say they are unavoidable. They argue there is a limited field of directors from which to choose. 'Since we rate the largest corporations and financial institutions in the country,' McDaniel said, 'that is naturally a place we would find some of the best thinkers.' Since Moody's rates virtually every publicly listed corporation, he asks, who would you propose should serve on their Board of Directors who would not have a current or past relationship with a rated entity?

Managing potential conflicts of interest

McDaniel admits, 'We do not deny there are latent or inherent conflicts of interest in our business. The important thing is, how do we manage those potential conflicts?' All three agencies say they adhere to strict codes of conduct, such as prohibiting any link between the pay and bonuses of their rating analysts and the fees that come in from the companies those analysts rate. The CRAs say they already have strong internal controls designed to minimise mistakes or conflicts, including codes of conduct.

Stephen W Joynt, President and CEO of Fitch Ratings, addressed the issue before the SEC in November 2002. The conflict of interest that critics point out 'should more appropriately be classified as a *potential* conflict of interest, that is, something that should be disclosed and managed to assure that it does not become an actual conflict'. As to the perceived conflict of interest in the 'issuer pays' model, he said Fitch already manages this through a range of policies, including separating business development from credit analysis, and not allowing those employees who assign ratings to handle fees or discuss fees with issuers. Moody's and S&P would concur with this approach. In truth, there is no realistic alternative to the current model of agency-issuer-investor relationships.[5]

Fed study supports agency position

Finally, in support of their position, the agencies can point to a 2003 study by two economists at the Federal Reserve who found 'no evidence' that ratings are affected by conflicts of interest. Instead, the agencies 'appear to be relatively responsive to reputation concerns and so protect the interests of investors'. What the Fed calls 'reputation concerns' is indeed what keeps the agencies honest in their dealings with their clients. Any whiff or taint of influence peddling would be deadly for their franchises. Nonetheless, the charges persist.

Conclusion

Some of the accusations against the agencies appear to have merit. Some of the allegations are simplistic and journalistic, where the reality is a bit more complex. It is hoped that regulators can tell the difference. Investors may have mixed feelings about the integrity of the internal controls the agencies have, but investors looking for an estimate of default risk have no other choice than seeking CRA opinions. Next up is how the regulators have responded. The story is ongoing.

---

[1] A number of smaller CRAs are recognised by the US and European authorities, but their markets are limited. Examples include Kroll Bond Rating Agency, DBRS (Canada), Japan Credit Rating Agency, Capital Intelligence, HR Ratings (Mexico) and Scope Ratings. Kroll was established in 2010 and quickly gained market share in the structured finance side of the business, capitalising on the lingering scepticism of Moody's and S&P in the wake of the credit crisis. Many CRA critics say more competition in the industry will reduce the impact and power of the Big Three. Ironically, all the new compliance rules imposed on the CRAs by the SEC are making it more costly and difficult for smaller agencies to enter the market and compete; barriers to entry have risen not fallen.

[2] Gaillard, N, *A Century of Sovereign Ratings*, 2011, Springer, pp. 133–35.

[3] 'Free speech or knowing misrepresentation', *The Economist*, 5 February 2013.

[4] www.businessinsider.com/moodys-analyst-conflicts-corruption-and-greed-2011-8?op=1#ixzz2lhPwYCyb. The environment Harrington describes was seconded in the Report of the Financial Crisis Inquiry Commission (January 2011) when it wrote (p. xxv) that 'the three credit rating agencies were key enablers of the financial meltdown'. The forces at work at Moody's behind the financial breakdown were 'flawed computer models, the pressure from financial firms that paid for the ratings, the relentless drive for market share, the lack of resources to do the job despite record profits, and the absence of meaningful public oversight'.

[5] There are two alternatives to the current issuer-pays system. One is an investor-pays model, such as that employed by two relatively new rating agencies, Egan-Jones and RapidRatings International. This approach may be workable in some markets but not in the near term or on a US-wide or global scale. The other is a government owned and operated CRA, which would be unlikely to function effectively in any market because it is open to political influence and unable to make timely rating decisions due to bureaucratic delays.

3.5 Regulating the raters

Ratings were started by John Moody. In 1909, he published a book about American rail-road securities, using letter grades to assess their risk, and other manuals about securities. Investors looking for more certainty liked the idea, and the Moody business took off. S&P likes to trace its history back to 1860, the year that Henry Varnum Poor published *History of Railroads and Canals of the US*. Poor was concerned about the lack of quality information available to investors and embarked on a campaign to publicise details of corporate operations. Poor's Publishing Co began rating corporate debt in 1916. John Fitch entered the rating business in 1924. Ratings were not paid for in the early days; it was the income of the manuals that sustained the cash flow.

Background to the business

In the 1930s, bank regulators in the US were frightened by the Great Depression and wanted to keep banks solvent. One means to this end was to require banks to hold high quality assets, not bonds deemed 'speculative'. But who would determine that quality? The regulators decided that banks rely on the 'recognised ratings manuals' existing at the time, that is, from existing rating agencies. Banks, whose very business is assessing credit quality, were thus instructed to outsource the job.

Rating agencies began taking the place of banks as credit assessors, and they have since remained virtually untouched by government interference in their business. Financial institutions were permitted to own only highly rated securities, and many capital requirements were keyed to ratings on the institution's holdings. Ratings had acquired the force of law. The CRAs now had a guaranteed audience for their ratings, one that grew beyond financial institutions to other participants in the bond market who wanted to know the ratings for their own investment and competitive purposes.

In 1969, a rating cut by S&P precipitated the bankruptcy of the Penn Central Railroad Corporation. This downgrade suddenly raised the profile of the long-sleeping rating industry for a much broader cross-section of capital market participants. The subsequent jump in demand for ratings allowed S&P and then its competitors to begin charging debt issuers for ratings during the 1970s. The justification for this move was that increasing demands on the agencies required much higher staff and compensation levels than could be afforded through sale of publication subscriptions alone. Income from rating fees quickly eclipsed amounts previously earned from subscriptions.

Then in the late 1970s came the offshore 'invasion'. Governments in Europe and Asia looked to the US market for their large borrowing needs, bringing vast new rating opportunities for the CRAs. The US market, the largest in the world, had near unlimited opportunities to place and trade large bond issues. Their investment bankers (broker-dealers) were pleased and said, 'First, let's pay a visit to the rating agencies.'

The ensuing boom in CRA business was followed by the agencies' expansion into Europe and Asia in the 1980s, where they acquired a much better understanding of local markets, the workings of political environments, overseas accounting systems, and local issuer management. The practice initiated by Fitch of imposing unrequested ratings on borrowers in these settings opened up vast new opportunities to earn fees (see Chapter 2, 'Unsolicited ratings').

Agency role imbedded in law

Ratings became perceived as an 'official litmus test of asset quality' and embedded in rules by state insurance commissioners, federal pension regulators, and broker dealers. Only securities of a certain credit quality (investment grade) can be held by financial intermediaries like pension funds, insurance companies, broker-dealers and banks. And it is the agencies that determine which securities are 'safe' enough to hold, giving them immense power in the market. Over time they became the gatekeepers to the capital market.

Then in 1975, the SEC embedded agency roles even further by formally designating ratings organisations as nationally recognised statistical rating organisations (NRSROs), giving them an official stamp of approval. This institutionalised a pattern of reliance by regulators on ratings. Rating agencies became 'deified' and the perception grew that they were the only source of bond information. This regulatory imprimatur gave the rating agencies a prosperous 'free ride'. As the New York Fed wrote:[1]

> Regulators, like investors, value the cost savings achieved through the use of credit ratings in credit evaluation. As a result, they have come to rely on a variety of specific letter ratings as thresholds for determining capital charges and investment prohibitions.

By placing its stamp of approval on CRA opinions, the US Government has effectively restricted the *supply* of new ratings (by limiting only certain CRAs for approval) and increased the *demand* for ratings (by mandating their use). It should not come as a surprise that the rating agencies as a government created cartel became very profitable.

In sum, over the past 80 years, the agencies have been partially sheltered from market fallout because: (i) issuers must have ratings and there are no reliable alternatives to CRAs; and (ii) the regulatory authorities required the use of their product, giving them immense power in the market. The CRAs are like quasi-public authorities with a government guaranteed market for their opinions. 'Ratings in regulation have been an indirect government subsidy to the rating industry.'[2]

Then as the 20th century drew to a close, a number of rating errors grabbed public, investor and regulator attention. First, there was the Asian financial crisis in 1997 to 1998 when Moody's and S&P combined were forced to downgrade precipitously the foreign currency ratings of a number of governments (Korea a record 16 notches, Malaysia 10 notches, Indonesia 8 notches, and Thailand 8 notches). Ratings do not change three or more notches at a time unless: (i) the agencies make mistakes in their initial assessments by failing to see weaknesses; or (ii) the issuers had not been completely candid with the CRAs about their finances. In the Asian crisis, it was a combination of both.

The agencies (and in particular S&P) had missed a number of key indicators that should have acted as early warning signals that a liquidity crisis was brewing, for example, the build-up of short-term debt, opaque accounting, withheld information, and quality-impaired 'policy loans'.

Then a few years later, the CRAs failed to issue warnings prior to the collapses of Enron (2001), Worldcom (2002) and Parmalat (2003), which again bludgeoned their reputations in the financial markets and called into question the credibility of their ratings elsewhere. The

Frequently asked question

'Is there a supervisory body that inspects rating agency decisions? Do the agencies report their activities to an independent body?'

Quis custodiet ipsos custodes? (Or loosely, who rates the raters?)

Answer:

No single directorial body reviews the rating decisions of Moody's, Fitch or S&P. The agencies are independent commercial enterprises, their survival dependent on their explicit legal mandate and on their maintaining credibility in the market. They do report to their own private sector shareholders, but reporting requirements are focused on financial results rather than the quality or accuracy of ratings, or the integrity of the rating process. However, given the rating scandals of recent years, their ability to regulate themselves in a laissez-faire mode has drawn to a close. Regulatory authorities in the US and Europe have passed new rules that restrict agency operations, monitor their methodologies, and require greater transparency in procedures.

CRAs' role as the financial system's primary and pristine monitors of company, bank and sovereign creditworthiness was suddenly open to question.

Following the Parmalat collapse, François Veverka, Executive Managing Director at S&P in Paris, wrote to the *Financial Times* on 24 December 2003, it is 'extremely unfair' to blame S&P for not uncovering the financial fraud and downgrading the company weeks, if not months, earlier. 'Rating agencies are not auditors or investigators and are not empowered or able to unearth fraud. To function effectively, they depend on truthful audited public accounts and honest private information from the entities they rate.' In the case of Parmalat, 'both these requirements were sorely lacking'. Audited year-end and half-year accounts, he maintained, were 'utterly misleading'. The CRAs do not undertake to verify the information provided by a company; that is not their role. This is a reasonable defensive declaration, but it convinced few.

Bringing this epic of agency errors and government engagement up to date, the CRAs stuck triple-A ratings on huge swathes of mortgage-backed securities throughout the housing bubble without bothering to ask a basic what-if question: what if house prices were to fall dramatically? The agencies tell us they perform these scenario-type questions as stress tests. Apparently not in this case.

Lawmakers and regulators in the US and EU arose from their torpor and decided it was time to 'do something' to protect investors. The first response was tougher oversight. In 2002 the SEC was empowered to look more deeply into the rating agencies. The SEC's choices were: (i) to increase accountability to the regulatory authority by imposing stricter operational guidelines on the agencies; (ii) to ease up current entry restrictions to allow more rating agencies to compete, allowing the market to determine an agency's worthiness; and (iii) to do a bit of both. They chose option (iii).

The next step was the passage in 2006 of the Credit Rating Agency Reform Act, which focused on mandatory disclosure of the rating agencies' methodologies; the law did not, however, permit the SEC to regulate the *substance* of the credit ratings or to mandate the use of certain procedures and methodologies. The result was that the CRAs were forced to undertake greater compliance efforts and risk management procedures. The gated community was breached.

In December 2008, the SEC unanimously adopted additional rules for the rating agencies that were designed to enhance disclosures and rein in business practices that contributed to the global financial crisis of 2007 to 2008. The SEC voted to require greater disclosure and to ban agencies from rating securities they helped issuers create or structure. These new rules were designed to stem conflicts of interest and provide more transparency for the ratings industry. The rules also ban the rating agencies from advising investment banks on how to package securities to secure favourable ratings.

The Dodd–Frank Act, 2010

The next step followed quickly. In July 2010, Congress passed and President Obama signed the Dodd–Frank Wall Street Reform and Consumer Protection Act (Dodd–Frank), which, among other things, expanded the regulation, accountability and transparency of US CRAs. An Office of Credit Ratings (OCR)[3] was created to oversee the practices of the rating agencies, to promote accuracy in credit ratings, to ensure that credit ratings are not unduly influenced by conflicts of interest, and to ensure that CRAs provide greater disclosure to investors. However, neither the legislation nor the SEC defined 'accurate ratings'.

As a result, the CRAs are now subject to annual examinations by the OCR and visits by the regulators to ensure that they comply with their internal policies and procedures and that they conform to SEC rules, including transparency and consistency in rating methodologies. The OCR issues an annual public report on the NRSROs. The agencies can be fined for non-compliance and even de-registered if adequate internal controls are not maintained. Dodd–Frank required the SEC to adopt rules that would require development of an extensive compliance and reporting infrastructure at the CRAs.

Here are the main requirements of the law and other proposed rules.

- Rating agencies must disclose their methodologies, disclose whether they use third parties for due diligence efforts, and their ratings track record over multiple years. They must show their qualitative and quantitative methodologies and the assumptions used. They must disclose why initial ratings were changed or withdrawn.
- Investors can bring legal action against ratings agencies for their 'reckless failure' to conduct a reasonable investigation of the facts or to obtain analysis from an independent source.
- To reduce possible conflicts of interest, the law installs a new requirement for the agencies to conduct a one-year 'look-back' review when one of their rating employees subsequently goes to work for an underwriter of a security previously rated by the agency or for an entity rated by the agency in the previous 12 months.
- CRA analysts would be required to meet qualification requirements, which would likely include passing qualifying exams and having continuing education.

- Half the members of an agency's board of directors must be independent, with no financial stake in credit ratings. The boards must have specific oversight responsibilities on agency rating procedures and conflicts of interest.

On the subject of all the imbedded rules that require the use of credit ratings, Christopher Cox, Chairman of SEC, had it right when he stated in an open hearing in June 2008:

> To the extent that the marketplace views the SEC's references to credit ratings in our rules as giving those ratings an implied official seal of approval, our own rules may be contributing to an uncritical reliance on credit ratings as a substitute for independent evaluation.

Therefore, the SEC intends to reduce or remove many statutory and regulatory requirements that mandate the use of credit ratings in order to decrease over-reliance on ratings and to encourage investors to conduct their own analyses of creditworthiness.

During the SEC's annual examination, the regulator will inquire of the CRAs: did you adequately state your methodology and did you follow it? Is there an internal control structure for creating and reviewing methodologies? One purpose is to uncover conflicts of interest, such as analysts helping negotiate fees for ratings or influential RC chairmen directing how analysts should vote in a rating committee depending on whether the issuer is paying fees on time.

An example of the latter found its way into the public press. A former Moody's credit analyst and vice president sued the agency for wrongful termination. In August 2009 he claimed he was fired after complaining to the Compliance Department about his manager who blocked a company's upgrade, arguing that the company 'doesn't pay us'. The credit analyst argued for an upgrade of the company in a rating committee meeting based on the company's improved performance. The committee voted 5 to 2 in favour of the upgrade but then his manager, also the committee chairman, called for a re-vote saying the company 'doesn't pay us and they don't visit us and they don't deserve our upgrade'.

The analyst protested but the committee reversed itself and voted 6 to 1 against the upgrade. The next day the analyst complained to the Compliance Department saying this was a breach of the company's conflicts policies. He was fired one week later.

No reasonable alternatives

Dodd–Frank seeks to reduce the reliance of investors on ratings, but simply put, there is no workable, low-cost alternative to the agencies' professional opinion on credit risk. The provisions mandating the use of ratings have been in place for decades and lifting them would leave an uncertain vacuum. Investors and issuers benefiting from the current rating regime oppose changes that would bring uncertainty to the whole framework.

Central banks, investment groups and international banks do not have the desire or resources to conduct extensive independent credit analysis, so ratings and the current framework remain the most expedient alternative. The current system is an easy shortcut for everybody. Nonetheless, by the end of 2013 requirements had been removed from some state and federal statutes.

To ensure consistency in the CRAs' approach to ratings, the SEC has forced the agencies to lock down, memorialise and disclose their rating methodologies so that a rating decision can be understood and examined in the future. The SEC is demanding a more transparent approach by the agencies, one that can be reviewed and critiqued by the SEC. The agencies need to document their data sources, interpretations and conclusions rigorously – all in the interest of greater agency accountability and protecting investors. Regulators in the US visit the agencies to ensure they are adhering to methodologies and models. Any deviation needs to be explained. Dodd–Frank is not imposing a methodological cookbook with precise recipes, but the new regulatory disclosure framework is intended to give a reader insight as to how the agency reached a conclusion and the evidence used.

It is much too early to see if a higher degree of SEC oversight will indeed give investors new and better information so that fewer ratings are 'wrong'. It is too early also to determine how issuers will benefit. What is certain is that the new administrative hurdles have added to the red tape of running a rating agency and have raised the cost of business by requiring more agency staff to comply with the new demands. One compliance officer subsequently observed, 'We are now in an age when compliance is as important as other aspects of the business.'

Shift in methodology

Dodd–Frank has encouraged a shift in methodology by the CRAs. To make rating decisions more transparent and replicable and the agencies more accountable, analysts in all issuer categories are increasingly using a checklist or 'scorecard' approach in determining rating recommendations. Analysts fill out matrices and weighted score sheets that add up to a likely rating outcome over a range of several notches, say BBB+ to A+. The score sheets go before the rating committee along with the lead analyst's written recommendation. These documents are discussed and the proposed rating range tweaked and narrowed down based on the analyst's assumptions and the qualitative expertise of the analysts. What is new over the past decade is that the initial pass on any rating, for a new or existing issuer, can be couched in terms of matrices and superscores.

There are two views on the use of the matrix-based approach to ratings. Those in favour say that it allows for more internal debate on a greater number of issues. 'Methodology is just the starting point of a discussion,' remarked a Moody's official. It forces the RC to be certain they are covering all the relevant factors and it makes the whole process more transparent to the market. It also ensures consistency within categories, such as within the industrials category or among commercial banks. Specific rating models have not been forced on the CRAs, but the regulatory requirements have generated the score-card driven model, allowing the agencies to explain more clearly and publicly how they arrive at a rating decision.

Those opposed argue that score sheets force segmentation in the rating analysis in an artificial way. The variables affecting creditworthiness are by nature interactive. 'Models, matrices and checklists should be auxiliary tools, not a decision maker,' argued a current CRA analyst. He misses the dynamism and debate of the pre Dodd–Frank approach.

There is too much focus on paperwork and less focus on creative thinking about credit risk, he maintains. With ratings being 'methodology driven', the 'craft' of ratings is being submerged.

For example, in sovereign analysis if one is required to check a scorecard on fiscal policy measures in one compartment and a scorecard on the trade and current account variables in a different compartment, this approach forces artificial division of naturally interacting variables. In the real world, these two compartments are not separate; they are inextricably linked.

Similarly with banks, a scorecard methodology that forces a segmented approach tends to compartmentalise the financial analysis rather than bring it together. For example, statistics in one compartment might show a widening net interest margin at a bank which points clearly to a positive development. Yet deeper, more inter-compartmental analysis might show that the wider margin actually indicates management's higher risk appetite as shifts have occurred in the earning asset mix.

At all major CRAs, the approaches to risk analysis have become quite similar due to the demands from regulators to be able to replicate the analysis years later when a question arises. Increased scrutiny by regulators on accountability and transparency has forced homogenisation and uniformity on how to do the rating business. It is still early days under this new score card approach, so we will have to wait to see how it evolves in actual practice and then assess what improvements, if any, it brings for investors and issuers. In the meantime, the CRAs continue to voluntarily update their methodologies,[4] meaning that issuers need to stay alert.

Current agency officials were asked in interviews, what are the biggest changes you have seen in rating agency procedures and practices over the past 25 years? Their answers uniformly were 'the changes mandated by the SEC: greater demands for accountability, transparency and methodological purity'. Certainly in the structured finance area of ratings but also in other rating areas, the agencies have undertaken a more formulaic, deterministic and model-driven approach. Regulators have required more codification of rating factors and public dissemination of just what goes into a rating.

The cast of culprits

At the same time, investors cannot escape some responsibility for the recent market calamity. When they blindly assumed the rating agencies had it right and purchased securities based on the ratings of a complex assortment of sub-prime mortgages, the odds of a financial meltdown greatly increased. Not only were the sub-prime loans untested as packaged securities, they were also issued to borrowers who could not have qualified under the more stringent guidelines of the past, making it hard to judge how the loans would perform in an economic downturn.

Here is a crucial factor often missed in criticisms of the rating agencies' performance in the housing crisis – how government policies directly affect the market and indirectly affect ratings. Embedded laws and regulations prevent the market from 'clearing' by interfering with normal market incentives. Public policy can cause any number of distortions in the financial markets, such as giving incentives to market participants to act contrary to their own interest or the public interest. For example, tax laws can encourage the accumulation of debt while discouraging the accumulation of equity capital on balance sheets. The US government can (and did) over-promote home ownership which contributed greatly to the 2008 housing market collapse.

While public attention focused on the errors of the rating agencies in the ensuing financial fiasco, the cast of culprits was much broader:

- the Congress for overzealously pushing home ownership and for not doing its duty of overseeing and reforming mortgage institutions;
- predatory lenders for taking advantage of unqualified and sometimes vulnerable home buyers;
- home buyers for getting in over their heads based on implicit or explicit assurances from lenders;
- the regulators for letting banking regulations become too loose;
- finance executives for selling products they did not understand while enjoying outsized profits;
- the Federal Reserve Bank for keeping interest rates historically low; and
- short-selling hedge funds for betting on doomsday, thereby ushering it in.

A characteristic common to most of these participants is the elemental motivator – greed. Think of all the investors seeking that extra spread, the investment banks pursuing those additional fees, the mortgage banks that relaxed their know your customer (KYC) rules to maintain or enlarge market share, the mortgage brokers who pushed obligations onto their customers, consumers who lost their common sense when offered 'no income verification' loans, and the rating agencies who profited mightily from the huge volume of securitised sub-prime mortgages they rated.

Overseas oversight

We move now to developments in rating regulation outside the US. The International Organisation of Securities Commissions (IOSCO), based in Madrid and established in 1983, currently represents 205 securities regulators around the world and sets standards for financial markets. In October 2004, IOSCO published a code of conduct for CRAs and ruled that they will be able to police themselves under this code. The code was not intended to be 'rigid or formulistic'. CRAs are able to maintain a degree of flexibility to deal with the different legal and market circumstances in which they operate.

Moody's, Fitch and S&P all welcomed the news, saying they were already largely in compliance with the code's provisions anyway. These provisions deal with such matters as conflicts of interest, transparency of ratings, and fair dealings with clients. The agencies were not alone in seeking a light application of rules; prominent financial market associations also sought a flexible regulatory regime.

The IOSCO code of conduct was perhaps the first international attempt to impose some discipline and disclosure rules on the agencies. CRAs are required to report to the market if they fail to adopt any of the code's 52 sections. On 2 June 2005, Moody's did its part, publishing an updated Code of Conduct, reflecting the IOSCO recommendations. This followed just two years after Moody's created its first compliance department in anticipation of greater SEC oversight.

The European Commission and other G20 countries have been demanding more accountability from the rating agencies, because they have so much influence in their economies. Hiding behind a freedom of speech defence, as they do in the US, is not going to play well. As a ratings colleague expressed it, 'influence without accountability' offends against natural justice, just like 'taxation without representation', no matter how legal it might be.

Some national authorities, especially politicians in France and Germany, believe the agencies have too much power and too little accountability. Journalists said the CRAs have too much gullibility, implying that the agencies do not probe a company's financials deeply enough and that they take as gospel what company management tells them. Some European critics pilloried the 'Anglo-American' approach to business that the CRAs supposedly take. The EU parliament began looking into the creation of an EU ratings authority to monitor the agencies, thereby 'strengthening investor protection'.

The agencies' response to the EU initiative was captured by Paul Taylor, group managing director at Fitch, who told the *Wall Street Journal* in early 2004 that Fitch is not opposed to mandatory registration of the agencies but feels the agencies are already held accountable – by the market. This is a tough enough policeman, he believes. Some years earlier Moody's President John Bohn voiced the same opinion, 'you can't regulate judgement'. He said the marketplace imposes enough controls on the ratings industry. 'If we're not useful, the market stops buying our stuff.'[5]

EU authorities thought differently several years later when the euro debt crisis threatened southern European sovereigns and drove many countries into recession. It was time to strengthen the regulatory framework relative to CRAs.

EU rules on CRAs

First, a new entity was created, the European Securities and Markets Authority (ESMA) which is exclusively responsible for the registration and supervision of credit rating agencies in the EU. Then the European Commission put forward proposals to reinforce the regulatory framework surrounding CRAs, and these proposals entered into force on 20 June 2013.

There are currently 30 rating agencies registered with ESMA to conduct ratings business in Europe. EuroRatings was the first pan-European rating agency, and after it failed other attempts have also foundered over the political demands of various EU countries and owners. ESMA scrutinises all rating-related matters and makes sure that methodologies are codified and policies and procedures are documented. ESMA does the onsite inspections of CRAs in Europe, the result being that the agencies are better organising themselves. In November 2013, ESMA wasted no time in warning the major CRAs that they could face fines or withdrawal of licence if found in breach of ESMA rules.

Michel Barnier, EU Commissioner for Internal Market and Services, spoke about the new law:[6]

> Under the new legislation, credit rating agencies will have to be more transparent and accountable when rating sovereign states. The new rules will also contribute to increased

competition in the ratings industry currently dominated by a few market players and will reduce the over-reliance on ratings by financial market participants. This is an important step towards restoring financial stability and trust in financial institutions and will help to avoid further crises.

These general statements are meant to show that the EU was 'taking action' to deal with irregularities in the European financial markets, but they also revealed that policy differences in the European Parliament prevented a tougher regime. Here are the principal features of current EU regulations with respect to CRAs.

1 *Reduced overreliance on credit ratings.* The new rules are intended to reduce financial institutions' automatic or mechanistic reliance on external ratings and to require financial institutions to strengthen their own credit risk assessment procedures.
2 *Improved quality of ratings of sovereign debt of EU member states.* To avoid market disruption, rating agencies will set up a calendar indicating when they will rate member states. One proposal is that sovereign ratings will only be published on Fridays after close of business and at least one hour before the opening of trading venues in the EU. Furthermore, investors and member states will be informed of the underlying facts and assumptions on each rating. The rating agencies will have to follow stricter rules which will make them more accountable for their actions and be more transparent when rating sovereign states.
3 *Credit rating agencies will be more accountable for their actions.* The new rules ensure that a rating agency can be held liable in case it infringes intentionally or with gross negligence the CRA Regulation, thereby causing damage to an investor or an issuer.
4 *Reduced conflicts of interests due to the 'issuer pays' remuneration model.* The CRA Regulation will improve the independence of credit rating agencies and help eliminate actual or potential conflicts of interest. There are limitations on the shareholding of rating agencies. For example, might Fitch Ratings' 50% ownership by the Hearst Corporation, a large US information and publishing company, be questioned by the EU?
5 *Publication of ratings on a European Rating Platform.* All available ratings will be published on a European Rating Platform, available as from June 2015. This will improve the comparability and visibility of ratings of financial instruments rated by rating agencies registered in the EU.

In addition, the new regulations contain these features [author commentary follows].

1 They prohibit a credit rating company from issuing a rating on a security when it also advises, underwrites or sponsors the structuring of the security. [All right, this is in line with SEC thinking and does help prevent a conflict of interest.]
2 They bar employees working on ratings from engaging in discussions about fees or from receiving gifts from corporations or underwriters worth more than US$25 from clients [This is already the policy at the major CRAs where their marketing arms discuss fees.]
3 They require that the agencies annually disclose statistics on upgrades and downgrades for each type of asset they rate. [Mostly done already, so only a minor increase in effort and disclosure.]

4 They require rating agencies to make publicly available the data and history behind 10%
of their ratings so that investors will have access to 'a statistically significant amount of
information'. [This is not overly burdensome for the agencies, the CRAs have these data
anyway, and they get to choose which ratings to report on. Nonetheless, no agency wants
to do unpaid work.]
5 The agencies must publicly disclose the name of every entity that paid for a credit rating
and provide more information about income earned from companies they rate. [This
amounts to more disclosure than the CRAs are used to, but at least the disclosures are
quite general statements.]
6 They require the agencies to describe the steps they take to verify information used
in ratings. [This will take each analyst ten minutes to list the steps without revealing
any secrets.]

From the above, it is clear that the new EU regulations will not be as stringent or restrictive
as in the US. These steps are simple, relatively non-invasive and doable by the agencies. They
have 'more bark than bite'. The agencies support these rules. They increase transparency
and accountability but are not revolutionary. They should assuage some critics of the ratings
process who question its integrity. However, the whole regulatory framework in Europe is
a work in progress and its practical impact is unknown. As the CRAs appoint compliance
officers to liaise with ESMA, the situation will become clearer over time.

The most that has been achieved with regard to CRAs is to get them to agree on more
transparent methods and greater accountability to regulators. Fortunately, the clumsy and
desperate attempt by European politicians to force the rating agencies to tell governments of
rating changes ahead of time so they have time to adjust and adapt did not succeed. That
approach risks leaks and worse, it risks the politicisation of ratings and contravenes the
rule that everyone in the market should know at the same time of rating changes regarding
any issuer.

Finally, governments have created another international institution to make recommendations on how to deal with the rating agencies. It is the Financial Stability Board (FSB),
established in 2009 in Basel by the G20 major economies plus the European Commission.
Its overall mission is to monitor and make recommendations about the global financial system. Inspired more by emotion and politics than by pragmatism, the FSB has
drawn up principles and road maps to reduce reliance on CRA ratings in standards, laws
and regulations.

The principles aim to end mechanical reliance on ratings by market participants and
establish stronger internal credit risk assessment practices instead. The problem, of course, is
that investors are not able to easily develop their own credit risk capabilities. They simply
do not have the resources, the will, the staff, or the know-how to do it. The reality is they
cannot invent and implement a new system, nor do they want to.

In August 2013, FSB produced a progress report[7] that admitted to little headway in
all these areas. The report did say that implementation of the Dodd–Frank Act in the US
has made the most advances in encouraging transparency at the agencies. In the author's
opinion, the FSB program will continue to be a work in progress with minimal impact on
investors and issuers.

Conclusions

In classical physics, inertia is the tendency of a body to maintain its state of rest or its uniform motion unless acted upon by an external force. With regard to fundamental structural changes to the rating industry, inertia is the operating force. Governments do not easily revoke long-standing rules. Laws are not quickly overturned or revised. US and EU regulations will discomfit the agencies but will not be a game changer. The bond market will remain wholly dependent on the accuracy of credit ratings because there are few if any institutional alternatives to the current situation. The rating agencies live for another day, buoyed by the growth of the global economy, the free flow of capital across borders, and the rise of bond markets in Europe, Africa and Asia – all of which reinforce the utility of credit ratings.

As one current CRA executive phrased it, 'We're fine with being regulated as a financial services company. Most regulation is quite benign.' From his point of view, the main impact of more oversight has been that they document things a lot more carefully, treat data in a more systematic way and communicate their position more clearly. This helps all participants in the fixed-income markets. He said that the only regulation that would cause severe problems would be one that curtails our opinion in the market.

Given the entrenchment of ratings in the global financial system, the regulators have little choice but to rap the CRAs' knuckles rather than behead them. The agencies have not been emasculated by severe legal redress or by punitive payments. Nothing here suggests a radical transformation of agency practices or an incentive for the agencies to change their business model. The agencies will survive much as they are today without much structural reform because their value and mandate are hard-wired into the regulations of the global financial system.

Authentic change would mean removing requirements about ratings that are embedded in the regulatory scheme of things, including in the Basel accords. To reduce reliance on CRAs materially, investors would actually have to do much more due diligence on securities themselves rather than rely almost solely on the agencies' pronouncements. The prospects for a change this radical are minimal since investors do not want to shoulder the attendant costs and responsibilities. The inconvenient truth is that as financial instruments continue to become more sophisticated and complicated – and as assessing the risk underpinning these instruments becomes more costly – CRAs will continue to wield great power in the financial system.

Ratings are part of the fabric of global capital markets. Government oversight in the US and EU will continue with incremental changes to improve CRA transparency and methodological faithfulness. Central banks, investment groups and international banks do not have the desire or resources to conduct extensive independent credit analysis, so ratings remain the best and cheapest alternative.

The biggest change the CRAs face is greater government oversight at home and abroad. So far the agencies have had little trouble complying with the requirement of more transparent processes and rationales. It has been more of an expensive nuisance for them. The medium-term impact on issuers and investors is unknown.

Those in the US who write the laws and regulations governing the rating agencies are the Congress and the SEC, neither of which fully understands the issues or is immune from political pressures, according to a former SEC staff member. The same is most certainly true in Europe. At worst, the regulations make life more difficult for the agencies and detract focus from the real business of ratings.[8] They amount to an additional hurdle for new agencies attempting to enter the business due to the compliance function and the need to document everything.

Observations for issuers

1 Issuers at all levels worldwide cannot count on governments anywhere to tighten the reins meaningfully on agency practices. If regulators pull too hard on the reins, there will be market confusion and counterproductive aftereffects, not the least of which could be less timely responsiveness by CRAs to issuer inquiries and investor requests.
2 Issuers still need a strategy for managing their ratings and their relations with the agencies. Issuers have not been relieved of the burden of managing the rating agencies. A more transparent CRA has emerged but not necessarily a more issuer-friendly one.
3 In the face of the agencies' vast authority, global reach and regulatory roots, issuers still need to use whatever leverage they can in order to level the playing field, optimise their ratings, and assure equitable treatment by the agencies.
4 From a legal standpoint, even if a plaintiff could prove that 'wrong' ratings were the result of negligence by the agencies, it would be virtually impossible to prove criminal behaviour. Legal penalties would be difficult to impose (although not regulatory ones), so issuers and investors cannot expect legal redress through the courts.
5 The CRA bureaucracies grow, and the impact on issuers is yet to be determined in terms of: (i) the pricing of ratings due to higher compliance costs; (ii) the accuracy of ratings as measured by default studies; and (iii) the speed at which rating decisions can be taken.

None of the alterations so far in the rating process are game-changing for the agencies. They amount to modifications and shifts in emphasis. The CRAs will make good efforts to clarify their thinking in reports and press releases. The fundamentals of the rating process will remain in place. The main consequence is that CRAs will now have a higher level of accountability to government and investors.

---

[1] Richard Cantor [now at Moody's] and Frank Packer, 'Multiple ratings and credit standards: differences of opinion in the credit rating industry', Federal Reserve Bank of New York, Staff Reports Number 12, April 1996, p. 1.

[2] Thomas J McGuire, Executive Vice President at Moody's, in a speech before the Securities and Exchange Commission in Washington DC, 'Ratings in regulation: a petition to the gorillas,' 28 April 1995, p. 8.

[3] The OCR currently comprises 25 lawyers, accountants and examiners, including the director, Thomas Butler. For more information on the Office of Credit Ratings, go to www.sec.gov/about/offices/ocr.shtml.

[4] A recent example was S&P's announcement on 11 December 2013 that the agency was updating its global criteria for rating corporate industrial companies and utilities. In the process, they expect about 5% of corporate ratings worldwide to change. Such updates and refinements can come without warning.

[5] Quoted in Anne Schwimmer, 'How far is too far', *Investment Dealer's Digest*, 12 February 1996, p. 19.

[6] http://europa.eu/rapid/press-release_MEMO-12-911_en.htm.

[7] www.financialstabilityboard.org/publications/r_130829d.pdf.

[8] In some cases, regulations have an even more punitive effect, as Alan Greenspan opined: 'My concern about regulation is that it's more vindictive than curative.' *Time*, 4 November 2013, p. 72. One could also point to the adoption in December 2103 by US bank regulators of the convoluted 953-page Volcker Rule aimed at reducing the likelihood of future financial crises, but instead it adds complexity and ambiguity – an example of the belief by regulators that more complicated regulations will yield a safer financial system.

Part 2

Managing the rating agencies

Chapter 4

The rating meeting

Précis

When an issuer's most important interface with the rating agencies is the annual due diligence meeting, it pays large dividends to prepare thoroughly and appropriately for the meeting. This chapter offers guidance on how to prepare, how credit rating agencies' (CRAs) perceptions of an issuer's performance play a large role, what to do and not do in the actual meetings (tactics and strategy), the best format and content for the meeting, and what information to provide the analysts that best meets their needs and benefits the issuer as well.

We supply some questions you may be asked in the meeting and some that you as an alert issuer should ask the agencies.

If I had eight hours to chop down a tree, I'd spend six hours sharpening my axe.
Abraham Lincoln

4.1 Proper preparation is paramount

The best opportunity to influence agency perceptions of management competence is in the due diligence meetings. No other occasion exists during the year when you can draw upon all your key people and devote time and resources to addressing all their concerns and telling your story in full. An onsite meeting on your premises has all the advantages. Sending the CFO or finance minister to visit the agencies in New York for an hour-long update does not compare with the leverage you have during their one or two-day visit on your turf, where you have the 'home-court' advantage.

The rating agencies' framework, contracts and criteria set the tone and substance of the rating relationship from the beginning. The rules are made by them and imposed on issuers with hardly a protest from their paying customers. When due diligence meetings take place, it is the agency agenda that is followed. Although the timing of visits can be negotiated, the topics to be covered are generally provided by the agencies based on their own list of standard issues plus whatever news there has been lately. In this environment, preparation is paramount.

> By failing to prepare, you are preparing to fail.
>
> *Benjamin Franklin*

Essential steps

Since the annual due diligence meeting is an issuer's best opportunity for making its case for an upgrade, careful planning for this meeting is vital. Start with a proactive and assertive mindset, aiming to take charge of the relationship. Here are a number of essential steps.

- Set internal objectives: what do we want to accomplish; how can we do it?
- Send the CRA a comprehensive briefing book as their preparation homework two weeks prior to their visit. The book will permit the agency to ask more informed questions and will reduce misunderstandings.
- Initiate information flows, telephone calls, and meeting schedules.
- Ask to see their rating criteria and reports on your peers.
- Ask for a meeting with the CRA to discuss specifically rating 'drivers' – the key factors and ratios they consider in assessing your issuer class.
- Monitor their public statements and develop a file on everything they say and write.
- Set the topic agenda for the meeting and agree to it with the agency. The agenda may or not coincide with the list of topics and questions the CRA sends you ahead of time.
- Ask for the biographies of visiting analysts and, if appropriate, question their lack or appropriateness of experience.
- Choose the most advantageous dates for a meeting so that you will have fresh data to reveal, time for preparation and the right senior people available.
- Understand how the agency thinks about your industry and what they deem to be the key variables so that you can explain these particular areas fully.

- Recognise the agency's issues and concerns and develop responses.
- Determine the agency analyst's likely questions and develop cogent answers.
- Prepare peer comparisons on a number of dimensions and present them during the meeting, because the agency will have prepared (or will prepare) its own set of peer metrics.
- Arrange for the right senior officers to make presentations.
- Confirm what the working language of the meeting will be. It may not be English. Ensure your representatives speak the language sufficiently well so that there are no distractions and misunderstandings.
- Organise an inter-divisional or inter-ministerial meeting prior to the agency visit in order to co-ordinate strategy. Ensure the overall approach and prepared answers are consistent. You do not want the agency to hear contradictory stories. With your CRA co-ordinator agree on what each presenter will hand out and speak about.
- Consider hiring a good ratings adviser, one who will review your documentation for consistency and completeness and help develop responses to the agencies' worries.
- Hold one or more dress rehearsals, especially if there are new officials involved on your side unfamiliar with the agencies.

Frequently asked question

'Do the rating agencies form their opinion on a rating *before* their team visits us for the due diligence meeting, perhaps on the basis of certain pre-determined parameters?'

Answer:
Analysts do indeed have views of an issuer's creditworthiness prior to their visit. The views are based on their own research and on the documents the issuer has sent them prior to the meeting. Their opinions are also pre-cast by your country's sovereign rating and by their understanding of the risks of your industry nationally.

For example, if the request for a rating comes from a sub-Saharan African country where most existing ratings are in or close to the 'B' category, and a B rating is defined as 'offering poor financial security' because 'assurance of payment of obligations over any long period of time is small' (per Moody's), then the visiting analyst approaches the rating assignment in this frame of mind.

Such a preconception is also the result of the analyst's own academic and pre-agency background. However, this early perspective may not be a well-informed one or a firm one. This is where issuers have the opportunity to shape fuzzy views, to counter the misperceptions present in the media, and thereby influence the rating outcome.

What the agency hears from issuer management onsite (ministers, CFOs and CEOs) can shift their opinion in a favourable direction. Can this 'favourable feeling' last through to the convening of the rating committee (RC) itself, which could be weeks later? See Chapter 6 for a three-step strategy that helps make that happen.

The rating outcome will be determined to a significant extent by the agency's confidence in management, which turns largely on the competence, openness and determination shown by officials before, during and after the meeting. The busy agency analysts appreciate an issuer that takes the whole exercise seriously and takes the time to prepare properly. It makes their work easier by filling gaps, and it provides material that may well make its way into the analyst's recommendation to the rating committee.

Direct questions

A competent ratings adviser will supply his clients with a list of questions the rating agencies will likely ask in your next due diligence meeting. Armed with these questions ahead of time, issuers have a head start in preparing for the meeting.

All issuers can expect the agencies to ask the standard questions about their financial statements, revenues, liabilities, governance, and so on, that is, about the types of issues shown in Chapter 3. They will be direct and probing. However, there could also be some unusual questions about your creditworthiness and your country-specific risks that you have not heard before and that could have a determining effect in the rating committee.

Be prepared for these types of questions from the CRAs, who are not worried about offending you. In fact, they are curious about how you react.

1 What structural difficulties do you have (in your industry, in your country) that are so overwhelming as to swamp even the best economic and financial managers, for example, intractable political divisions, the tax code, strict regulations, labour unions, an entitlement mentality?
2 Given your relative lack of transparency, how much corruption must we assume exists?
3 What past instances of mismanagement or misapplication of resources affected your liabilities and your ability to repay and service debt?
4 What extreme set of circumstances might force you to renege on an obligation? What probability do you assign to these circumstances?
5 How can we be assured that the information you have supplied us is trustworthy?
6 Do your management information systems (MIS) permit timely flows of information both up and down the organisation? Give us an example.
7 What will your owners or the government do if you are close to default?

These questions all have a negative bias and are typical of the idiosyncratic element that can enter rating decisions.

Lesson for issuers

The issuer needs to help the agency prepare well ahead of its visit and then perform professionally in the due diligence meeting. Proper preparation will make a big difference in how the agency analysts perceive the overall economic, competitive, regulatory and financial environment in which the issuer operates.

Conclusion

Agency visits cannot be taken for granted. Once you have made a positive impression, it is easier to reinforce it on the next visit than it is to erase negative impressions from the previous visit. It is essential to ensure that the few hours you have to impress the agencies during your meetings are maximised in terms of your performance, including your ability to withstand probing questions.

Thorough preparation raises the odds for an optimal rating, involves a good disciplinary exercise for management and staff, generates useful materials for other audiences, and makes updating for next year easier.

4.2 Your critical performance

Of all the factors that enter into a rating decision, the most important one is the perceptions of the agency analysts regarding the performance of senior managers or government officials whom they meet across the conference table.[1] Whether the meeting is in Paris, Tokyo or your home base, the analysts not only focus on the substance of the message you and your colleagues are making, but they also pay close attention to the manner, style and confidence with which you present your message. The agencies want to hear your story, and they appreciate one that is well done. It makes their analysis easier.

Frequently asked question

'Don't the agencies determine the rating outcome, not us?'

Answer:
The agencies determine the final outcome, but it is up to you to present your story in a way that represents the best outcome for you. What you say and do not say in due diligence meetings and how you say it influence the rating outcome. How you manage relations with the agencies in-between meetings also affects the rating result. Part of the rating decision is based on factors over which you have some control. By taking a more active stance, you stand out as exceptional among your peers. You *can* influence the rating decision. The benefit of the doubt in the rating committee goes to those issuers who take an active interest and a proactive approach.

Perceptions of performance

The reality is – you are 'on stage' with the agencies. Once the economic and financial data are analysed and compared with those of your peers, *their impressions of your competence determine the rating outcome*. All the data and peer comparisons may justify a rating increase, but if your senior managers do not impress the agencies with their experience and determination, then the merits of the case will be overshadowed by the agencies' inference of 'lack of will'.

Weak performances by officials who are unpersuasive or for some reason ill-prepared on that day can and do influence analysts' perceptions about the capabilities of the client. In the meeting, if the issuer exhibits an indecisive manner, a stumbling style, or a wavering answer, it will cast doubts in the agency's mind on the ability and willingness of decision makers to effect changes in the desired direction, to meet targets or fulfil a strategic plan.

Many agency questions are designed to fill in the gaps of knowledge regarding your business, your industry and your competitors. At the same time, the CRAs like to pose hypothetical questions to learn how issuers might react to sudden events or various trends. How these questions are answered tells the agencies how management thinks and how they plan for contingencies. If a question seems 'off base', issuers should understand that the analyst may have other motives for it.

The Ministry of Finance can have the most coherent plan for cutting budgetary expenditures and corporate management can describe in fulsome terms a way to restructure a corporate division, but if the agencies do not believe you can really accomplish the task, then they attach a higher level of uncertainty to the future and less credibility to your management.

Naturally, the higher the uncertainty they feel about bondholder protections, the lower they set the rating. Your aim should be to convince the analysts that you have a credible plan and will follow through. Make no mistake – poor meeting performance affects the rating decision.

Obviously, issuers have to have actual, measurable successes to point to as evidence that policy and plans are on track and management knows what it is doing. You have to show concrete evidence that there has been progress in meeting sales, budgetary targets, in reducing non-performing loans or current-account deficits. A show of bravado with no substance behind it will not win the day and will only undermine the credibility you are trying to build. The analysts are not fooled by Potemkin Villages or misled by malarkey. If you try to trick the agencies with financial legerdemain and they discover it, it will take years to undo the damage. They will remember your attempted hoax in future rating committee meetings.[2]

An unnamed official at Moody's once said, 'Issuers are talented at pitching themselves. That's what they do at road shows. We have absolutely no responsibility to believe it. Our role is to be independent and poke at it.'[3] Moody's stance is not really that extreme.

The weight the agencies place on management presentations varies by agency and by each analyst's degree of scepticism based on his education and natural temperament. The agencies certainly pay close attention to the quality of management and their ability to create cash flow or generate healthy operating margins. For sovereigns, they ask: will this government be able to meet budgetary targets given political pressures, or will they have to borrow more? The more volatile and uncertain the sector, industry or region is, then the more cautious the agencies are in accepting management's views.

Corporate or government officials often provide subtle, unintended, but telling clues about their management style by the manner in which they conduct their agency meetings and the type of materials they provide in the due diligence process. For example, when one bank held its meeting with Moody's, the bank arranged to meet in a special room set up like a court room, with the Moody's analyst on a raised dais acting as 'judge', while senior management acted as witnesses to be called onto a special chair. This behaviour told Moody's how management ran the company, and it was more compelling than any 'evidence' given in the proceedings. It also tells the agency a lot when the issuer delivers his message from the fancy charts already published in the annual report rather than through a meaningful discussion of strategy.

Lesson for issuers

How you deliver the message is almost as important as the message.

Frequently asked question

'How much weight do the views of the visiting agency team carry with the rating committee?'

Answer:

The agency analyst who meets with you carries a lot of influence into the rating committee back in New York, London or Tokyo. He or she brings back to the committee first-hand knowledge and insights and opinions of issuer management. If, in addition, the analyst's written rating recommendation has been clearly and logically drawn, this combination is usually the determining factor in a rating decision.

Evidence for this is that the outcome of rating committee deliberations seldom differs by more than one notch from what the senior analyst recommends. Most analysts' rating recommendations are adopted as presented to the rating committee or decided with a difference of only one notch higher or lower. The primary purpose of the rating committee is to ensure: (i) that all significant variables and questions have been addressed; and (ii) that the rating outcome makes sense relative to other already-rated peers. (An unspoken purpose is to ensure the rating outcome does not violate common sense, the other agencies' rating result, and the market's expectations.)

It is almost always the case that an issuer's efforts to influence the rating outcome are most effectively directed at the senior analyst with primary responsibility for the rating and/or at his immediate supervisor. There are appropriate and inappropriate means of exercising this influence, which we will present later.

The ABCs

The secret to better performance is a confident approach on your part – a confidence gained by understanding the agencies' ABCs, that is, their Agenda, Biases and Concerns, both in general and in relation to your specific circumstances. In your due diligence meetings, issuers should choose presenters who are cognisant of the agencies' ABCs. For example:

- if certain of a company's lines of business are suffering from a slowdown in sales, then the division managers involved should be at the table with credible fixes and forecasts;
- if a commercial bank experiences a trend in bad loans and write-offs, then the relevant credit officers need to be ready to explain how the impact on net profit is going to be minimised and how loan standards have tightened; or
- if a country's budgetary balances are deteriorating, the head of the budget office at the Ministry of Finance should prepare and present telling arguments that explain how the problem is being addressed, for example, increase in the VAT.

Part of the planning for the meeting discussed earlier was to agree with the agency ahead of time what topics will be covered and how much time will be allocated for each. If this has not been settled, there is a risk that once the meeting has begun, the agency may put pressure on the issuer to move quickly through the presentations since they have a plane to catch or some other pressing reason. An issuer must ensure they have enough time to make all their necessary points and not be forced to rush through discussions.

If a new lead analyst has taken over the responsibility for your credit, issuers should view this as a good opportunity to teach him or her the fundamentals of your business, to make another good first impression and to start with a clean slate. If issuers listen carefully to the new analyst's questions and comments, they can determine where his or her prejudices and misunderstandings lie and correct them on the spot. If the issuer has a new minister or CFO, the meeting presents an opportunity to explain how new policies will address the agency's specific concerns. What will change and what will stay the same?

Just as the agencies loathe surprises from the issuer that make them look unprepared or incompetent to their bosses or to the market, so should issuers make it clear to the agencies that they want a 'no surprises' relationship that could hinder achieving an optimal rating.

---

[1] The perception of the competence of government officials can be too coloured in favour of the issuer as well. There was the famous incident when a CRA sovereign analyst on a trip to South Africa met Nelson Mandela and was reportedly so impressed that she could not argue for less than investment grade rating in the RC.

[2] 'Creditors [and credit rating agencies] have better memories than debtors.' Benjamin Franklin, *Poor Richard's Almanack*, September 1736 [brackets added].

[3] 'Rating the rating agencies', *Treasury & Risk Management*, July–August 1994, p. 32.

4.3 Presentation format and tactics

Each agency visit is important for the impressions gained by the analysts. Once you have made a positive impression, it is easier to reinforce it on the next visit than it is to erase negative ones left behind. It is essential to ensure that the few hours you have to impress the agencies during their visits are maximised in terms of your performance. That requires a strategy to begin with and solid preparation for each agency visit, as we have argued.

The agencies come to the meetings with concerns and issues in their minds that they want clarified or want some assurance on, because these concerns are what investors (or the rating committee) may ask them about. If not clarified, these worries could become the basis for the senior analyst's ongoing apprehensions about your credit quality.

As we have seen, there is an art to presentation. There is also a skill in using legitimate tactics successfully in a formal due diligence setting. Here are 15 suggestions and tactics that will enhance and improve your relationship with the agencies and enhance your chances for an optimal rating.

Fifteen tactics

1 *The meeting site:* the location you choose for the due diligence meeting conveys the degree of importance you attach to the occasion. Issuers are judged by the surroundings they keep, so it is wise to use board rooms, investment centres and senior level conference rooms for your meetings with the rating agencies.[1] These meetings should be chaired throughout the day(s) by a senior official who is in a position to give overviews and perspective on the issues, someone who can control the agenda, the pace, and the content of the meeting. Using a senior person to chair the meeting tells the agencies you take the exercise seriously. It does not, as one issuer supposed, give the impression that 'we will appear worried enough to have to bring in the big guns'.

In the early days of international ratings in 1977, Hans van den Houten, Vice President and Director International of Moody's, was invited for a review of the Republic of Austria in Vienna. A large number of Ministry of Finance officials brought him into a room in the Hapsburg Palace where the Ministry was located. The room was more appropriate for a fancy ball and contained tables and chairs that were centuries old. He looked around and the display of gold on the walls made him wonder, he recounts, why on earth is this exhibition necessary and what is the message going to be from the Austrians? How did this relate to the country's performance and future growth prospects?

After the welcoming statement by the Head of Treasury, the Moody's man replied: 'Gentlemen: the gold in this room alone tells me that you have enough wealth to be able to meet your future commitments. May we now start the meeting and hear what you really have in the coffers of State!' The rest of the meeting was a solid presentation, but Hans say he will never forget the opulence of the room and its conflicting message. The lesson for issuers is that vast displays of wealth can set the wrong tone and leave the wrong impression.

2 *The welcoming speech:* the most senior official available (the CEO or a government minister) should start the day with an introductory speech, one that welcomes the visitors, makes a

few light comments, and then strikes key themes. The official should identify the half dozen or so major points you want the agency to depart with at the end of the day. You do not want to start off the day with a series of naïve statements or inopportune asides that have to be explained away later.

If the issuer is a government, then a senior political figure can be a valuable ally in the due diligence meeting if your goal is to impress the agencies with the commitment behind policies and to give positive impressions of the political dynamics at work.

3 *The note-taker:* someone should be appointed the role of note-taker for all the meetings. His/her job is to record all the questions the rating agency analysts ask as well as their solicited and unsolicited comments about your creditworthiness. Note should be taken of any remark they make regarding peers, the state of the national economy, the nature of competition in your industry, international commodity prices, and so on. Sometimes the analysts do not volunteer these views, and you have to dig them out. However, it is well worth the effort since gems are often hidden away in their remarks that point to special biases or leanings.

After the meeting, the note-taker's written record of agency questions and comments will alert you to a number of important points:

- the kinds of issues the agency is concerned about, both generically and on this occasion;
- the kinds of issues the other agency will likely raise at their next meeting;
- the hidden agenda behind their questions;
- trends in agency thinking from year to year; and
- an individual analyst's strength and weaknesses, which can be exploited.

The notes are a very useful tool in managing the rating process year round. The knowledge gained can be applied to future calls, mailings and face to face sessions. For example, you can quote back to them next year something they said this year that amounts to a contradiction, a flimsy rationale, or an inconsistency. If they do not correct it, at least they will admire your attention to detail.

Over the ensuing year you can work to raise the analyst's comprehension of certain fundamental relationships or problems where you sense he has a weakness. Issuers can gain more leverage through this simple process than they imagine. Take particular care, at both formal and informal sessions, to record verbatim any comments by the agency officials present.

In fact, even offhanded comments by the CRA visitors can trigger an opportunity for issuers. There was one occasion when an analyst mentioned to a petroleum client that he had never visited an offshore platform and could not imagine the size of such on operation relative to the enormous costs to construct one of these mammoth things. The issuer quickly arranged for the CRA team to fly to Stavenger, Norway where they spent a full day on a platform in the Ekofisk oil field in the North Sea. They left having a much better understanding of the financial investments and commitments required and were able to transmit that knowledge to their colleagues on the rating committee.

4 *The presentations:* senior officials with both the greatest expertise in the subject area (for example, budgets, loans, investments, external accounts, liability management) and

the requisite presentation skills should be called upon to make the substantive presentations. Key aides and assistants should be present as well since quite detailed questions are sure to arise. It is best to have only two or three people participate on the issuer's side during each separate topic-session. Too many people in the meeting room might imply insecurity or lack of confidence in the subject area. Large numbers do not always connote strength. Make sure the core line people are available, not just the treasury or planning people.

Each presenter should give the agencies a quick overview of his topic so the analysts will have a framework in which to place all that the presenter says. Distribute to the agency analysts a one to two-page summary or outline of the key points you will be making. Identify the key themes and messages at the outset. Prepare ahead of time the key points you want to make, and then repeat them. Attach copies of any charts or tables used. By giving them prepared materials, the analysts will not have to spend so much time taking notes and can concentrate on listening to your message. The summary pages you provide also give them easy reference for later follow-up as well as a basis for their written reports.

When the agencies cite an obvious problem, a good strategy is to acknowledge that, yes, that is a difficulty, but we have the right policy framework in place to deal with it. Go right down your list of accomplishments since their last visit, and show how these achievements directly address the concerns the agencies may have had, for example, about competitiveness, market shocks, sales fluctuations, tax avoidance, industrial relations, a highly leveraged balance sheet and so on.

Usually not residents of your country, the analysts may ask questions that appear naïve and show little understanding of local nuances. The questions may seem to have little relevance to the issues at hand. Presenters need to show patience and assist the analyst to come to the conclusion you want. Finally, each speaker should stay within the time limit allotted. The high-level welcoming speaker should not monopolise the dialogue, which leaves the impression that underlings cannot perform. It also connotes a dictatorial leader.

5 *Charts, graphs and format:* visual presentations make deeper impressions on the brain than verbal ones. Use a variety of presentation formats, charts, displays and graphs to highlight your main points. Make the data easily understandable. Interpret all handouts for the analysts. Do the work for them, in a sense, by easing their task of interpretation.

The meetings should be devoted to covering broad issues and trends that can be summarised in simple text and graphics. Straight text is acceptable for the background material that you send to the agencies ahead of meeting time, but reams of straight text in the meeting itself is a waste of your time and theirs. It tends to direct attention toward minutiae and away from key issues. Dealing with broader issues rather than getting mired too deeply in numbers permits you to control the pace and content of the meeting.

A former analyst at Moody's offered this advice: 'Put weapons in the analyst's hands. You can't assume the analyst has the time to do the comparative charts, so provide them so he won't have to spend time creating them. He can walk into a rating committee with them and they could make a difference. Provide materials that are organised in a manner the analyst can easily digest and reproduce in his recommendation to the rating committee.'

A word of caution

Do not overwhelm the analyst with so much information and detail that a clear picture is drowned out. Build a case relative to your peers, but be careful you do not leave the impression that you think the agencies cannot do their own thinking or are too incompetent to make their own comparisons.

---

6 *Forecasts and projections:* an important part of any presentation to the rating agencies is your view of the future. Come to the meetings with economic and financial projections that are realistic, ones that have built-in sensitivities and conservative assumptions. Analysts like to see that you have considered upsides and downsides, not just a single bullish outlook.

Rule One is that any forecasts and projections you provide them should, above all, be realistic. Forecasts should not be based on wild or improbably optimistic assumptions. The official outlook on any issue should not be abstract or extreme. The agencies think, 'if their scenario building is not realistic, how can policy advice or objectives be sensible?'

Rule Two is that all assumptions behind forecasts should be mentioned openly. Unclear or improbable assumptions immediately cast doubt on the whole forecasting exercise... and on your ability to plan. Share with them government plans and solutions to key social and economic problems or your corporate plans, as the case may be. Acknowledge possible downsides. Provide them with hard copies of the forecasts and the underlying assumptions.

Your task is to convince them that even in a worst-case scenario, existing policy will limit the negative fallout and/or that you have such-and-such backstops built in to recover quickly. In this respect, be equipped to answer 'what-if' questions, such as what if the economy does not recover quickly, or what if competition in your industry grows, or what if XYZ law passes?

7 *Use the negative to your advantage:* one tactic is to put the negative facts up front. This way the agency does not have to dig them out and does not feel cheated or fooled. You want the analysts to feel confident in your level of disclosure and to perceive you as forthright. With the negatives out of the way, you can then get on with the credible plans you have for correcting the imbalances and moving forward.

8 *Take the offensive:* analysts respect issuers (banks, companies, sovereigns) who are assertive about who they are and positive about the correctness of their policies. Issuers should not be reluctant to say to an agency, 'I don't agree with your analysis *for these reasons*.' If a good dialogue opens, then the agency might just think, 'Perhaps we didn't place enough weight on that. We need to go back and think this through again.' The lesson: do not be bashful but do not be arrogant either, leaving the impression that the agency analysts do not know what they are doing.

Proactive issuers (see Exhibit 6.1) should provide the CRA with several pages of comparisons that properly position themselves relative to rated peers, showing strengths and weaknesses as well as relevant metrics. This will help the analyst do the hard research of digging out those important facts.

9 *Feedback:* during each segment of the presentation, put questions to the analysts to see if they understand the points you have just made. Encourage immediate feedback. Now is the time to correct their wrong impressions or assumptions. Discuss peer comparisons openly. Soliciting their views will help keep the analysts awake.

The analysts tend to nod their heads in agreement as you speak, but that does not necessarily mean they understand what you said. It may simply mean they are hearing you. Nodding in supposed agreement is also their subtle way of signalling that you need not follow up with a question to them that would uncover their lack of knowledge in this area.

Analysts may be too embarrassed, especially if their boss is in attendance, to admit they do not catch your point. Yet, we do not want them to go away confused or uncertain about key subjects. You have the right to have your full story heard and understood by the agencies. Risking their embarrassment is a small price to pay for clearing up confusion during the meeting. Do not wait until a week or two later when the context is different, the momentum is lost, and you have fewer resources at your immediate disposal to deal with the issue.

10 *Your questions:* questions you should ask the analysts directly during your presentation include: do you see the point I am trying to make here? Do you agree with our way of looking at this? How do you see the issue in our competitive environment or in an international context? Does this trend exist amongst our peers as well? What else can we provide to make the point clearer? Does this allay your concern about our financial results? If the agency answers 'Yes' to this last question, the note-taker should be sure to record it for future reference. Quoting back to the agencies statements they made earlier gives you a powerful weapon when making a point in your favour.

If the issuer has prepared properly and listened carefully during the meetings, then you will not have to ask – what areas of policy or performance will help us improve our rating? You will already know the answer.

When issuers confront the analysts directly on questions of agency policy or on their assumptions, the analysts tend to resort to hedging and obfuscation. They sometimes try to be vague, so as to reinforce the mysterious aura surrounding their business. They do not like to be pinned down. Yet you have the right to ask them to explain responses that are cloudy or contradictory. You have the right not to be intimidated by agency image and verbiage. It is a matter of your persisting in the face of their smoke and mirrors. Ask for explanations of anything that is cloudy or contradictory. In fact, if you are a particularly proactive issuer who has studied the agency's methodology, you may want to base the day's discussions on the agency's methodology itself, rating factor by rating factor.

Finally, the matter of Q&A comes up. Issuers should arrange enough time in the meeting schedule to allow time for mutual questioning at the end of each segment or presenter. Questions by either side should not be left until the end of the day, where the context and momentum will have changed. Do not permit the visiting CRA team to insist on questions at the end. Issues should be addressed as they are raised. Encourage immediate feedback from the visiting analysts with pointed questions; do not wait until sum-up time at the end of the day.

11 *Eye contact:* maintain strong eye contact with all agency analysts throughout your presentation and during the Q&A period. This tactic shows confidence, firmness and determination on your part – factors that count heavily in their subjective assessment of government leadership and policy implementation. Strong eye contact also sends a subtle signal: it makes some analysts a bit more reluctant to question your reasoning and hence more willing to accept it.

12 *Body language:* be aware of the body language of the analysts. Be alert for signs of fatigue, boredom, loss of concentration, or misunderstanding of a point. If you sense any of these, pause and allow some silence, and then ask them directly if that point was clear because you would be glad to elaborate. Even if they say, 'No, that's clear', it would be wise to repeat the point. It may be time to allow them to take a stretch break or coffee break. Upon return, make a note to reiterate your main points where they may have been confused or inattentive.

13 *Conclusions:* each presenter should conclude his or her section of the meeting with remarks such as, 'So that sums up the evidence on this subject. We think it's clear and compelling and answers your concerns (or addresses the issue you raised). We hope this clears up any lingering doubts. Do you have any questions? No? May we take that to mean you have no further concerns on this issue?' They will likely respond, 'No further concerns at the moment but maybe later. We'll get back to you if we do.' At that point, you need to get them to commit to inform you of their concerns on a timely basis (that is, before announcing the rating result or a Credit Watch).

14 *The lunch break:* the midday break for lunch is an opportunity for a needed change of pace and locale. In this interim period, you may introduce the analysts to other senior bank or corporate personnel not involved in the actual presentations. A catered lunch of sandwiches, fruit and soft drinks is appropriate, preferably taken in a private room other than the main meeting room. The analysts are not necessarily impressed by your hosting an expensive luncheon at the best restaurant in town; they see lots of good restaurants in their travels. Besides, a big lunch will put everyone to sleep – not a good strategy when everyone needs to stay sharp.

During the lunch, you should feel free to raise broad questions about the analysts' background and interests. Do not hesitate to query them on rating agency policy. Remember, you have the right to hear clear rating policy statements and the reasons behind them. Take the time after lunch to walk around outside, if possible, so all will be refreshed for the afternoon sessions. Post-luncheon meetings can be unproductive (and even risky to your credit health) if one side or the other is not alert.

15 *Follow-up:* after the meetings, follow-up is vital. Be sure to keep track of outstanding questions and open issues that were not answered in the meetings. Write them down. Establish

responsibility on your end for getting the requisite information together and on their end for acknowledging its receipt and processing it. Your competence will be judged by how rapidly and completely you meet your post-meeting obligations. Ensure there is appropriate follow-up by both sides. Finally, ask for and get a reasonable estimate from them as to their timetable for analysing the data, coming to a rating conclusion, and writing their report. You have the right, of course, to read and correct their report before it is published.

In terms of longer term follow-up, we recommend establishing regular, periodic contact with the CRAs from whom you have ratings. Make contact at least every quarter (telephone is preferred over email) to keep the analysts up to date on events at your end and to learn the latest agency thinking about your credit and that of your peers. Use the conversation as an opportunity to gauge what questions or issues are on the analyst's mind. Prepare for this conversation by anticipating the agency's concerns and having answers ready. As an issuer you should also have a set of questions designed to elicit the analyst's level of understanding and underlying assumptions about your credit quality. The analyst will respect your hands-on engagement and co-operation in the process. This proactive approach gains more 'points' than an aloof or benign approach (see Chapter 6).

Summary of key points

- In the rating meeting, *do*:
  - expand on the written material you have provided to the agencies already; do not read it or rehash it;
  - emphasise issues and strategies, not myriad details;
  - explain scenarios, plans, solutions;
  - be candid about risks and exposures; do not hide the skeletons;
  - answer questions directly, not evasively; admit you do not know something but will find the answer… and then do it immediately;
  - provide hard copies of slides so that the analysts can take notes on them;
  - aim for the right rating, given your financial goals, not the highest rating; and
  - make the most of this opportunity.
- In the rating meeting, *do not*:
  - wait until last minute to prepare;
  - waste time on presenting material that drowns out your main messages, amounts to a sales or marketing pitch, or glorifies your institution's history;
  - reproduce fancy charts from the annual report or data designed for equity analysts;
  - base forward planning on wishful thinking;
  - hide your problems; acknowledge weaknesses;
  - blame misfortunes on external factors, for example, competitors, government, volatile market;
  - exaggerate the likelihood of best case outcomes; or
  - lie – be open and honest.[2]

After the rating meeting, you have these rights:

1 to reject the rating or appeal an initial rating;
2 to request that the agency withdraw an existing rating, which you will not pay for;
3 to hear a clear rating rationale for the rating and to question matters you do not understand;
4 to challenge any public statement or private assurance from the agencies;
5 to be a demanding customer, not a passive consumer; and
6 to consider shifting your business to another rating agency if the relationship is not beneficial or fair.

---

[1] When an issuer visits the agency's headquarters, the agency chooses the meeting site, usually a special conference room set aside for such meetings. One visiting issuer with a macabre sense of humour looked at the meeting room and asked, 'You chose this conference room so that they won't hear us scream, right?'

[2] 'If one tells the truth, one is sure, sooner or later, to be found out.' Oscar Wilde.

4.4 Useful and non-useful information for the agencies

A number of surveys and interviews with current and former rating agency analysts over the years revealed what they consider the most useful and least useful information provided them by issuers. Their answers are effective in telling issuers what the CRAs want and what they expect to see in terms of documents and preparation.

The two lists here, which should be self-explanatory, will guide issuers so that they do not waste time and effort in preparation. The agencies benefit from having available to them the kind of information they need to do their job effectively. Issuers benefit from showing the agencies that they understand agency needs and are willing to assist them.

What is most useful to the rating agencies

1   An emphasis on goals, strategies, forecasts and process. Show how successful strategies have played out, and describe the options available in cases of the unexpected.
2   How management will deal with changes in the marketplace and how the company intends to stay competitive.
3   The CEO's vision and philosophy.
4   Bringing coherence, focus, direction and personality to the presentation exercise.
5   Insight into plans, forecasts, assumptions, projections, contingencies.
6   Explicit financial goals and how you expect to attain them.
7   Organising documents in digestible form.
8   Presentation materials that are focused on issues that have a credit impact, for example, leverage, margins, cash flow, those that are tied to the agency's metrics and key rating factors.
9   Products and asset quality (the bases of any business).
10 Where the business is heading in different product areas and how you are going to finance it.
11 Plans for protecting and enlarging the franchise.
12 Your view of structural changes in the markets and how you define your markets; how you plan to stay competitive.
13 Showing how you insulate various revenue streams from shocks.
14 Being prepared to answer 'what-if' questions.
15 How you intend to deal with the things the agencies worry about, and giving straight answers to the questions the agency deems most important.
16 For banks, highly detailed asset/liability data which help the analyst construct a series of key revenues and costs over time, plus loan portfolio schedules, problem loan schedules, reserve reconciliation.
17 Admitting your problems up front and not ignoring them in hopes the agency will not notice, and then explaining how you are managing them (but not blaming others).

What is least useful to the rating agencies

1 Overwhelming the analysts with information in unimportant areas, such as an exhaustive breakdown of subsidiary activities, or IT systems, or monthly imports by product.
2 Too much detail, a 'data dump' that does not show a clear picture, micro-managing the numbers.
3 Duplicating or reformatting information already available in the public domain, for example, the annual report or press releases.
4 Not answering questions or concerns posed by the agencies ahead of time.
5 Praising one's computer systems and MIS framework.
6 Sales and marketing materials, public relations materials and propaganda.
7 Long-winded and glorious histories of your institution.
8 Presenting promotional campaigns and bland statements extolling the enterprise.

Frequently asked question

'What kinds of financial projections should we show the agencies?'

Answer:

First, all classes of issuers should make a permanent habit of providing the rating agencies with projections, whether of line items, prices, and costs or of budgetary outcomes, current account balances, and gross domestic product. These projections should be chosen carefully to align with the key ratios the CRA uses. This exercise has at least two benefits: it shows the agencies you have a planning orientation, and it helps the issuer uncover important sensitivities at the agencies.

Second, the best *timeframe* for financial projections, such as budgets, net income, and trade balances, is forward two or three years. It should not be 5 or 10 years which no one can project realistically and which no one believes anyway.

Third, the best *framework* is a most likely case, a best case, and a worst case. All assumptions *must* be made explicit. The agencies will judge management on the degree to which forecasts are realistic, not just hopeful. The most likely case should be based on reasonable assumptions, not super-optimistic views, and it should represent your opinion of what stands the best chance of being achieved. You should also present a worst-case scenario that gives you the opportunity to argue, for example, that even if recessionary conditions prevail, your profitability is relatively unaffected, especially relative to peers, and therefore your credit rating should not be impacted. It is not a good idea to construct forecasts that are easily achievable so that next year you can show the agencies how 'conservative' your planning was.

A major objective of your relationship with the agencies is to establish and maintain your credibility. The agencies readily identify poor or unrealistic assumptions and forecasts, and you do not want to be forced to defend them. The agencies will think that if you are irrational in this area, other areas of your presentation may be suspect as well, not to mention senior management's hold on market-based realities.

Steps to take and questions to ask

Steps to take now:

1

2

3

4

5

Follow-up questions to ask:

1

2

3

4

5

The rating committee

Précis

One question that issuers and other involved parties frequently ask rating advisers is, how does the rating committee (RC) work? This chapter deconstructs the content, agendas and membership of rating committees. There is a discussion of the dynamics of decision-making, and the role of both objective and subjective factors in a rating decision. Caution and conservatism rule in the RC.

The extensive time and effort spent by issuers in pursuit of a rating that coincides with their financial goals is well worth it. However, in addition to an issuer's own possible short-comings from a credit standpoint, there are other constraints to an upgrade or an optimal rating. These constraints are the result of credit rating agency (CRA) fundamentals, analysts' shortcomings, and the forces at work within a rating committee. Issuers need to know these possible hurdles and how to remove or alleviate them.

Once the due diligence meeting is completed and once the RC has met and decided the case of credit quality before them, and once the issuer has been informed of the rating decision, the next step is the agency's dissemination worldwide of a press release about the rating. Issuers have the right of appeal in limited circumstances, and we disclose the difficulties and consequences of going that route.

The analysts are not paid to be right; they are paid not to be wrong.

5.1 How the rating committee works

The image that many issuers have of rating committees at Moody's, Fitch and S&P is that of a mysterious and permanent assembly of financial wizards sitting on high in the caverns of Wall Street making judgments on the creditworthiness of trembling issuers.

In reality, the RC is an amorphous, ad hoc body that convenes as needed to decide usually straightforward, but sometimes complex, rating issues. Ratings are not done by mechanical formulae, as one myth about the agencies supposes. They are done by intelligent analysts trying their best to provide investors with a set of consistent and globally comparable ratings that reflect credit quality.

RC procedure at all three agencies remains primarily a democratic discussion and then a vote, with each RC member getting one vote no matter his or her rank within the agency. Ratings are decided by majority vote. Tie votes seldom happen since each RC contains an odd number of members. Decisions can take 30 minutes or many hours, even days for a first-time controversial rating. If the rating decision is particularly contentious or debatable, then the committee may reconvene with one or more new members, but one that still includes the senior analyst in charge of the credit. The senior analyst may need extra time to seek additional information on the issuer.

The RC usually comprises anywhere from five to nine analysts and officers (maybe more), depending on whether the decision is an easy confirmation of an existing rating or a highly sensitive and divisive downgrade, say of a major sovereign, or a set of major banks and insurance companies, or something that could jolt the financial community.

For example, an RC meeting to determine a sovereign rating will likely comprise the lead analyst, backup analyst, other sovereign analysts (several from other regions of the world), one or more managing directors, the group managing director, the chief credit officer, and analysts from non-sovereign sectors. The internal deliberations and identities of those who sit on an RC are kept confidential and not disclosed to the issuer. Notes are taken and votes are recorded as part of the RC due diligence.

Caution rules

Senior management at a rating agency is inherently more cautious than the analyst, because they are charged with maintaining the integrity of the rating system and the agency's reputation. Thus, while the analyst pushes his recommendation in the RC, the role of the senior members of the RC is to probe, be sceptical, ask tough questions, and be assured the analyst has done his homework. If there are doubts on the part of the senior members or the analyst does not make his case convincingly, then either the recommended rating change will not happen or the analyst will be asked to do some more research.

During RC deliberations, a premium is placed on the oral presentation skills of the lead analyst, that is, on his ability to convince the committee of the 'correctness' of the recommended rating. The analyst must be certain of the data supporting the recommendation and certain he or she has followed the agency's methodology for that class of issuer. If the analyst is insecure or overwhelmed by other RC members, he or she is not likely to make a 'sale' of the recommendation. A pattern of unsuccessful or overturned recommendations prompts the analyst to start looking for another job.

Not all RC meetings are long-winded or contentious. With some sovereigns, banks and industrial corporations, rating conclusions can be co-ordinated by an analyst and his immediate boss and be brought to the RC for pro forma presentation and ratification, especially if no rating change is anticipated. In the old days decisions were known to take place in elevators and hallways, albeit infrequently. Under SEC scrutiny the RC process has become more rigorous and mechanised.

Issuers should ask their credit rating agency(ies) to explain clearly how the more mechanised and somewhat deterministic rating process works. How has government regulation altered their previous determination of ratings, especially from a methodological standpoint? They should ask them to provide a written description of the committee process, which can vary by sector and geography.

Qualitative versus quantitative

RCs use objective data from private and public sources and organise them into 'rating factors'. This exercise tends to place an issuer within a certain category, such as single A, but the final determination of the rating (A+, A, A–) is quite subjective. Veterans of rating committees, drawing on experience with different issuer classes, rely on a 'feel' for where the credit belongs. The data will get you in the neighbourhood but professional judgment gets you to the front door. Or, as S&P's managing director Marie Cavanaugh put it, 'Quantitative is where you are, and qualitative is where you're going'. Numbers are a guide to what in the end is a qualitative decision.

Continuing on this theme, people ask whether objective or subjective criteria hold sway in RC meetings. Are ratings a numbers game or a judgment call? We have already demonstrated in Chapter 2, 'Inherent subjectivity' that ratings on balance are not statistically driven. Let us amplify on those observations with direct statements from those agency analysts the author interviewed.

Bank analysts

'Qualitative factors prevailed in our meetings, even in the numbers-oriented banking sector. What often carried the day were opinions on the outlook for the real estate market, or quick judgments on a bank's asset quality without thorough examination of the loan book.'

'The qualitative is emphasised for downgrades and the quantitative for upgrades. This means that downgrades are a matter of subjective assessment, while the numbers have to be there to support an upgrade.'

'The higher the degree of disclosure by an issuer the more quantitative the assessment becomes, the less disclosure, the more qualitative. When there is inadequate information on which to base a rating decision, the bank is down rated for qualitative reasons. Foreign banks may rank lower than US banks because their degree of disclosure is less. They do only what's required in their home countries.'

'Qualitative factors outweighed quantitative but the two are not discrete. It depends on how the issues are raised in the RC. There's usually a good mix and one doesn't dominate.'

'The language is quantitative (statistics, economics), but the arguments and considerations are qualitative.'

'The qualitative prevailed over the quantitative at Moody's, because the numbers are history, and the rating depends on how the RC feels about an issuer's ability to perform in the future. The RC makes a judgment call on this and since it doesn't want to be embarrassed if management doesn't perform as expected, the RC shades the rating down or hesitates to grant an upgrade without evidence already of performance.'

Sovereign analysts

'As to determinants of rating changes for sovereigns, it's the usual stock and flow approaches: how much debt, current account deficits, budget balances, and so on. A broader determinant was the terribly fluffy gut feeling of the analyst and the credibility of the decision-makers on the other side. It's all pretty inchoate.'

'Both, but on balance it's qualitative. You discuss the facts and ratios which are disputed and then you move on to policy. You ask, "how credible is their policy?" and this is a gut feel call. The large credit calls require more inherent understanding and adjustments.'

'The qualitative prevails. We believe ratings should depend more on an analyst's skills of interpretation and superior judgment, not on the numbers.'

'Moody's is more quantitative than people think. We publicly emphasise the qualitative to promote the image of mystery, black box. The huge qualitative component is comprised of a call on political risk and a subjective sense of where the credit "belongs."'

'It's qualitative more than quantitative in the sense of interpreting the data. Everyone has the same data, but what does it mean? This is open to debate and interpretation. It's the analysis that's important, for example, how much weight should be put on the contingent liabilities of the government?'

Corporate analysts

'The quantitative is the starting point. It gives a broad benchmark and points to an initial basket of relative risk. Then the quantitative has to be qualified and challenged and even in cases ignored by the judgment and qualitative points of view of the RC.'

'The quantitative is given more weight in our RCs, even heavily, but in the following context. The numbers are done first and then the analyst is asked to *interpret* them, to adjust them based on his experience and qualitative knowledge. In the end, the agencies look at adjusted numbers.'

'The qualitative always given more weight (maybe 70/30) because you're forecasting management actions and strengths, industry trends, off balance-sheet risks.'

'The qualitative is more important, and here we're talking about preconceived notions and personal biases. At the same time, there are some qualitative issues that are important, such as the quality of management, company strategy, and competitive advantages. Qualitative does not have just a negative connotation. You start with the quantitative side in the RC and you've got the rating within plus or minus two notches. Then you look at the qualitative aspect.'

The rating committee did what?

There are instances where the rating committee has been less than democratic, unbiased and methodical. Agency analysts pointed out examples where rating decisions were outside the norm – ones influenced by eccentric behaviour, time constraints or human factors.

1   Because the major CRAs are juggling tens of thousands of debt issues at any given moment, the time available for RC meetings is at a premium. Some ratings can only be given cursory attention. RC meetings in such situations are hastily arranged and may include only two analysts and the last minutes.[1]
2   'It's late in the day; time to wrap things up and go home.' Or, 'We have to do four ratings this afternoon and be out of here by 5:30.'
3   'I've got other meetings and commitments I need to attend to,' the RC chairman might say.
4   'We need to hurry and issue our press release before the competition does.'
5   'We on occasion had to rush a rating decision because the market was waiting for it. We had no luxury of exhaustive consideration.'
6   RCs are comprised of whoever is available to meet that day, and this affects the decision.
7   There can be RC members who have not visited a country and do not really understand the nuances but are committed to vote on issues or issuers in that country.
8   An RC can be poorly prepared because its members have not read the pre-meeting materials distributed by the analyst. Time is wasted within the RC, especially by senior members who skim the material for the first time at the meeting itself, delaying the meeting and hence constraining the amount of time available to consider the case. They are not ready for the debate and have not considered the merits.
9   Other larger issues (for example, a major external shock affecting an industry different from the one being considered) may distract management's attention from the case at hand such that peremptory consideration is given to the case or it is placed on the deep back burner.
10 There could be personal bias in the RC, for example, against the investment banker who brought the client in or against company management because the 'CEO wore white shoes'.
11 Sometimes weaker analysts would wait to see how the senior people voted before casting their votes. In fact, perceptive RC chairmen could see this and in cases where they wanted to influence the outcome, they would vote first and then allow the others to be drawn into concurrence. It is clear that rating determination is a group activity, subject to all the nuances, personal and psychological, of group dynamics. Now, senior RC members vote last.
12 Some managers (as everywhere) are pessimistic and negative; their temperament is always to look for the worst and only grudgingly recognise improvement. Their natural tendency is to 'low-ball' the ratings, which happens to fit with the protective tendency of both the agency and individuals.
13 One former Moody's sovereign analyst noted the following hidden agenda. Senior RC members always wanted its ratings to be one notch lower than S&P's, to promote the

idea that Moody's is more conservative. Senior management was fully conscious in rating committees of inter-agency rating distinctions, and this made the difference in some cases.

14 An autocratic RC chairman has a fixed notion about the issuer's industry or credit quality and will not compromise despite the senior analyst's sound reasoning and recommendation.

15 To ensure a rating decision he wants, a managing director may 'stack' the RC by bringing in his own people to vote his way.

16 It was common practice at Moody's in the 1980s, regardless of the composition of the RC, for the RC chairman in the Financial Institutions Group to 'push through to unanimity' a rating decision he deemed right, given his own perception of the health of the industry or peer group that included the issuer.[2]

17 Senior members of the RC have been known to lobby other members of the RC prior to the meeting in order to influence the outcome.[3] Hardly ethical or proper procedure.

While these behaviours are certainly the exception to the rule of properly run RC meetings, it is nonetheless instructive to see that unconventional, if not unethical, practices can have a role in rating determinations. No one knows when such anomalies will pop up in an RC context. Apparently there has been progress in how RC meetings are run because current agency analysts, when told of this list, say these occurrences are rare if not non-existent.

David Beers, while Head of Sovereign Ratings at S&P in the 1990s, offered his candid opinion: 'We aspire to have good analysis and to have categorical, objective standards. But in the end, ratings are opinions and interpretations and observations. The RC system cushions but does not prevent human mistakes. There is no objective truth. The rating scale is an invented one. We're dealing with uncertainty. That's the nature of the beast.'

Lesson for issuers

Issuers need to ensure the lead analyst has the right facts and interpretations in mind because you cannot control how the RC may proceed.

---

[1] 'We had a colloquial term for that,' said W Bruce Jones, a former Moody's official who works for a small competitor, Egan-Jones Ratings Co. 'We called it a water cooler rating.'

[2] An insurance company analyst who worked at both Moody's and S&P in the late 1980s and early 1990s summarised the RC procedures at that time in this fashion: 'At S&P votes were by simple majority. At Moody's votes were "managed to consensus" or to unanimity if possible. If Moody's is a dictatorship, then S&P is a chaotic democracy. These are two opposite poles of mismanagement.' According to current analysts: (i) this distinction no longer holds; and (ii) heightened SEC oversight has prompted more RC documentation and hence more consistent and open procedures.

[3] Moody's Executive Vice President, Thomas McGuire, powerful Chairman of the Rating Committee, walked into the office of a new hire in the corporate department and said, 'Nestlé, Siemens and Diageo are important to our European strategy so don't mess it up.' The analyst could not decide if this meant 'do a good job on these key credits' or 'don't even think about downgrading them'.

5.2 Constraints to an upgrade

Since getting an upgrade is the goal of most CFOs and ministers of finance, one of the most frequently asked questions put to a rating consultant is 'What can we do to enhance our chances for an upgrade?' This book attempts to answer that question with suggestions for issuers. A longer answer would require another book with advice specific to the issuer in question.[1]

What is not as frequently asked is, 'What are the constraints or roadblocks to an upgrade that will hinder my achieving that goal?' In addition to an issuer's own less than expected financial performance, there are a number of factors, both inside and outside the agencies, which act as a check on higher ratings. They can sidetrack or delay indefinitely upward movement on a rating. Let us examine these constraints and follow them with *lessons* for issuers.

For example, on the issuer side, is there sufficient management interest in getting an upgrade? Are they willing to pay the price by: (i) devoting resources to managing the CRAs; and (ii) running a more conservative balance sheet, to wit, lower debt and more liquid assets?

Also, there is the case of being non-investment grade (BB+) and trying to get to the lowest investment-grade rating of BBB–. That one notch is a bigger hurdle than any other one-notch upgrade. A lot of investor behaviour hinges on that one notch.[2] The evidence suggests that if an issuer loses his investment-grade rating, it will be difficult to regain it for some years.

Now we will break down the constraints to upgrades by rating agency fundamentals, by lead analyst competence and disposition, and by barriers within rating committees themselves.

Constraints relative to rating agency fundamentals

- Fixed income analysts are trained to look at downsides. The agency will weigh negatives more heavily than positives, always looking for disasters.[3] Agency conservatism rules.
- When it comes to a credit whose fundamentals and ratios are improving, the instinct at the agencies is to say, 'Well, it won't hurt to wait a quarter or two to see if improvements persist. We've got nothing to lose by waiting and more to lose by upgrading too soon when the seemingly positive changes may prove ephemeral.'
- Expressed another way, the CRAs cannot do an upgrade fast but they can do a downgrade fast. There is a lack of symmetry. For example, 10% deterioration in a key measure could trigger a downgrade, but a 10% improvement in that measure would likely not trigger an upgrade.
- There is an inherent reluctance in agencies to grant an upgrade without a degree of certainty that the company can sustain performance over time. Perversely, they do not need that same degree of certainty to decide on a downgrade.
- It may take only two quarters of deterioration to 'earn' a downgrade, but it could take five or six quarters of improvement to merit an upgrade. The changes in issuer performance are measured against the CRA's own projections.
- A former chairman of the RC at Moody's told the author that 'a high visibility company (measured by the volume of its debt rated) gets more analytic power assigned to it.

Conversely, little debt outstanding means little attention by the agency.' In other words, small to medium-sized rated issuers are given less consideration at the CRA in terms of time and manpower because their rating is less important to the agency's reputation in the market.

Constraints relative to the lead analyst

- The analyst may be weak without the strength of his convictions, which will affect the content and tone of the recommendation he or she has written for the rating committee.
- The analyst's biases, personality, ambition and location on the optimism–pessimism scale all affect what he brings before the RC to consider. The lead analyst is often more positive about 'his' credit than the rest of the RC, and his task involves convincing the 'outside analysts' on the committee.
- Analysts see their role as professional sceptics, but there can be unjustified levels of scepticism, such as when an analyst may be unwilling to listen to or accept an issuer's story. This tendency is only reinforced when issuers do not present their cases well.
- There are times when an analyst gets behind in his work and just cannot give proper consideration or time to an issuer's case, no matter how worthy it is. The size of an analyst's portfolio can hinder timely consideration.[4] When everybody gets too busy, what can be delayed is delayed.
- All humans (including rating agency analysts and RC members) are prone to cognitive dissonance, holding a belief plainly at odds with the evidence, usually because the belief has been held and cherished for a long time. An analyst can be 'in denial'. Fortunately, this analyst will not be employed by a CRA for long.
- Rating agency analysts, like everyone else on Wall Street, regularly miscalculate probabilities. Analysts assume that outcomes that are very probable are less likely than they really are, that outcomes which are quite unlikely are more likely than they are, and that extremely improbable, but still possible, outcomes have no chance at all of happening.
- It can be difficult to convince four to eight other members of the rating committee, especially if they are newly hired or tired, biased or opinionated, regarding the issuer's improving conditions. It takes more convincing for upgrades than for downgrades.
- Analyst turnover can be high[5] and new analysts need time to learn about a particular credit and get comfortable it.

Constraints relative to rating committee dynamics

- The rating committee process has a built-in conservative and sceptical bias that retards upgrades more than it does downgrades. Therefore, it may take time for the RC to be convinced that an impediment has been removed, that the change is fundamental and not ephemeral, that a major transformation in circumstances has occurred. The RC does not want to be forced to reverse its decision in the future. And their greatest fear is that a 'free-fall' in the rating could occur. This leads to caution.

- There is no advantage for the agency or the investor in liberality. For the agency, too high a rating could embarrass the franchise; for the investor, too high a rating does not provide the appropriate risk premium. Thus, the RC becomes inherently biased toward scepticism and cynicism. That is why the upgrade slope is harder to climb than the slippery downward slope.
- Agencies want to make sure their own downside and back side are protected. 'As an agency analyst, you're not looking for an opportunity to raise a rating; you're looking for risks.'
- There is a truism at the agencies – 'the weakest link drives a rating action' – which means the agency must act first on the weaker credits because they can hurt them. The credits that get the most attention are those that are deteriorating with the most debt outstanding. 'We'd better do it now before the situation gets worse and then we're accused of not moving fast enough.' An agency will act later on the stronger credits which can wait. If an issuer is a candidate for an upgrade now, he still should be in a month or so.
- Ratings are supposed to be valid and robust over various scenarios over the medium term (say two or three years), so the shortage of time since the last rating change can be a hindrance to an upgrade.
- Analysts and rating committees do not have unlimited time to do a rating. There is only so much research one can do and present to the RC, and RC executives have a busy schedule. Would an extra day's research really bring that much extra value to the rating decision? Usually not, so the committee usually meets under time-constrained circumstances. In fact, on any given weekday, Moody's, S&P and Fitch will together announce dozens of ratings in all categories, which means there are many rating committee meetings every day.
- The new compliance requirements of the SEC are a burden to fast decision-making.
- RCs now contain participants external to the particular credit category being considered – an 'outside' voter from elsewhere within the rating agency. These professional observers of due process might be a senior administrative executive attending an RC meeting on a structured finance rating or a vice president in municipal ratings attending an RC meeting about a sovereign. The purpose is to ensure that consistent internal procedures are followed and that the letter and spirit of rating standards are adhered to – noble goals but undertaken partially due to regulatory pressure. It is very likely that a member of the RC will have no prior experience with the type of credit in question.

The advent of this outsider, or 'cross-participation' as S&P labels it, was actually prompted by two external events: the 2008 global financial crisis when critics of agency procedures demanded better transparency of methods, and the decision of regulators in the US and Europe to step up oversight of agency practices. For the agencies, the result has simply meant more bureaucracy, more record-keeping and a slower moving, more mechanical process. The CRAs have to be sure now more than ever that they are complying with what the regulators want. The point is that if RCs act more slowly, then the new regulatory regimes imposed since 2008 could themselves be a constraint to an upgrade.

A current agency analyst complained that 'more time is spent on administrative staff and stuff than on useful debate'. He worries that stiffly codified procedures and mechanistic *règle du jeu* (rules of the game) will take away from the natural argumentative give and take of RC meetings. He worries that more stringent measures are in the offing.

Lessons from all these constraints

1 Upgrades take work; downgrades can happen suddenly. It is usually easier to suffer a downgrade than it is to earn an upgrade. Hence, issuers need to help analysts get the rating right in the first place... and then work to keep it optimal over time. They need to position themselves to defend their rating under any circumstance, and that means knowing what the 'triggers' are in the agency's mind that could change an outlook or a rating.

2 An issuer must develop a strong relationship with the lead analyst and his team and work to maintain it. Issuers have to take the initiative here because it is your credit and the analyst does not have time to monitor a particular issuer daily or even weekly.

3 Make it a priority to build trust with everyone at the CRA by taking ratings seriously and by meeting financial targets. This trust will smooth the way to an upgrade when the time is right, while lack of confidence in issuer management will constrain an upgrade if not precipitate a downgrade.

4 Issuers need to make their case clearly to the analysts to ensure that their job of collation and scrutiny is easier. RCs run more smoothly if the analysts are well prepared... with your help prior to the RC meeting.

5 There are both overt and subtle ways for issuers to avoid some of these obstacles. One of them is learning how to communicate better with the agencies. That topic is covered in Chapter 6.

6 Issuers need to keep the agencies informed but not overwhelmed. Issuers need to persist with their point of view but with solid reasoning and evidence. Too aggressive an issuer can alienate the analyst and strain the relationship. One agency analyst explained it this way. 'Issuers don't often realise this, but analysts can get irritated if an issuer pushes too hard for an upgrade. It feels arrogant and out of place. First, there are no magic formulas or ratios that drive an upgrade. There are no decisive rating determinants. Issuers should not expect a CRA to give an easy answer to the question – how can we get an upgrade? Second, analysts feel as if aggressive issuers are trying to tell them how to do their job.'

7 On the other hand, analysts appreciate it when issuers made a good comparative case on their own behalf. 'A good case and a smooth presentation are like a lawyer arguing a case before a jury. Analysts tend to give extra points for a case well-argued.' Find the right balance between pushing too hard and pushing not enough.

8 There are limits to the kind of proactive approach that we recommend for issuers. Over-eagerness backfires. Calmly arguing your case wins. Knowing what buttons to push is critical. Timing matters.

9 Issuers should ensure that the person at their company, bank or ministry responsible for agency relations is sensitive to rating issues and credit-related concerns.

---

[1] Such as the author's *How to get an Upgrade*, with advice primarily for governments but much of it applicable to other issuers.

[2] 'Not all notches are created equal', a truism expressed by Guido Cipriani, senior sovereign ratings officer for 15 years at S&P and Moody's.

[3] The story goes of a Soviet general on the Kremlin planning staff who always forecast war for the next year. When asked why year after year he forecast a war for the following year, he replied. 'If I predict war and there

is one, I get promoted. If I predict war and there is none, no one cares or listens. If I predict no war and there is none, there is no need for my job. If I predict no war and there is one, I'll be shot.' Moral: there is an institutional bias toward forecasting risks even when they are not there.

4 A former Moody's European bank analyst covered 42 banks at the same time. When he left, his portfolio of credits was split among three analysts. On the corporate side, an analyst may be responsible for anywhere from 12 to 60+ companies, or about 20 days per year per company for a light load and 4 days per company for a heavy load. Subtract from that the amount of time an analyst spends travelling and report writing, and the time available for original research is reduced by at least half. They do not have time to check every company assurance for accuracy. This is not an excuse for rating errors, but it is one explanation.

5 Pay scales at the CRAs are significantly lower than elsewhere on Wall Street, so once they have CRA experience on their CV, some analysts jump to investment banks where there is greater upside earning potential. Here is a more recent factor that could force faster analyst turnover: just as an analyst has a good understanding of a credit, regulators in Europe are considering a rule to force more rapid changeover in analysts for fear that too many years following a single client could foster too close a relationship between them and thus make analysts less willing to change their views. Critics of this view would label such a rule 'regulatory hubris'.

5.3 The press release

Once a rating has been determined by the RC, the CRA will send a draft press release to the issuer to be sure that there are no proprietary or incorrect facts included. The draft will include the principal considerations underlying the rating decision. Since the issuer will need to review the draft within an hour, it is important that appropriate staff be available to approve the release.

Once the issuer has had the opportunity to review the press release, the rating decision is almost always made public immediately via various media because the rating agency cannot withhold confidential insider information from the market. In the worst case, there could be a leak, but that is so rare as to be unheard of. New issuers may appeal the rating, although that happens infrequently.

When to announce the rating decision over electronic media is not debatable. It must be made public shortly after the rating decision is made by the RC since it consists of 'material non-public information' under SEC regulations. Drafts of a press release are often brought to the RC for final amending and approval once the rating decision is made. It is here that the actual wording of the press release is decided.

The reasons why an RC votes to upgrade or downgrade an issuer or confirm the rating may not coincide with those they wish to state in the press release. The language is often not explicit but deals in generalities with enough substance to justify the rating change. Press releases are cautiously crafted and can at times be imprecise.

There is an open message in the press release and a hidden message. The first is a message of risk – the letter rating and rationale. That is what investors and issuers look for. The second message is a veiled one – the message of credibility. Will this rating fly in the marketplace? Will it enhance or undermine our franchise?

Absolute candour has not always been the definition of most press releases, especially if management of the rated entity appears at fault for a downgrade. This fact may be hidden or some other way will be found to express it to allow the paying client to save face. The CRAs are not in the business of insulting their clients (knowingly). What is left unsaid can be important, especially if it deals with the agency's lack of faith in management.

Hidden motives and euphemistic language are found commonly in press releases dealing with rating changes at corporations and banks where relations with senior management are more sensitive. Such covert language is seldom found in press releases dealing with sovereigns. In fact, successful government policy is often directly alluded to, as in references to 'disciplined economic management'.

In the case of sovereign downgrades, some euphemistic language does creep into press releases. For example, where the government has let the fiscal accounts get out of control, the press release speaks of 'burgeoning public sector deficits' or 'the inability to control expenditure'. These conditions are clearly in the power of the authorities to correct, but press releases never point a finger directly at the finance minister or castigate a specific government.[1]

Crafting equivocation

With the regulatory spur to a more codified framework, the agencies must now reconcile any rating change with the methodology used and also state which rating factors drive the outcome. Senior management at the CRAs have also determined that more transparency in their operations and public statements will bring benefits. This shift is a significant improvement over press releases as recent as six or seven years ago, when a press release could be vague and give few clues to issuers about what key factors to pay closer attention to in the future.

Nonetheless, the agencies are still able to craft semi-ambiguous or imprecise press releases for these reasons.

1 The agencies do not wish to appear prescriptive, telling issuers what policies they should pursue. Astute management can read between the lines anyway.
2 The real reasons might constitute a breach of confidential, insider information supplied by the issuer. The agencies cannot disclose non-public data.
3 The issuer may have failed the agency's internal 'stress test' or the severe 'haircuts' to determine vulnerabilities to worst case scenarios. But the press release does not allude to that.
4 The agencies prefer to use euphemisms for management incompetence or for their own lack of trust in management policy or personnel.
5 The agencies may wish to send a veiled 'signal' about their approval of certain credits vis-à-vis other credits.
6 The real reason for a rating change is poor past performance, but the press release is worded with the future outlook in mind.
7 They may want to hide past rating mistakes or realign peers within an industry, for example, S&P's realignment of the Australian States' ratings in 1991, so they use general or murky language.
8 They do not want to give a false sense of precision; after all, the real world is subject to sudden and unexpected events.

Lesson for issuers

If an issuer suspects lack of candour, he should contact the lead analyst directly. It is the issuer's right to do that. Issuers need to know the real reasons for the rating change, so that they can take the necessary steps to either protect or boost their current rating.

---

[1] Interestingly, former S&P analyst Philip Alexander stated that in 2006, after S&P downgraded Italy, the finance minister at the time sent the S&P sovereign team an email thanking them, saying he had been warning his government for years that it could happen. Creswell, J, Story, L and Wyatt, E, 'Behind S&P's downgrade, a committee that acts in private', *New York Times*, 8 August 2011.

5.4 The appeal process

The international rating agencies have similar policies with regard to a bond issuer's appeal of an assigned rating. The policies are intended to display their fair-mindedness yet also to discourage frivolous and time-consuming appeals. Let us look at the major agencies' practices with respect to appeals.

Moody's Investors Service has always wanted to be perceived in the broad investment community as decisive and never subject to outside pressure. They do not want to appear to have made a mistake. It is in Moody's DNA to be tough and unyielding. If not, the flood-gates could open to unending pressure from issuers, tarnishing their image as independent authorities. As a result, in the past Moody's did not permit issuers to appeal their ratings. Then in the early 2000s the real world caught up to Moody's. Along came:

1 heightened SEC scrutiny of agency practices;
2 European pressure for greater transparency; and
3 demands for a code of conduct.

Failing to comply with these demands would have meant even greater government over-sight. Thus, Moody's responded quickly with: (i) a section called 'The Appeals Process' in its Sovereign Rating Methodology Handbook (February 2004); and (ii) a code of conduct (April 2006) which had a section on rating appeals. Here is a summary of Moody's current policy from these publications.

There are limited occasions when an issuer can bring an appeal to Moody's.

1 Issuers can appeal only on a *new rating*, not an existing one. In other words, no appeal after a downgrade or upgrade.
2 Moody's will consider a rating appeal if an issuer can provide new, significant, relevant and material information that could possibly lead Moody's RC to reconsider the rating. Moody's is very strict on this criterion.

Formal appeals are infrequent at Moody's because the lead analyst works with the issuer throughout the original rating process to make sure that all relevant information is brought forth and considered prior to the convening of the RC. If new information supplied by the issuer is *material and sufficient*, a RC will discuss it and either make a new rating decision or confirm the existing one. Appeals beyond this are very unusual, maybe non-existent.

Standard & Poor's Ratings Group has publically written that 'it is S&P policy, as part of the rating process, to allow the issuer to respond to the rating prior to its publication by presenting new or additional data'. S&P is willing to reconsider a number of things: the rating decision itself, the weight placed on the components of the analysis, and the rationale behind the rating. The objective is to have available the most important information affecting a rating, thereby ensuring the most accurate rating.

What constitutes 'relevant and new' data is a matter of opinion, of course. Once the rating decision is taken, there is no second appeal at S&P. If a *new* issuer does not like his rating, he can reject it and it will be kept confidential. If an *existing* issuer is about to be downgraded, he can appeal to S&P, in which case his case will either be: (i) reviewed quickly if a transaction is pending; or (ii) placed on Credit Watch Negative for a month or so until the situation is resolved. In either case, the issuer needs to bring new information to the table.

Following an appeal, S&P's RC has been known to change its mind. In the late 1990s, a senior S&P official admitted to the author: 'A material number of appeals have been successful, perhaps 15% to 20%.' It is unlikely to be that high today.

S&P at one point even allowed sovereigns and other issuers to argue their case in person before the RC. There was the prominent instance some years ago when S&P revised a sovereign rating downgrade from two notches to only one notch following personal intervention in New York by senior treasury officials of the government in question. That is certainly not the usual outcome, however.

Fitch Ratings retains the right to turn down any issuer request for a review of its rating. However, if an appeal is accepted, the issuer needs to provide new information. If the material then supplied is deemed 'new and material', Fitch will convene a new RC comprised of the main analyst and the backup analyst as before plus new members to add a different perspective.

To quote their written policy, 'Fitch shall review any rating action when requested by an issuer to do so if the issuer provides to Fitch in a timely manner [within two business days after hearing the rating decision] new or additional information that Fitch believes to be relevant [and material] to the rating'. In cases where the review of an existing rating is not finalised during that period, the rating is typically placed on Rating Watch.

Like the Big Two, Fitch will not accept issuer appeals on outlook changes or Rating Watch actions which are merely indicative of trends, not rating decisions per se. Appeals are rare at Fitch and seldom successful. Second appeals are not permitted.

Overcoming the hurdles

There are a number of significant barriers to appealing a rating agency's decision.

1 No agency wants the perception abroad that ratings are open to outside influence. An appeal could be perceived as an opportunity for issuers to influence the agency unduly after they have already come to a decision. *It is fundamental that ratings are not negotiated.*

2 Issuers do not appeal ratings very often. Many potential appeals are indirectly discouraged before they become 'formal' appeals, perhaps by the agency analyst who for personal reasons does not want to take the time or energy to revisit what (s)he knows is a lost cause for the issuer. The lead analyst may also fear that his supervisor will ask, 'Well, why didn't you have this information before?'

3 The appeals task can prove daunting in itself. An issuer's hurdle is to get the agency to admit their analysis involved misplaced weights or invalid assumptions – that their analysis was in effect wrong. Even if an issuer presents 'significant new facts' (which is quite rare to begin with), the agencies may simply say, 'We don't believe that these facts are relevant in your case.'

4 Issuers that appeal the rating decision face the risk of ending up with a rating lower than the one they are appealing. The new facts you present may not have the intended

effect. After all, you are asking the agency to re-think their assumptions and review the data again.

5 The success of rating appeals is very low. Knowing this, issuers may not want to devote time and resources to the effort.

6 Some advisers to issuers (principally some of well-regarded investment banking companies) have priorities that override an individual issuer's interest, and thus they may not suggest or encourage an issuer to appeal. An appeal will likely delay an issuance which means a delay in receipt of banker fees.

7 Some issuers so dislike the agencies or are so intimidated by the process that they avoid 'unnecessary' involvement with the agencies. Of course, avoidance is not the right strategy for those who want to optimise their ratings. Proactive management is the right strategy. More on this subject in Chapter 6.

So how does an issuer overcome these hurdles? The short answer is – *do not arrive at the point where you have to appeal your rating*. Well, you may say, that is easy to say, but how do we do it? Again, the short answer is you need to directly address the agencies' concerns and meet their needs, and you need to have prepared and performed as indicated earlier. Doing so will make rating appeals unnecessary.

If you maintain regular contact with your assigned analysts and their relevant team, if you are aware of their current concerns, if you are able to anticipate agency apprehensions about your credit, and if you present your well-prepared story to them at least annually (with informal talks more often), then you have done what most issuers do not take the trouble to do.

If despite these odds an issuer does decide to take the appeal path, then here is a strategy that might work. Send high level officials in person to the agency's headquarters. Treat the agency analysts with respect, not disdain for not understanding your case. Argue that their rating decision was based on cyclical factors not structural long-term ones. Argue against the weight placed on the components of the analysis. Question the rationale behind the rating.

Chapter 6

The proactive approach

Précis

If there is one factor that can help an issuer achieve an optimal rating and one factor that credit rating agency (CRA) analysts appreciate because it makes their own work easier, it is continual communication between issuer and agency.

An issuer must develop a strong relationship with the lead analyst involved and work to maintain it. The issuer has to take the initiative here because it is their future, and the analyst does not have time to monitor a particular issuer or to initiate contact unless there is a concern. Good advice is to treat the CRA as an ally not an adversary. Build trust.

Issuers have a number of rights vis-à-vis the CRAs, but these are generally unknown and seldom exercised. We list two dozen of them and recommend taking a proactive approach to CRA management rather than a sitting back, hands-off approach.

The rating agencies will appreciate an issuer's deeper involvement in the process, and issuers need not fear some kind of ratings retaliation for speaking up. Speaking up does have its limits, however, as some outspoken government officials learned to their chagrin. Emotional rants and frustrated fulminations backfire.

To raise the odds for an upgrade or to achieve an optimal rating, there is a simple procedure issuers should follow – the strategy, performance and persistence (SPP) formula, explained here. The one sure way not to be successful in this regard is to 'whistle in the dark', that is, make excuses for doing nothing to improve relations with the CRAs.

If you don't control your own destiny, someone else will.

6.1 Communicating with the agencies

One topic that former agency analysts like to talk about is the importance of issuers' communication with the rating agencies. The passages in quotation marks are the actual statements of these analysts during interviews.

The ex-analysts uniformly say that in their days at the agency, issuers made their life easy or hard depending on how often issuers stayed in touch with them. Those that made the effort to communicate regularly with S&P and Moody's have found a more receptive audience at the agency than those who did not. For issuers, managing the rating agencies and optimising ratings begin with good communications. The agencies value candour, honesty and willingness to co-operate. Send them information that cannot be found in the newspapers or online. Alert them early on to both good and bad developments.

Open communication is a necessity

The basic principle is that issuers need to have full and open communication with the agencies in all important matters. For sovereigns, 'important matters' comprise any developments relating to the economy, fiscal policy, debt, or political issues. For banks and corporates, it is any development affecting leverage, cash flow and profitability. Immediately notifying the agencies of these events deepens agency trust in treasury or company management. Openness helps promote mutual trust and favourable inclinations at the agencies. These can certainly be beneficial in the analysts' subjective assessment of the credit and can be decisive at the margin if there is a 'close call' in a rating committee (RC).

As difficult as it may be on occasion, issuers should see relations with the agencies as a co-operative and consultative venture, not an antagonistic one. Issuers should view agency relations as part of their investor relations function. They should work closely with the agencies, helping to create an atmosphere of mutual confidence. Treat the agency as an 'insider' to be trusted with confidential information. Issuers also need to be accessible and straightforward – as do the agencies. The alternative is not conducive to good ratings. 'It's hard to be fair if you suspect incomplete disclosure,' admitted a former analyst. 'If issuers don't communicate openly, the agencies get suspicious.'

Allies, not adversaries

Hans van den Houten, a former Vice President and Director International at Moody's, wrote that issuers should treat the rating agencies as allies, not adversaries.[1] Management should utilise the rating agencies as *part of* their business strategy. In other words, they should view the agencies as independent and impartial assessors of their own financial performance and learn from them. They should embrace the agencies as part of their team, which is much better approach than to view them as adversaries or roadblocks or time-wasters. Harmony should replace animosity. 'Don't fight them, embrace them!'

He gives a good example: by paying careful attention to an agency analyst's questions, a company can draw insightful inferences with direct impact on company operations. In their conversations with the agencies, management should be able to garner new insights about more effective strategy and marketing. Company officials can even voice certain questions back to the agencies with the intention of getting independent answers to those issues and questions currently facing management. Thus, the benefits of a rating are more than just access to international markets at cost-effective rates. It would cost an executive's annual salary to hire someone to generate this type of intelligence and yet the agencies are doing it for you for no incremental cost.

Both the quality of the dialogue and the information provided to the rating agencies are important. If the information is pertinent and timely, then the analyst and the RC tend to give the issuer the benefit of the doubt on matters at hand. With these issuers, the RC reaches a 'comfort level' and feels 'ahead of the curve' or 'on top of' the credit. In this situation, the agency concludes there is less chance of their being surprised or blindsided by events, which could embarrass them if the rating is too high. At the margin, this feeling of confidence can influence a rating by one notch. It also enhances the chances for an upgrade or minimises the damage in a downgrade.

For example, while being downgraded progressively in 1991, India sent reams of material weekly to S&P. The deputy minister of finance actually stopped by their offices regularly. This pre-emptive approach, urged by their ratings adviser, limited the extent of the downgrade.

Issuer alerts

Issuers need to alert the agencies at an early stage to pending developments, especially if there is bad news coming. Analysts want to stay on top of their credits and sincerely appreciate efforts by their issuer contacts to help them do this job. They do not want to read online about events they should have been alerted to earlier. Analysts hate surprises. The worst thing that can happen to an analyst is that his boss comes in and says 'What's the impact of this recent event on the credit?' If the analyst has not been informed, then he is angry and embarrassed and his trust in you is severely strained. Keep the dialogue and information flows going. The alternative is for the agency to think there is sudden heightened credit risk, which could lead to a lower rating.

Put in a more positive context, an experienced sovereign analyst suggested that 'timely reporting and updating of information on economic performance is key. There could be a good story evolving, but if the agency does not hear about it soon enough, the issuer misses an opportunity.' This lesson applies to corporates and banks, too. They should always inform the agencies of rating-relevant news prior to its public announcement, such as mergers and acquisitions, asset sales or major accounting write-offs.

One former agency official urged issuers, 'Give us a sense of the predictability of financial management, that is, that you will do what you say you will do. We need to have confidence that management can manage an economic downturn and won't get caught with a large spending program underway when the recession hits.'

And beyond that, 'convince us that even in the worst-case scenario, the progress to date will be preserved'. Analysts like to see issuers well-equipped to answer 'what-if' questions, such as what if the housing market slumps, what if the competition lowers its prices, what if the opposition gains power, or what if unemployment stays high? How will these affect your business?

Frequently asked question

'The agencies have completed their visit to us, have written their reports and have confirmed our ratings, so what else do we need to do?'

Answer:

There is much you can do between now and their next visit. That is what 'managing' the agencies means. Since most issuers ignore the agencies in between due diligence meetings, a strategy of active involvement with them will make you stand out by comparison. First, it is important to know how the agencies think and which arguments are useful to make to them. Second, you should know what the agencies need to hear and also what they do not like to hear. Finally, your institution needs to implement a consistent pattern of contact with the agencies that fits your particular strengths and weaknesses.

Contact person

Provide information constantly to the analysts, especially in bad times when many issuers avoid going to see the agencies. Make sure you have good communicators in charge of this. Just because a person is a CFO or a senior bureaucrat does not mean he or she is the right person to be the liaison with the agencies. The right person needs to understand the rating agencies' agendas, issues and concerns and needs to make the goal an optimal rating.

Does the contact person have on file every report, comment, and press release written by all the agencies about their credit as well as those of their peers? There are important clues therein about what causes upgrades and downgrades, and what each agency considers pertinent and rating-sensitive. Such a robust file will also help in learning what corporate actions are needed to position the company or bank for an upgrade. By creating a strategic plan for the next three years showing the steps to take toward that end, you will be far ahead of what most companies do.

Issuers need to understand how the agency thinks about their credit 'class' (banking, corporates, sovereigns, insurance, and so on) and what the agencies deem important so that they can tell their story in the most appropriate manner. 'Emphasise *goals and process*, and how your strategies have successfully played out. Keep in close contact and anticipate our concerns,' urged one analyst. 'Call us and say we have a problem. Don't try to slip it by the analysts. Show us you're working on it; don't hope the agency won't notice anything. If we do notice, some of us could be angry and unforgiving.'

Build credibility over time with the agency. 'It's dangerous if the agency feels you are not levelling with them or are always putting a positive spin on everything you say. View the relationship with the agencies as a life-time affair, not just an annual song and dance. And, importantly, assume the agency will remember all you tell them.'

In your regular communications with the agencies, remember to be honest with them and put the negative facts up front. The benefits of doing this are:

- you will be perceived as forthright and honest and not hiding the dirty linen;
- the agency will not have to dig out the negatives themselves or feel they have been fooled; and
- you will be putting the negatives behind you and can move on to more positive subjects.

Here is a telling case of poor communication by a rated entity and the consequences. In mid-November 2004, Moody's, S&P and Fitch all downgraded the pharmaceutical giant Merck two or three notches from AAA, a very rare instance of multi-notch downgrades from the top rating. Merck faced substantial potential liability from one of its products, Vioxx, which was associated with increased incidence of adverse cardiac events, many leading to death. A veritable flood of lawsuits followed, claiming total damages in the billions of dollars. The downgrades followed. The risks associated with Merck's products were likely known by the company but were not disclosed, perhaps due to worries about the effect on its share price.

Lesson for issuers

Keep the agencies apprised of bad news; they do not appreciate surprises such as the one described. For years afterwards, the agencies will ask themselves, I wonder what else they have not told us.

The two-way street

Do not be bashful. Agencies tend to respect companies who are assertive about who they are and about why what they are doing is right. Issuers should not be reluctant to say, 'I don't agree with your analysis for these reasons.' If a good dialogue opens, then the agency might just say to itself (not to you), 'Perhaps we didn't place enough weight on that. Let's go back and think this through again.'

At the same time, do not be insistent and obnoxious about an upgrade, constantly hammering the agency about being more creditworthy than your peers. That tactic can backfire in resentment that you are taking up too much analyst time.

Maintain good relations beyond the lead analyst by initiating conference calls with members of the RC and heads of departments. This tactic is especially beneficial if you sense the lead analyst does not appreciate your case. In fact, taking this initiative a step further, a proactive issuer should ask the CRA to meet periodically to discuss their rating relationship in general and the rating factors that specifically could lead to a change in rating or outlook.

Do not outsource your active communications to your investment bankers or your public relations company or your investor relations team which tend to focus on the equity community. They rarely have the sensitivity or the information that is of interest to the fixed income community.

In sum, the *benefits* of full, open communication with the agencies are:

- the building of trust with the analyst;
- a more confident analyst going before the RC;

- a greater 'comfort level' on the part of the RC; and
- the benefit of the doubt in a difficult situation.

Conversely, the *drawbacks* of not communicating regularly with the agencies include:

- the assumption that information not supplied is information deliberately withheld;
- surprises sprung on the analyst that destroy his trust in your desire to co-operate;
- a long institutional memory summarised by 'once burned, never forgotten'; or
- delays or lost opportunities for getting an upgrade, or an overreaction on the downgrade side.

You need to treat the agencies as travel companions in the capital markets, as allies not opponents, and that means regular and open communication. The key to a successful relationship with rating agencies is open communications – but you as the issuer will have to take the initiative. You need to tell the agencies:

> It's a two-way street; we will be responsive to your requests for data; you need to be responsive to our requests about how you determine ratings and the global assumptions you bring to the table. As paying customers, we expect due process. Our borrowing costs depend on it.

---

[1] Email to author, September 2005.

6.2 Issuer rights and leverage

What should an issuer expect from the rating agencies? That they provide a fair hearing and due process, that they be good listeners and ask good questions, that they follow consistent policies, that they put aside the arrogance and condescension that still hangs over the industry, and that they co-operate as equals.

However, there are certain facts of rating life that complicate that expectation.

- The rating agencies can be secretive, unresponsive, and impenetrable.
- Their agendas, methods and procedures can be unclear.
- The rules are made by them... and imposed on issuers.
- They set the timing of visits, reviews, meetings and rating changes.
- The impact of ratings on issuer finances can be large.
- Ratings are judgments, hence fallible, which gives issuers opportunities to alter the outcome.
- Issuers do have rights and leverage vis-à-vis the agencies.
- However, these rights are mainly unknown and unexercised.

Ideally, the relationship between issuer and rating agency is one of peers. However, too often the relationship is perceived by both sides as superior and subordinate – 'Us versus Them'. The relationship does not have to be that way. Changing it, though, will require action on your part, that is, 'active management' or more strongly put 'assertive management'. The 'benign' approach shown in Exhibit 6.1 does not work. It implies weakness or indifference.

Yet issuers tend to acquiesce in what the agencies say and do, assuming that agency policies are an irksome but necessary part of the debt issuance process or because of some unspoken or misplaced fear on their part of ratings 'retribution'. We will deal with that worry in the next section.

Assertive management means knowing your rights as an issuer vis-à-vis the agencies and exercising them. It means devoting resources to meeting their needs and your own. It means making credit agency relations a priority. It means ensuring the commitment of senior management. It means seeking a reasonable justification for your rating.

Assertiveness means not losing sight of your focus and your intended message despite the intrusion of extraneous issues. It means asking the agencies questions about their policies and then persisting if their explanation is too glib or unclear. Issuers sometimes worry that a more active and demanding posture might alienate the agencies. On the contrary, they respect issuers that display pride, confidence and dynamism.

Assertive management means being proactive, for example, understanding and anticipating the credit implications of future policies and financing decisions. It means sharing information with the agencies regularly through ongoing dialogue but also requiring that they reciprocate. Issuers need to re-educate the agencies constantly, as personnel and concerns change on both sides of the table.

The key to a successful relationship with rating agencies is open communications – but *you* will have to take the initiative. You need to tell the agencies: 'It's a two-way street; we will be responsive to your requests for data; you must be responsive to our requests for information on how you determine ratings, the global assumptions you bring to the table, and feedback on our performance. You want a "no surprises" relationship – so do we.'

Exhibit 6.1

Managing the rating agencies: two schools of thought

Facet	Benign school	Proactive school
Issuer attitude	Passive, confused, intimidated, defensive	Confident, assertive (but not combative or argumentative)
Communications	Irregular phone or email contact	Same, but more probing for underlying concerns
Agency methodology	Accepts agency framework with no questions asked	Questions and learns agency methods; probes for weaknesses
Peer comparisons	Accepts agency peer group model	Does own comparisons; shapes to own purposes
Preparations for the annual rating meeting	Last minute rush; updates last year's materials	5 to 6 weeks in advance; develops new materials; uses adviser if necessary
Annual meeting	Accepts agency agenda and timetable	Uncovers covert agenda; sets amenable timetable
Credit watches, negative outlooks	Panic, anger; bad result seen as unavoidable	Calm and probing; looks for contradictions in agency writings and statements
Fees	Pays unquestioningly for all issues; does not negotiate	Negotiates contracts; does not pay for unrequested ratings
Issuer rights	Does not realise or utilise	Exercises rights fully

Source: Author's own

List of issuer rights

If an issuer's rights are to be respected by the agencies, issuers must employ a more assertive approach than perhaps they are used to doing. Assertiveness begins with choosing the best agency for your needs, controlling the agenda of meetings (the topics, speakers, and pace), and working with the agencies throughout the year. Remember, issuers pay for the rating service and have the right to demand good and full service.

What are issuer rights and what strategies and tactics are appropriate to level the playing field, to redress the balance? Here is a list of issuer rights. They range from the general to the specific and from pre-meeting to post-meeting. Elaborations on these rights appear throughout the book. They appear in one spot here as a summary and to facilitate their application.

1 The right to use your inherent leverage as a borrower in the capital markets.
2 The right to be a demanding customer, not a passive consumer.
3 The right to take charge of the relationship with the agencies.
4 The right to proactively influence the perceptions of agency analysts.
5 The right not to be intimidated by agency image and jargon.

6   The right to object to those agency policies you do not find applicable or fair.
7   The right to challenge the agencies' procedures and practices.
8   The right to contest any public statement or private assurance from the agencies.
9   The right to know the backgrounds of the analysts and senior credit officers making assessments.
10 The right to see clear rating criteria and clear rating policy statements.
11 The right to challenge how they apply their methodology.
12 The right to challenge the analysts' economic biases and assumptions.
13 The right to be aware of the agencies' real agendas, concerns and issues.
14 The right to understand the functioning of the rating committee.
15 The right to ask why you can rest assured that your rating will be correct.
16 The right to demand that the agencies explain past rating errors.
17 The right to choose the most advantageous time for an agency visit.
18 The right to have your full story *heard* by the agencies.
19 The right to have your full story *understood* by the analysts.
20 The right to review and correct credit reports before they are published.
21 The right to pressure the CRA for a quick decision when On Review or CreditWatch.
22 The right to protest and appeal a rating.
23 The right to refuse to pay for a rating you did not request.
24 The right to a clear and reasoned rating opinion about your creditworthiness.

Issuers that take this list seriously can ask and 'demand' of the agencies all they like, but they need to be aware that the agencies, uncomfortable at the prodding, may push back. It was related that one curmudgeonly agency official replied to an inquisitive issuer: 'I'm the one who asks the questions here!'

6.3 Rating agency retaliation

The bi-monthly magazine *Treasury and Risk Management* carried an article in late 1994 with the intriguing title, 'Why everyone hates Moody's.' The article was based on a survey of corporate treasurers in the US who often complained of arbitrary and capricious actions by the rating agencies that left CFOs feeling powerless, unfairly treated and fearful.

In such surveys, CFOs have admitted they are reluctant to speak openly or 'on the record' about their relations with the rating agencies. They say frankly they fear the agencies will somehow 'retaliate' if they criticise the agencies, so they request anonymity in return for candid comments. Have there been actual instances where an agency has 'retaliated' against an issuer, such as assigning a punitive rating for reasons not related to real issues of creditworthiness? Let us examine the question.

Checks and balances

First, there are a number of safeguards that prevent punitive ratings against an outspoken issuer or one who is unco-operative or one who refuses to pay rating fees.

- A rating agency needs to maintain its reputation with investors, and precipitate, unjustified rating changes will undermine that reputation.
- A rating agency cannot invent a rationale for a downgrade that does not fit the realities of the marketplace or the agency's credibility will suffer.
- An analyst must take an unbiased approach in the rating committee if he or she is to maintain credibility and reputation both at the company and with clients.
- SEC rules and agency operational policies are designed to separate the analytical side of the business from the revenue and fee-paying side. The analyst responsible for a particular credit is seldom, if ever, aware of the issuer's contribution to agency revenues.
- Rating committees include members not otherwise associated with the credit in order to enhance objectivity and promote internal continuity.
- Issuers pay the agencies for their ratings according to their contract. Issuers' fees comprise about 80% of agency revenues (the other portion being non-rating activities such as data collection and dissemination and on-line rating subscriptions). No business can afford to alienate its main client base.
- Issuers always have the option to appeal to senior management with a legitimate complaint.

Do these safeguards against punitive ratings really work? Do the agencies' inherent checks and balances prevent 'retaliation'?

Over the past two decades the author has spoken with former senior rating agency officials at Moody's, S&P and Fitch about so-called 'ratings retaliation.' Their conclusion was consistent and unvarying: never in their five decades of experience at the agencies had they encountered a case where there was even talk of ratings retaliation, let alone an actual downgrade. No matter how abrasive or outspoken a CFO may be, the agencies simply do not respond to public criticism. One source said, 'It's not a good use of their time, and it would compromise their image of impartiality.' More importantly, punitive ratings, if ever discovered, would fatally undermine the agency's franchise.

Safeguards are effective

Another said, 'It's poor performance over a lengthy period by a whole company, not the words of a single headstrong treasurer, that determines whether a downgrade occurs.' A third source said, 'Business relations between the company and the rating agency may be affected if fees are not paid, and personal relationships may suffer if a CFO publicly criticises an analyst or an agency, but these factors don't affect the rating.' The checks and balances appear to be quite effective in preventing corrupt rating results.

Still, if the rating committee is aware of taunting behaviour by an issuer, might not this affect the rating? Can senior officers use their power to force a lower rating without revealing to others why they are doing so? Could they not simply maintain in their exalted position that the credit just does not 'feel right'? And do not junior members of the committee traditionally defer to more senior members?

All this sounds plausible, especially since rating committee deliberations are secret. However, this type of 'revenge' on issuers is clearly not within the experience of those former agency officials we interviewed. Assuming there is any kind of ratings 'retaliation' at all, at most it might take the form of not returning phone calls to issuers, of not co-operating with an issuer's request, of not accommodating on meeting schedules, and of not giving the issuer the benefit of the doubt on key concerns and leveraging matters. It would certainly not take the form of an all too obvious rating downgrade.

To be clear, we are not referring here to issuers who refuse to disclose necessary information. Where the data are incomplete, the rating committee will take a conservative approach and assign a lower rating in order to capture the uncertainty caused by insufficient information. In today's capital markets, however, there are not too many issuers who do not co-operate when the agencies request material. Issuers know that their data and strategic plans are secure in agency files. Moreover, they have little choice if they want to augment their funding in the fixed income markets.

There is any number of reasons why a rating might end up lower than anticipated, but an agency's retaliating for criticism in the media is not one of the reasons. A low rating can be the result, for example, of a legitimately marginal call on the part of the rating committee. These close calls usually result from internal disagreement over trends and forecasts affecting the issuer.

Theoretically, an agency could punish an issuer by withdrawing an existing public rating, making the issuer suffer the consequences of having unrated paper in the market. This particular debt obligation could suffer a decline in value if investors were forced by their own regulations not to hold unrated paper. Or, an issuer might find it more difficult and costly to sell new debt. However, this kind of action is so rare as to be non-existent. Ratings are only removed when an issue is fully paid, redeemed or matured, or when there is so little outstanding that it is not worth the agency's spending time to monitor it. It may also be withdrawn if current information is not forthcoming to allow the annual review or contemporaneous surveillance. In these circumstances, the withdrawal of coverage is publicly announced.

Suppose an issuer refuses to pay for ratings it did not request, or refuses to pay for an increase in annual fees when there is no clear value added by the agency to justify the increase. Will the agency seek retribution in some fashion? No, again that is not how the system works. There have been a number of issuers in the past who have stood firm on such matters, and there has been no agency response beyond cajoling and persuasion.

Conclusion

Rating agency retaliation is theoretically possible and may enter the rumour circuit, but it does not happen in real life. That the topic is even raised by issuers (or their bankers) is testimony to the power of the agencies. Issuer anxiety on this matter is clearly not merited.

6.4 The tipping point

Malcolm Gladwell wrote an interesting book called *The Tipping Point*[1] that dealt primarily with how social 'epidemics' (disease, crime, teen smoking, the success of VHS over Betamax) gain momentum with just the smallest change in behaviour. The 'tipping point' is a sociological term that refers to that dramatic moment when some unique idea, message or product becomes common. Trends start to grow once a critical mass is reached. The phrase has taken on broader meaning now and has become almost a cliché.

In the ratings arena, we could define a tipping point as that critical moment when a rating decision is made by the rating analyst or the rating committee as a result of an event or trend in the issuer's environment that solidifies previous views or that causes a fundamental shift in thinking and opinion. It is a *decision moment* that leads directly to a rating conclusion. Here are two examples.

The due diligence meeting

First, there can be a tipping point in any *due diligence meeting* with the agencies, whether it is on the issuer's home-court or at the agencies' headquarters. A particularly cogent argument made in the meeting by a CFO or minister of finance can tip the scales in favour of an upgrade (or away from a downgrade), whichever was in the mind of the senior analyst when the meeting began. Remember that analysts do come to meetings with predetermined leanings and perceptions.

Similarly, the inability to respond adequately to analyst questions can confirm in the analysts' minds that 'these guys deserve a downgrade' or 'they don't deserve the upgrade we were considering'. One naïve or inappropriate statement can do just that, as former agency analysts can testify. It obviously pays to be well prepared so that any tipping point is in your favour.

Rating committees

Second, tipping points occur in a *rating committee*. As the discussion about an issuer's creditworthiness proceeds in the committee, a consensus (or a strong majority opinion) emerges due to: (i) the analysis and presentation of the senior analyst; or (ii) the probing and sceptical questions of his colleagues. At some juncture, the rating conclusion usually becomes obvious to all around the table.

The information on which that rating decision is based depends to a large extent on what the analyst has learned and deduced from the issuer. The analyst processes this information and develops a numerical as well as subjective forecast of the issuer's willingness and ability to pay obligations in the future. That forecast depends on the analyst's training and experience and on the credibility and completeness of what the issuer has told him.

All banks, companies and countries face challenges on a daily basis in both their domestic and international markets. These challenges, all of which affect their credit ratings, run the gamut from political and economic, to fiscal and monetary, and to legal and regulatory. Despite the complexities of analysing all these variables, there is one common thread, which determines the rating at the end of the day. It is the agency's opinion about the ability of management to recognise, deal with and solve the problems they may face.

For a *sovereign*, the tipping point can be the presentation of a sound fiscal plan based on realistic assumptions (or the reverse, the inability to demonstrate how recurring deficits will be reversed).

For a *bank*, the tipping point can be the demonstration of adequate risk management systems (or the lack thereof) that protect solvency.

For a *corporation*, the tipping point can be a deep and refined SWOT[2] analysis or a demonstrated failure to understand the competition in the marketplace.

What do all these tipping points have in common? Answer: *the central role of management*. Management's policies, demeanour, performance and persuasiveness *are* the tipping point in ratings. Decision makers in an institution have the power to 'make or break' a rating outcome. It is their effectiveness in running their business or country that determines a rating.

The choices of management

The choices are myriad and the matters complex, but here is a sample of what management in various issuer categories must accomplish to assure the tipping point goes in their favour.

Sovereign officials need to show fiscal rectitude in order to prevent the rise in domestic and foreign debt. They need to demonstrate their ability to cope with the social and political challenges of globalisation. The inability of the US government to agree on budgets and deficits for several years prompted S&P to downgrade its AAA rating on US debt in August 2011 by one notch to AA+.

Bank managers need to demonstrate they understand and practice 'effective enterprise risk management', as S&P terms it, in everything from market risk to operational risk. In the light of 'rogue' trading activities at certain international banks, for example, Société Générale and Barings, the rating agencies are taking a much closer look at operational risk, which according to Basel II regulations, is 'the risk of direct or indirect loss resulting from inadequate or failed internal processes, people and systems or from external events.' Examples include internal fraud, fiduciary breaches, and management information system (MIS) failures.

Corporate managers need to generate cash to adequately cover outstanding obligations, and this depends on the skills and ability of management to make wise use of existing resources and market opportunities, and to respond effectively to adverse conditions that might arise (for example, technological developments, regulatory changes, new competition). They also must assure analysts that they have adequately covered operational risk, such as damage to physical assets and workplace safety.

---

[1] Gladwell, M, *The Tipping Point: how little things can make a big difference*, 2000, Little, Brown and Company.

[2] SWOT is a planning and evaluation method that stands for 'Strengths, Weaknesses, Opportunities, Threats' and is used to evaluate a project, a business enterprise or an industry. It helps one identify the internal and external factors that are favourable or unfavourable toward achieving objectives. Presenting an honest and thorough SWOT matrix will show the agencies that you know your business and are less likely to be caught out by surprises.

6.5 What not to say and do

Rated issuers of all stripes around the world have a habit of speaking critically and publicly about the rating agencies when they receive an unwelcome rating. These outbursts may relieve some political or stakeholder pressure, but they certainly do not have any positive effect on the rating itself and only negative effect on relations with the agencies.

Let us begin with an example of a government. Following a recent series of downgrades of Japanese debt by the three major rating agencies, the Japanese government issued stinging statements and letters of rebuke to the agencies. (Japan is one of 13 sovereigns to have lost its AAA over the years.)

In 2002, the Japanese Ministry of Finance wrote to Moody's, S&P and Fitch castigating them and blasting their assessments of Japan's creditworthiness. The ministry called on the agencies to explain their reasoning behind the ratings, 'which are already too low... your explanations regarding ratings decisions are mostly qualitative in nature and lack objective criteria, which invite questions about the larger issue of the reliability of ratings itself (sic)'.

It is not accurate and only illustrates the naïveté on the part of the ministry to say: (i) the ratings 'lack objective criteria'; and (ii) Moody's downgrades are because 'they're doing it for business reasons'. Such criticism never has a positive consequence, except perhaps in the realm of domestic public opinion. In many instances, the rating agencies are being used as scapegoats for inept macroeconomic policy settings and failure to address fiscal challenges.

A missed opportunity

Then when Moody's downgraded Japan's yen-denominated debt two notches to A2 on 31 May 2002, the Japanese Ministry of Finance went apoplectic. The downgrade put Japan's creditworthiness in local currency at the same rating level as Cyprus, Israel, Latvia, Mauritius and Poland. The government tried to deflect criticism onto Moody's and away from itself, typical of the Japanese government's ongoing denial of its deep-seated financial problems.[1]

Actually, if the Japanese government had chosen to be astute, they could have used the downgrade as a political opportunity and an incentive to justify domestic reform, saying, 'Look what outside experts are saying about our financial vulnerability; now we really have to change our policies and fiscally consolidate.'

This 'foot-in-mouth' disease is not limited to the Japanese, of course. There have been other instances where displeased government officials have crossed the line and uttered inappropriate, naïve or overly aggressive statements publicly. Here are five more examples.

Example 1 Malaysia: after Moody's and S&P both downgraded Malaysia in July 1998 (Moody's three notches, and S&P one notch), Prime Minister Mahathir Mohamad of Malaysia was forced to postpone an international bond issue of US$2 billion just before officials were to embark on a road show.

Mahathir responded with this retort on 4 August: 'It is clear [the agencies] did this to prevent us from reviving our companies and banks. This was deliberately done. When they knew we were about to borrow money, they reduced our credit standing.' The prime minister was suffering from a basic misunderstanding of how the agencies think and operate. Or, he may have understood very well but chose to castigate the outsiders to shore up domestic political support.

In the interest of keeping investors informed of their latest thinking, it not uncommon for the rating agencies to change an outlook or a rating just prior to a bond issue because that is exactly *when investors need the latest information on default risk.*

Example 2 Turkey: in the mid-1990s, both Moody's and S&P downgraded Turkey several times. Just prior to the agencies' next visit the following year, government officials publicly criticised the agencies for not having upgraded their debt in the preceding 12 months in the light of 'the improvements in our economy'.

The Governor of the Central Bank said they had 'applied to a third rating agency, and we will apply to a fourth. Then S&P and Moody's will have to raise our rating.' What was the bank's line of reasoning here? He explained it as the agencies' 'fear of undermining their reputation for accuracy if they do not [raise the rating]'.

This line of logic showed little understanding of agency criteria and operations, and it certainly did not impress or intimidate the Big Two. In fact, in the absence of fiscal consolidation, disinflation, and structural reforms, the agencies downgraded this country two more times over the next 20 months. After one such downgrade, one cabinet minister demanded to know – who was paying S&P to downgrade us. The minister was quoted in the *Financial Times* as vowing, 'S&P will definitely not get away with this'.

Example 3 Cyprus: Moody's was about to establish an office in Limassol and had a then-confidential rating on the country that the government was unhappy with. The Central Bank sent Moody's a clear signal that the future conduct of business in the country would be facilitated if they would upgrade the sovereign rating! Moody's did not agree to this 'suggestion'.

If the Central Bank had known Moody's *modus operandi*, they never would have made such an offer (read: bribe). The Central Bank gave the appearance of blackmailing, or at least strong-arming, the agency. Moody's seems to have the final word in this instance – they publicly announced the confidential rating and proceeded to open their office, which still operates today.

Example 4 Venezuela: in August and September 1998, Moody's had just downgraded Venezuela twice and S&P had changed its outlook on Venezuelan debt to negative. The government's reaction, with statements by the Finance Minister, the Planning Minister and the Central Bank Director, was a broadside at both agencies. This is a good example of 'shoe-in-mouth' disease. Here are their statements [followed by this author's commentary].

- Latin America should rebel against the credit-rating agencies due to their lack of professionalism. Investors should take a closer look at the situation in the region and try to come up with their own analysis of our reality. [All right, the first part is bombast, but the second part is what the agencies urge anyway.]
- Venezuelan officials accused the agencies of contemplating more downgrades *despite* an unexpected appreciation of the local currency, the bolivar. The agencies 'were disoriented by the positive performance of the bolivar... We have not humoured them by devaluating, and they are irritated,' said the Planning Minister in response to the S&P negative outlook. [First, the minor fluctuations in a country's local currency have little to do with rating or outlook changes. Just read their press releases. So

this accusation is not grounded in reality. Second, 'irritation' has no role in rating committee deliberations.]

- The Finance Minister told Moody's that 'its analyses were no longer based on a careful review of economic variables but rather governed by a herd mentality and by the simplification of measuring all emerging markets by the same yardstick.' Moody's does not 'act in good faith with its hasty and indiscriminate downgrading of countries' credit ratings'. [Actually, it is appropriate to measure all emerging markets with the same yardstick since that helps ensure a consistent result and a suitable range of these countries' *relative* creditworthiness. The agencies' downgrades are often perceived as 'hasty' only by those downgraded, and they are certainly not indiscriminate.]

- The Finance Minister went on to say that the downward spiral of emerging markets stems from the uncertainty caused by their downgrading. The agencies then respond to the resulting situation by downgrading yet again the countries concerned. Downgrades become vicious circles of self-fulfilling prophecies due to the agencies' 'enormous clout'. [There is some truth in these statements. Investors do react negatively to downgrades, and the resulting capital flight can indeed provide less protection for bond holders and hence cause further downgrades. And yes, the agencies do have enormous clout, one which they have earned over a century of effort with credible rating opinions.]

- The Planning Minister questioned the suspicious decision-making processes of risk-grading agencies. He added that the error was that the financial and productive sectors had allowed such companies to acquire an undeserved reputation of infallibility, especially when subjective perceptions took precedence over objective data. [Since the Minister has not had access to a rating committee, it is doubtful he comprehends the process or appreciates the rigour of the analysis. Other caveats: (i) subjective perceptions weigh heavily in rating decisions but they hardly take 'precedence' over the data; and (ii) the agencies do not claim infallibility.]

- The credit-rating companies are passing harsh judgments on Latin America in order to atone for their excessive complacency while the Asian crisis was breaking out 14 months before. [Following the Asian financial crisis, critics accused the rating agencies of 'lagging the market'. The rating agencies defended themselves by saying, 'Our ratings are opinions based on information available to us at the time. Because of the region's lack of financial transparency and up-to-date accounting standards at that time, we underestimated the troubles in the banking and corporate sectors and the spread of market contagion. We were not the only ones feeling misled.' The agencies may have been somewhat complacent in Asia, but they were hardly compensating for this in Latin America.]

In the six years following this tirade, Venezuela due to its own policies suffered two more downgrades from Moody's, four downgrades from S&P and seven downgrades from Fitch. None were due to 'irritation'. Interestingly, the country was also upgraded by Fitch three times, but the government did not complain that these rating actions were 'hasty and indiscriminate'. It would appear that the agencies' methodologies are right for upgrades but wrong for downgrades.

Consequences

When senior government officials go public with these kinds of statements and challenges, one wonders, what is the impact of such criticism on the agencies? Does this kind of censure persuade the agencies to rethink their position? The short answers are 'none' and 'no'. First, no agency can afford to change its rating on the basis of pressure from those they rate. Second, the agencies are expressing an 'opinion' that is inherently subjective and subject to change.

Ironically, the officials are correct when they say, 'rating decisions are mostly qualitative in nature'. The agencies would agree with that. Issuer statements about ratings are usually seen by the agency as either naïve or threatening, which does not help their cause. In sum, there is zero persuasive impact.

Example 5 Telecom Italia: here is an instance of a very public complaint by a European corporate due to a Moody's downgrade. In mid-August 2003 Telecom Italia (TI) blasted Moody's for cutting its credit rating following TI's merger with Olivetti. TI issued a press release saying the Moody's analysis contained errors and calling the assessment 'inappropriate, mistaken and inaccurate, as well as without legal foundation'. Strong words indeed for the public forum.

TI explained its statement in terms of its 'responsibility to the market', but some analysts said TI's real reason for its unusual public action is that step-up clauses in TI's bond indentures had forced an increase in TI's coupon payments – some 25 basis points – due to the downgrade.

Another factor behind the TI complaint was that S&P and Fitch viewed the merger as positive and assigned higher ratings to TI. For example, S&P said, 'It will significantly increase discretionary cash flow (after dividends), thereby enhancing debt-reduction potential' and rated TI BBB+. Fitch assigned an A– rating to TI's debt, one notch higher.

Unlike the others, Moody's saw the glass as half empty, focusing on the negative aspect of the merger and noting 'the substantial increase in debt for TI's bondholders as a result of the direct assumption of Olivetti's debt resulting from the merger'.

TI management (and every issuer) needs to keep in mind that the agencies are expressing an 'opinion' that is inherently subjective and subject to change. Clearly, the issuer wants the best rating possible, but good advice for TI in this case would be:

- work with Moody's quietly behind the scenes and do not vent your frustrations publicly;
- start gathering evidence of the success of the merger so that after a few quarters you can counter the downsides Moody's raised; and
- do not forget that Moody's responsibility is to warn bondholders of credit risks. Since there are many examples of mergers gone wrong, Moody's is, on the one hand, being responsible to its main constituency and on the other hand acting conservatively. Unlike the other two agencies, they eventually may be able to say, 'we told you so'.

TI needed a better approach to its preparation since all three agencies looked at the same facts and came up with different conclusions. Since most issuers typically see the agency analysts only once a year, they have to make the most of that opportunity and provide the agencies with arguments and materials that: (i) meet their analytical needs; and (ii) tell their story in the best light possible.

On the lighter side, the Lebanese newspaper *Al-Mustaqbal* on 14 March 2001 quoted Mr Habib Abu Fadhel, Managing Director of Lebanon's United Trade Bank, as saying that S&P's rating practices are like 'coffee grounds reading'. (He was objecting to S&P's 'low' sovereign foreign-currency rating of B+ for Lebanon.) The comment is uniquely cultural in context; Europeans would say the rating emerged from a 'black box' and others might describe it as reading the tea leaves. The spokesman meant the analogy in a derogatory way, but in a sense he was right.

Conclusions

There are a number of broad conclusions that issuers should draw from these examples.

- Do not attack the rating agencies publicly. Open criticism of agency decisions by disgruntled issuers tends to backfire, only delaying any reversal of opinion.
- No agency can afford to change its rating on the basis of pressure from issuers.
- Such criticism never has a positive consequence for the sovereign issuer, except perhaps in the realm of domestic public opinion.
- If the public attack is very personal or emotional, then investors, who have many investment alternatives, may have second thoughts about the wisdom and rationality of management under pressure.
- Wild or unrealistic statements do not reflect well on the issuer, and they breed an atmosphere of distrust and disrespect between issuer and agency.
- The rating agencies (and often the IMF) are used by governments as scapegoats for their own inept macroeconomic policy settings and the lack of official responsiveness to internal or external shocks and challenges.
- There are no alternatives to the rating agencies, so it is wise to learn how to work with them. Their power is entrenched in market reliance on ratings and embedded in financial regulations around the world as well as in various bond contracts, such as indentures and triggers. Alienating them is a no-win situation.

Each agency needs to be treated as independent and unique. Moody's, Fitch and S&P all require a customised approach by issuers because the analysts have different backgrounds and biases, and the issues of concern can be different for each. Aside from the visiting analysts, there are people back at agency HQ that are part of the rating decision. Agency analysts and senior officials in London and New York have different perspectives on European corporates, banks and sovereigns. Issuers need to understand their roles in the process.

While on the subject of what not to do, here are a few final reminders.

- Do not deny or misrepresent systemic or structural problems.
- Do not ask bluntly, 'What does it take to get an upgrade?' If you have been communicating regularly with the agencies, you should already know.
- Do not be too aggressive or impatient about an upgrade; you appear desperate and not committed to taking the necessary actions.

- Do not constantly bombard the agency with peer comparisons; it is a waste of your time and their time.
- Do not appear to be telling the agencies how to do their job.
- Do not quote one agency approvingly to the other.

Let us turn to more positive suggestions.

---

[1] Two years earlier the *Financial Times* of 28 June 2000 reported that the Japanese finance minister Kiichi Miyazawa appealed to Moody's to refrain from downgrading Japan's yen-denominated debt. As the yen was weakening against the dollar, the finance minister was quoted as saying to Moody's, 'It would be best for Moody's to think and not do something which it might regret'. This despite the fact that at the time Japan's government debt alone was 130% of GDP, the worst in the industrialised world.

6.6 Raising the odds for an optimal rating

We have provided a number of basic truths about the rating agencies – their thinking, their analytical predilections, their operations. Understanding these truths will give clues about how to raise the odds for an upgrade. Here is a summary of these realities.

- The agencies are cautious and conservative and do not give upgrades quickly.
- As bureaucratic institutions, the rating agencies respond slowly to financial developments with respect to the credits they cover.
- They worry more about the worst-case scenario than the upside; hence, they tend to wait until the evidence is before their eyes rather than upgrade based on expectation.
- They are analytically predisposed to distrust what they hear from you.
- It is up to the analyst to 'sell' the case for an upgrade to the rating committee, but senior management on the committee is inherently more cautious than the analyst, because they are charged with maintaining the integrity of the agency's whole rating system.
- Rating agency analysts tend to be overworked and cannot spend more than one or two weeks out of the year concentrating on your particular situation.
- Ratings are ordinal rankings so rating shifts among your peers affect you.

Regarding this last point, ratings can go up or down depending on what your peers are doing. If the agency perceives a whole industry is deteriorating (for example, airlines, banks), then as part of that industry an issuer can be pulled down even if no material changes have occurred in its own finances. In one such case, in the early 1980s, Moody's felt the whole banking sector in the US was overrated and in one weekend, they dropped ratings on all the big banks, including Aaa-rated banks, just because they perceived that the industry as a whole would suffer from greater competition in a deregulated environment.

Lesson for issuers

Peer comparisons are inherent in rating assignments. Ratings are after all ordinal in nature. However, issuers can avoid being indiscriminately lumped in with peers by proactively managing the process and pointing out differences within your industry. Doing this assumes, of course, that the issuer knows exactly the peers used by the CRA.

Overcoming the obstacles

These realities amount to obstacles to obtaining an optimal rating. How should an issuer overcome them? Here are some tested ways.

1 The agencies base their rating opinions on their perceptions of events and trends, and their perceptions can be altered in your favour.
2 Issuers need to devote their attention to filling the analyst's informational needs so that he or she will feel comfortable and confident enough to withstand the pressures of the rating committee.

3 Issuers need to follow rating changes among their peers, build comparisons, and think how they might take advantage of them.

4 Issuers need to provide full, appropriate documentation to the agencies when requested and even when not requested; the analysts are gluttons for information. From their standpoint more is better.

5 An issuer can reduce the effects of agency bureaucracy by continuous proactive interaction with them. Since most issuers will not take the time to do this, you will stand out. Take the whole rating relationship seriously and manage it over time.

6 Have in place a well-considered strategy and a program to optimise your ratings. Do not wait until you are facing a downgrade or actively pursuing an upgrade.

7 Understand the agencies' opinions, outlook and underlying biases and constraints.

8 Be candid and forthcoming on all issues; give them 'alerts' to build trust.

9 Understand what aspects of the rating are within your control, and what aspects are not.

10 Think of issues the rating committee might raise in opposition to an upgrade (for example, peer performance, not enough confirming data) and develop counter arguments to these issues.

11 Convince the analysts that recent fortuitous events are not one-off but the result of previously implemented policies. For example, for sovereigns, an improved current balance is not the result of a cyclical spurt of demand from a major trading partner so much as it is the result of a more efficient export sector due to domestic structural reform. Or, that a revenue windfall is not the result of a one-time tax amnesty but the result of better and permanent computerised collection methods.

12 As we saw in Chapter 5, due diligence meetings are your best opportunity to make the case for an optimal rating. You have the leverage; this is the 'home-court' advantage where you can bring in your experts as needed. The agencies want to hear your story, and they appreciate one that is well done. Therefore, in these meetings take these measures:
   • control the agenda and the theme;
   • help new agency analysts up the learning curve;
   • emphasise issues, not numbers – the former have a longer life than the latter;
   • share your plans and solutions and alternative scenarios; it makes their analysis easier; and
   • present data in an easy-to-understand format – do the work for them.

Not taking these recommendations amounts to setting yourself up for a non-optimal rating.

A ratings success formula

The power and global reach of the US rating agencies are well known. In the face of this, issuers tend to acquiesce in the agencies' policies and practices, taking a passive approach to managing their agency relationships.

However, we have shown that issuers can influence agency views and the way the agencies approach their analysis. The projections and ratios pertaining to an issuer represent only half the picture of what comprises input for a rating. The other half of a rating decision is based on the agency's *perceptions* of issuers, particularly the strengths and strategies of management, and these perceptions can be altered or strengthened. The premise of this book is that the more you understand how the agencies operate, the more potential influence you can have over their ratings.

How do debt issuers shift the leverage in their favour? The process involves three steps, a formula that we will call 'SPP' for short. No, that is not an abbreviation for a chemical additive for petrol. And it is not a typographical error referring to Standard & Poor's. It stands for 'Strategy, Performance and Persistence'. A combination of these three factors, appropriately and consistently applied, *virtually guarantees* rating success, that is, an optimal rating, assuming exogenous events do not intrude.

Whether you are a central bank, a ministry of finance, a debt management office, a corporate or bank treasurer, success in the ratings game is generally defined as accomplishing one or more of the following:

- securing a rating upgrade at your own initiative;
- achieving a rating confirmation when on Credit Watch Negative or on Review for possible downgrade;
- alleviating pressures on existing ratings due to rating agency misperceptions;
- allaying and deflecting the agencies' economic and socio-political concerns;
- improving performance in meetings with the agencies;
- knowing your rights as an issuer and exercising them;
- taking charge of the relationship with the agencies;
- uncovering the agencies' inconsistencies in approach and methodology;
- challenging their biases and assumptions, their unclear practices and procedures; and
- seeing that the agencies' analyses are consistent with the story you have told them.

How many of these achievements can you as an issuer claim? Not many? Well, experience shows they are all attainable using the *SPP formula*.

Step 1: strategy

To succeed in any enterprise, one needs a blueprint or set of guidelines that sets out the goal in straightforward language and contains guideposts by which to measure progress along the way. As consultants like to preach, strategy is a way of organising resources to achieve some end.

With regard to rating agencies, a strategy for you translates into: (i) determining your exact needs in terms of a rating outcome; (ii) devising a plan that works toward meeting these needs over time; and (iii) implementing the plan assiduously. Executing the strategy entails institutionalising the commitment with a structure, that is, a person with a specific assignment and a set of targets, and accountability built into the process within your organisation.

Issuers should discard the passive style of relating to the agencies, and instead commit to an active management of the relationship. You need a proactive posture with Moody's, Fitch and S&P.

A beneficial by-product of setting this strategy in motion is gaining a clearer understanding of: (i) the generic types of concerns the CRAs have as part of their models of credit risk; and (ii) the particular configuration of concerns they have about yourself and your peers.

The latter set of concerns is not always the same as the ones they publish. As both their generic and their issuer-specific concerns become evident, your strategy should be refined.

Step 2: performance

Of all the factors that enter into a rating decision, the most important are the perceptions of the agency analysts regarding the performance of those senior managers or government officials they meet across the conference table. The analysts not only key in on the substance of the message you are making; they are also paying close attention to the manner, style and confidence with which you present your message. As we have argued, you are on stage with the agencies. Once the data you supply are analysed, their subjective impressions of your competence determine the rating outcome.

Agency visits cannot be taken for granted. Each one is important for the impressions gained by the analysts. Once favourable impressions on performance have been made, it is easier to reinforce them the next time than it is to erase negative ones left from before. There are standard tactics that enhance issuer performance in meetings. It is essential to ensure that the few hours you have to impress the agencies during their visits are maximised in terms of your performance. That requires a strategy to begin with (Step 1) and solid preparation for each agency visit.

As we saw in Chapter 4, 'Your critical performance', an indecisive manner or a vacillating answer can cast doubts on your ability and willingness to effect policy change in the desired direction. You can have the most coherent plan for cutting budgetary expenditures or restructuring a corporate division, but if the agencies do not believe you can really accomplish it, then the level of uncertainty they attach to the future outcome rises. Naturally, the higher the uncertainty over bondholder protections, the lower the rating.

Obviously, you have to have actual, measurable successes you can point to as evidence that policy is on track and management knows what it is doing. You have to show concrete evidence that there has been progress in budgetary or balance of payment (BOP) statistics or in non-performing loans. A show of bravado with no substance behind it will not win the day and will only undermine the credibility you are trying to build.

Step 3: persistence

After you have devised a strategy for managing the agencies and after you have maximised your performance during their visits, you need to stay focused and resist the temptation to let the momentum you have achieved abate. Between visits, issuers should concentrate on realising their rating goals and insisting that the agencies act responsibly toward them. This is the period for persistently exercising your rights as an issuer (see 'Issuer rights and leverage'). By continually anticipating the agencies' concerns about your creditworthiness and by taking care of their informational needs, you are assisting them to arrive at a more informed rating decision. A foundation of trust and mutual respect has to be built through your efforts.

Step 3 is often the most neglected one. There always seems to be something more urgent to do than to take the initiative and make that phone call to 'New York' or write that email requesting clarification of their policy or methodology. And yet, persistence is usually the key to success. Very few issuers put in the effort to make agency relations a year-round exercise, but those who do have better control over their ratings than those who work on the process only one or two weeks a year. Resolute follow-up makes all the difference. Issuers should not rely on their investment bankers to be the liaison with the agencies, because this may cause the analyst to wonder what you are unwilling to discuss; it could raise questions about your willingness to co-operate fully.

If you pursue these three steps as a regular part of managing your external relations, you are certain to achieve rating success, whether it is securing an upgrade or scheduling agency visits to suit your timing, not theirs. Do not wait until the shock of a Rating Review forces you into action. That can be too late to implement an effective counter-strategy. Start now.

How to avoid a downgrade (at least temporarily)

If an issuer finds himself on Review for Possible Downgrade by Moody's or with a Negative Outlook or on CreditWatch Negative by S&P, then it is time to take serious steps to dodge a downgrade. Former analysts suggest there are at least four steps issuers should take to ward off the dreaded lower rating.

1 Understand the specifics of why an agency may downgrade – its real concerns – and then develop counter arguments that can be presented at the right time.
2 Convince the agencies that the worrisome events they see are a 'one-off' and that changes have been put in place to stop the damage from occurring again.
3 During the due diligence meeting, spend time explaining the details on issues of concern so that the analyst is not misunderstanding or guessing later in the rating committee.
4 Find ways to *extend* the negative outlook or postpone an early rating decision. The purpose is to allow time to pass so that some of the CRA's concerns can be alleviated by events and by suitable explanations from the issuer.

(By following the SPP formula, you will not need to take these steps.)

There are many reasons why an issuer should make the management of ratings a year-round effort.

- It pays to retain your options and flexibility; you want to have a process in place such that you can mobilise resources when an upgrade opportunity surfaces or when a downgrade threatens.
- Managing the rating agencies should be part of your overall investor relations activities. Investor confidence cannot be allowed to diminish, and optimal ratings help support that confidence.
- Your national Treasury may find a need for funds during an economic slowdown.
- At some point, the time will come when every issuer will need to go to the bond market again.

There really are no excuses for not taking control of your ratings future. As British Prime Minister Benjamin Disraeli said, 'Success is the child of audacity'.

6.7 Whistling in the dark

Nonetheless, there are many excuses. In 25 years of discussions with senior commercial bankers, CFOs, and top officials in treasuries, central banks and national debt offices around the world, the author has heard a lot of wishful thinking and justifications for doing nothing to improve relations with the rating agencies. Putting on a brave face and whistling past the graveyard do not address the underlying issues that can constrain achievement of an optimal rating.

In the light of that, it will be useful to survey some of these excuses and show how a thoughtful and pragmatic issuer should respond to them. The intention is to remove some misperceptions and perhaps motivate some issuers to start improving their ratings and their agency relationships.

Seventeen excuses

The first excuse is a common one.

Excuse 1: 'We already have good relations with the agencies.'
Response: 'good relations' with the agencies is often a euphemism for the issuer's taking a passive approach, one that permits the agencies to set the rules and agenda by default. Good relations with the agencies are not sufficient; they do not get you an upgrade or immunity from arbitrary decisions. The agencies play by their own rules, and you need a framework for responding. You cannot just rely on their judgment and firm handshakes to get fair treatment.

Excuse 2: 'We feel confident and comfortable where we are right now with the agencies, and we feel we are adequately prepared and experienced.'
Response: first, one can never be too prepared to meet with the agencies or too knowledgeable about how they operate. The stakes are too high to be complacent. Second, given periodic volatility in the financial markets, issuers cannot rest assured that their rating is secure. In fact, some borrowers deserve a higher credit rating than they now have and some deserve a lower one. Finally, no matter how many years you have been making presentations to Moody's and S&P, there are always new people on both sides of the table and new issues or concerns that need attention. Last year's presentation will not work this year.

Excuse 3: 'We are doing a good job of dealing with the agencies.'
Response: even the most sophisticated finance officials in institutions around the world are probably not devoting sufficient resources to ratings management. It is often not seen as a top priority. Yet there is much to learn about how the agencies think and make decisions, and there are many ways to be more proactive in pursuit of your deserved rating. No matter how well you think you are dealing with the agencies now, there is more you can do to enhance your objectives.

Excuse 4: 'We have done our best with the agencies, and we do keep in contact. We arrange for them to see the best and right people when they are visiting.'

Response: that is a good start. However, there are probably a number of strategies and tactics you have not utilised that could improve your performance in due diligence meetings, as professional as it may have been to date and as talented as your staff is. The odds are that you are not fully satisfying the agencies' needs – both analytical and subjective. Your first step is to make the decision to adopt a proactive approach to managing the agencies so that you are more in charge of your ratings future.

Excuse 5: 'Representatives from both agencies say they appreciate their working relationship with us and are comfortable with the information they are getting on a timely basis.'
Response: the agencies typically make such weak statements. However, declarations of appreciation and warm feelings do not guarantee either fair treatment or an upgrade. Given their heavy workload, the analysts devote very little time to monitoring your specific credit situation, so there is always an opportunity to shape their views. By adopting a more proactive approach to ratings management, you become less subject to the agency's whims and relative lack of accountability.

Excuse 6: 'It's up to the agencies, not us, to determine the rating outcome.'
Response: issuers have the power to influence rating outcomes. Taking a passive role will lead nowhere. Issuers need a proactive approach, one that puts your rating destiny into your own hands. About half the rating decision is based on factors over which you have a great deal of control. Moreover, by taking an active posture, you stand out as exceptional among your peers.

Excuse 7: 'We cannot affect the agencies' subjective decisions.'
Response: the ex-agency analysts interviewed admit that issuers *can* influence agency views and the way the agencies approach their analysis. Half the rating decision is based on agency *perceptions* of issuers, and perceptions can be altered or strengthened. The more you understand how the agencies think and operate, the more influence you can have over their ratings. The agencies respect issuers who take ratings seriously and provide them with a challenge.

Excuse 8: 'The ratings we have are appropriate and fair, and we're comfortable with them.'
Response: there is enough capriciousness in the markets, within your peer group, and in the way rating agencies approach ratings that one cannot assume all is well. There are financial and reputational gains to be made from optimising one's rating, so one should not let complacency or indifference or even fear override one's best long-term interests.

Excuse 9: 'We cannot change the comparative ratios of our peers because they represent reality.'
Response: first, statistics are not always reality; they are subject to revision and interpretation. Second, issuers have the right to question agency data and challenge their basis; maybe the assumptions are wrong. Third, some statistics are more important to the agencies than others, and you should choose those that best illustrate your advantages. Finally, the ratios of your peers are in as much flux as yours, so who is to say at which point in time the comparison is relevant?

Excuse 10: 'The agencies have just completed their visit and their written reports and have confirmed our ratings, so there is little we can do now.'

Response: actually, there is much you can do between now and their next visit. That is what 'managing' the agencies means. Since most issuers ignore the agencies in-between due diligence meetings, a strategy of active involvement with them will make you stand out by comparison. First, it is important to know how the agencies think and which arguments are useful to make to them. Second, you should know what the agencies need to hear and also what they do not like to hear. Finally, your institution needs to implement a consistent pattern of contact with the agencies that fits your particular strengths and weaknesses.

Excuse 11: 'We need improved profit or budget performance before we can press for an upgrade.'

Response: financial performance is only part of the basis for an upgrade; there are a number of other conditions (necessary and sufficient) that need to be in place. It would be a mistake to wait for a rebound from the recession or to wait for the agencies' next visit before building your case. You are in a position *now* to influence their perceptions on an ongoing basis. The path to an upgrade starts early. It takes long-range planning and execution.

Excuse 12: 'The timing for trying to get an upgrade is not right.'

Response: an upgrade is part timing and part persistence by the issuer. An upgrade is based partly on luck and partly on skill, partly on economic performance and partly on peer performance, partly on objective measures and partly on subjective assessments by the agencies. There are appropriate and inappropriate ways to approach the agencies on the subject of an upgrade.

All of these considerations require careful handling by issuers; the nuances must be appreciated. An upgrade opportunity may arise suddenly, so one needs to be prepared in advance. Laying the proper foundation is essential for success. Now is the best time to begin implementing the procedures that will position you for an upgrade when the right moment appears. That may be a year or so away. The timing of upgrades is more in your hands than you may realise.

Excuse 13: 'A large share of our country's external debt is held by the private sector, mainly banks who borrowed to finance the trade of corporate clients. So why is our *sovereign* rating under pressure?'

Response: debt is debt and needs to be repaid, whether raised by the public or the private sector. The means to repay must come from the foreign exchange the country earns, and the central bank can decide to supply foreign exchange (FX) or not through the banking system. Thus, even if the private sector does most of the borrowing, all debt is ultimately a matter the sovereign has control over.

Excuse 14: 'External forces (for example, commodity prices, EC growth rates) determine our chances for a good rating.'

Response: even commodity-dependent countries can get an upgrade if they sell their situation properly to the agencies and if they understand the weight of all external factors in the analysis.

Excuse 15: 'We have already earned an upgrade on our own, so we know how to do it.'
Response: would you like to know how much luck and how much timing were involved in that upgrade and how much skill was involved? How much of it was due to your own efforts and how much was due to other factors? Knowing this will help you achieve your next upgrade. Keep in mind, too, that the higher your current rating, the tougher another upgrade gets. You need additional tools to assist in the process.

Excuse 16: 'We have no new borrowing needs and in fact we are paying down debt and thus don't need new ratings.'
Response: issuers must not neglect their credit ratings and assume that all is well. A 'stable' outlook is no reason for complacency. There are many reasons why an issuer should make the management of ratings a year-round effort.

- It pays to retain your options and flexibility; you want to have a process in place such where you can mobilise resources when an upgrade opportunity surfaces or when a downgrade threatens.
- Your domestic banks and corporates who borrow need the highest sovereign rating possible in order to minimise their own funding costs.
- Managing the rating agencies should be part of your overall investor relations. Investor confidence cannot be allowed to diminish, and optimal ratings help support that confidence.
- Your debt management team may at some point find it useful to issue new bonds to preserve liquidity in the market at certain maturities.
- Your Treasury may find a need for funds during an economic slowdown.
- At some point, the time will come when you will need to go to the bond market again.

Excuse 17: 'We're still a long way from getting an upgrade. Why start now?'
Response: because the path to an upgrade must start early. It takes long-range planning and persistent execution. By the time the objective conditions are ripe for an upgrade, your agency relationship must be appropriately fine-tuned. By the same token, if your rating situation is in any way precarious, you should ensure you have appropriate defensive measures in place to guard against a downgrade, which would put you even further away from a rating recovery.

Conclusion: issuers must not neglect their credit ratings and assume that all is well. As we saw earlier, a 'stable' outlook is no reason for complacency. There are many reasons why an issuer should make the management of ratings a year-round effort.

6.8 Cutting connections with the CRAs

It is very unusual for an issuer to end his business relationship with a CRA. Even when issuers do not have a good rating or good rapport with an agency, they usually persist in the relationship, because: (i) the fees are usually not onerous compared with other financing costs and some of them can be negotiated; and (ii) issuers want to avoid any potential misinterpretation by the market. For example, investors will probably get suspicious about your motives or they may suspect that you have something to hide or that you are expecting a downgrade. And indeed, that is often the case.

An issuer needs to ask himself some pertinent questions before cutting ties with a rating agency, for example.

- Why are you considering this option?
- What do you hope to gain?
- What are the possible consequences of such an action?
- Are the expected benefits worth it?
- What 'costs' are you willing to absorb?
- What benefits would a different rating agency bring to you?
- How will the market view the switch?
- How many ratings and agencies do you really need, given your financing needs and the markets you intend to access?
- Do you want to just stop paying their fees, or do you want a complete break with your existing ratings removed from the public domain?

In considering dropping your business relationship with an agency, you need to determine how likely it is that you will need a rating in the next several years. After all, certain bond markets require ratings from certain agencies. You may not want to burn the bridge completely. You may want to consider maintaining a dialogue with the agency but not pay their fees. A relationship can continue without fees being paid, but this strikes at the heart of the agency's business and is likely to lead to an indefinite 'adjustment' in agency perspective.

Negative consequences

If you are thinking about ending an existing rating agency relationship, consider the negative consequences – you are relinquishing: (i) ready access to the market; and (ii) the right to have your story disseminated to the market by respected independent analysts who have global credibility. Your 'passport' becomes invalid with that agency, and you often lose the ability to influence the content of the analysis that is published. The analysts will not incur the expense of a visit to your HQ or capital city, meaning you lose the advantage of drawing on all your resources in one place when wishing to discuss already-rated and outstanding securities. You cannot expect the full attention of the targeted CRA should you send representatives to their offices.

The CRAs maintain that they retain all rights with regard to what to do with ratings once they are published. An agency can maintain the ratings if sufficient information continues to be available in the market, regardless of whether the issuer's management (or government officials) participates in the rating process or pays fees. When issuer management declines to contribute to the credit assessment, then the agency will issue a press release that 'the issuer did not participate in the rating process other than through the medium of their public disclosure'.

You cannot prevent the agencies from expressing a rating opinion on any large domestic or cross-border security that you issue or have issued. It is common practice with most rating agencies that they will not withdraw an existing rating but will keep it in the public domain as long as the debt itself is still outstanding. The rating is then withdrawn when the debt matures or is retired. If you have just an 'issuer rating' without any outstanding rated debt, then this does not apply. An issuer cannot 'relinquish' a rating once it is assigned, since the rating is only an opinion based on publicly available data. An issuer cannot force the agency to stop its publishing of ratings.

The reasons for severing ties with an agency need to be clear so that the agency, your bondholders and your brokers do not misunderstand your thinking and come to the wrong conclusion. They may be concerned anyway if it happens when you are experiencing some trouble. You will need to give a clear explanation to the agency involved, perhaps along these lines.

> We (the issuer) have done a study of the marketability of our issues, and we have talked with our bankers. We have come to the conclusion that it is not cost-effective for us to maintain a business relationship with so many rating agencies [or with the one agency in question]. The cost to us in terms of fees and the management time required to maintain all these relationships exceeds what we reasonably wish to expend. In addition, we find that your ratings will not be useful to us in accessing the markets we consider most important for our future funding needs. Therefore, we have decided not to renew our contract with your esteemed agency.
>
> If your duty to investors is to continue to monitor our creditworthiness, then we will be glad to continue to send you our annual reports and other relevant documentation. However, we will be unable to accommodate onsite visits by your analysts.

You need to be certain that your contract with this particular rating agency permits you to stop paying their fees without penalties or other 'exit costs'. Does the contract say existing ratings will be removed if fees are not paid? Rating agencies cannot do much to clients who do not pay. The market itself provides the 'punishment' in the form of higher rates and limited access because you are now a less known and less traded entity.

To avoid a future unsolicited rating, you should make it clear in your correspondence that you will not accept future agency visits or pay for any future rating by the agency that is not requested by you. In order to discourage the agency from future billings, you should discontinue displaying the agency's ratings in your annual reports and/or budget papers.

Lesson for issuers

Ending a relationship with one or more CRAs is seldom done by issuers because the benefits of retaining the relationship are deemed to be greater than the drawbacks. The risks may outweigh the rewards unless it is handled properly.

Chapter 7

The sovereign setting

Précis

As the global economy has become more integrated, so has the expansion and flow of credit ratings around the world. Financings anywhere increasingly require credit ratings everywhere. Issuers that value their ratings and their unfettered access to markets must themselves take a larger role in managing the rating process.

The credit rating agencies (CRAs) hold a body of 'accepted wisdom' about how sovereigns govern and operate. From the supremacy of politics to the quality of a country's economic managers, the agencies' major tenets are explained. Fiscal policy is the best leading indicator of credit quality. The agencies favour economic structures and government policies that help generate wealth, because these increase the likelihood that debt will be serviced and repaid.

All governments have options and all governments face constraints. Ratings will reflect how effective the authorities are in choosing their options and in managing around those constraints. The agencies like to see an appropriate and flexible use of monetary and fiscal policy to pursue the two aims they deem important for creditworthiness: wealth generation and debt sustainability. The presence of official corruption will sidetrack the best of efforts in this direction.

While there are no formulae that determine when a sovereign is upgraded or downgraded, one can gather evidence of the most common reasons for these rating changes based on the historical record. We provide those reasons here.

> *De omnibus dubitandum.*
> *(Everything should be questioned)*
>
> *Karl Marx*

7.1 Globalisation and credit ratings

Sovereign government bonds, which represent more than 40% of the stock of bonds issued globally, are a significant asset class for investors, so issuers of these bonds should heed the advice in this chapter in order to optimise their rating and maximise the prices of the securities they sell.

The broad definition of globalisation is 'the process of economic integration of nations', specifically involving the flow across national boundaries of goods and services, capital, people, technology, ideas, and culture. Martin Wolf wrote that the forces driving globalisation remain powerful after three decades: 'They include the rise of English as a world language; the cross-border movements of people seeking better education and jobs; the rise of a planetary economic and business elite running global companies and living in global hub cities; and the trans-border flows of ideas, including religion.'[1]

The focus for us is the integration of financial markets, in particular the banking systems and bond markets of each country.

Erosion of sovereign power

While the World Cup and the Olympics engender nationalistic fervour and the nation state is alive and well, there can be no denying that the freedom of individual governments to set economic policy has progressively eroded in the past two decades as interdependence among nations has grown rapidly.

Two propellants are driving this important and irreversible trend.

1 Technological – the capacity of computers to transfer information past all national barriers in nanoseconds.
2 Financial – the ability of investors to move vast sums of money from one country and currency to another.

These two facts of modern life have the effect of erasing borders and reducing the power of sovereign governments to command their own fates. No government can evade the consequences of rapid flows of information and funds. The Soviet Union could not survive the communications revolution. Uprisings in the Middle East, dubbed the 'Arab Spring', were the direct result of the international tide of information and images.

Financial frontiers are so permeable that governments have lost much control, for example, over their ability to make monetary policy work. No country can hide from the collective judgment of the market regarding its economic policies. This judgment is translated instantly into exchange rate shifts and monetary flows. Central banks are then required to respond with defensive policies that can be at odds with domestic priorities, for example, raising interest rates when there is no inflationary threat.

As economic and financial barriers are dismantled and world trade and capital flows accelerate, there are several consequences.

- One country's missteps flow on to affect other countries, the so-called contagion effect.
- In a world where every country needs private capital to prosper, international investors have growing power to dictate economic policies.
- Bankers and traders everywhere are demanding more standardised rules of accounting and more rigorous audits of the accounts.
- International institutions such as the IMF and international standards, such as GAAP, intervene in what used to be domestic affairs. The financial markets thereby limit national freedom of choice.
- All issuers are now more than ever subject to the discipline of the external markets, which can swiftly reward transparency and conservative policy settings or punish corruption and mismanagement.

As a result, the ability of governments to determine their own fates has been compromised. A Canadian Finance Minister is said to have lamented, 'We have suffered a tangible loss of economic sovereignty', meaning his country is hostage these days to the volatile sentiments of global financial markets.

The ratings impact

What does all this mean for international credit ratings? Globalisation and inter-dependence have made the rating agencies rethink their approach to rating sovereign and non-sovereign issuers. Several years ago we spoke with the managing directors at Moody's and S&P in charge of sovereign ratings.

David Levey at Moody's argued that a country's capacity to manage its own affairs has indeed diminished as a result of recent global trends. Even if a country shows good fundamentals, it can still have a crisis engendered by external events. The risk of a future financial crisis is generally higher in emerging markets than in the advanced industrial economies, which can handle the technology and globalisation issues better.

Today, the triggers to fiscal crises lie more in public and private sector debt leverage and contingent liabilities than in external shocks. The CRAs thus pay considerable attention to the health of the banking system and the amount of corporate leverage when forecasting a sovereign's contingent liabilities. The quality of senior officials and corporate management becomes an even more important rating factor, because bank officers, company CEOs and ministers of finance make critical decisions that affect debt payment capacity. For Moody's 'management' now includes supervision of the banking system, not just those in charge of fiscal and monetary policy.

David Beers of S&P made several related points. Capital flight is not an independent variable acting autonomously somewhere out there in the world. It is linked to a government's financial policies and position. Capital flees when the market determines that a country's policy fundamentals are out of line. Financial contagion is due to investor behaviour, to widely divergent views of what constitutes default risk. It is not due to rating actions, which often lag market perceptions.

The expansion of ratings

In the 20th century, globalisation was driven by trade and foreign direct investment. Today, spurred by information technology, financial markets around the world are assuming broadly similar norms, procedures and practices. Ratings contribute to globalisation by facilitating the widespread adoption of common and easily understood symbols to denote credit quality.

Credit ratings have expanded to countries and markets around the world, as the agencies market their services and investors demand more credit opinions. Ratings transmit rapidly across borders, helping investors search for investment alternatives using a common relative risk standard. The agencies themselves have become internationalised; they are progressively more global in staffing and outlook. Due diligence meetings may be conducted in languages other than English, such as Arabic, French and Russian.

Finally, the rating business is being cloned worldwide as emerging markets establish their own rating agencies. These local rating agencies help build a local capital market and a culture of credit risk, but on a cross-national basis they cannot compete with the world view and franchises of Moody's, S&P and Fitch.

The rating agencies clearly benefit from the integration of financial markets globally, principally because there are no credible, established, franchised alternatives to their opinions on credit risk. New issuers have little option but to seek out ratings from the usual sources since the investors that issuers depend on for financing rely on the opinions of these agencies.

Ratings are a part of the increasingly global drive to greater transparency, broader market access and greater attention to risk assessment, management and control. The harmonisation of financial systems around the world means that the rating agencies' criteria, standards and methodologies are being accepted more and more. In a word, globalisation has increased the importance of ratings and hence the CRAs' power.

Thomas Friedman

Let us continue our discussion of globalisation with some selections from Thomas Friedman's book *The Lexus and the Olive Tree*.[2] He offers an interesting perspective on globalisation, providing many cogent, real-life examples. He also reinforces the arguments above. We will relate his views to the world of ratings (*shown in italics*).

Among his insightful descriptions are the following.

- Globalisation is not simply a trend, Friedman asserts; it is the international system that has replaced the old Cold War system. It has its own rules and logic that directly or indirectly influence the politics and economics of virtually every country. It integrates finance and trade and technology in a way that influences wages, interest rates, living standards, culture and job opportunities everywhere. (*The rating agencies have of necessity revisited their rating methodologies to account for this new reality*.)
- 'The driving force behind globalisation is free-market capitalism – the more you let market forces rule and the more you open your economy to free trade and competition, the more efficient and flourishing your economy will be.' (*And the higher your credit rating will be.*)

- 'The rules of globalisation revolve around opening, deregulating and privatising your economy, in order to make it more competitive and attractive to foreign investment.' The rules have become the widely adopted standard for creating economic growth. (*This is the standard around which the agencies build their decisions.*)
- Following these rules means authorities have fewer policy choices; they are constrained in what they can do, because if they deviate too much, investors will stampede away and economic growth will suffer. (*The agencies pay attention to the potential for capital flight.*)
- 'There is a direct correlation between the openness of a country's economy and its standard of living... If you close your country off in any way to either the best brains in the world or the best technologies in the world, you will fall behind faster and faster. An efficient, transparent and honest legal system... is essential for economic growth.' (*And for an investment-grade rating.*)
- 'Statistics show that as countries adopt liberal economic regimes, foreign investment increases.' (*And ratings rise; just ask the Finance Minister in any transition economy.*)
- 'Globalisation makes it very costly for any country to try to challenge or oppose the trend.' (*One of those costs is a low rating.*) Investors around the world, what Friedman calls the 'electronic herd', make quick judgments about whether countries are living by these rules and reward those who do and punish those who do not. Friedman calls Moody's and S&P the 'bloodhounds' for the electronic herd – those faceless stock, bond and currency traders sitting around computer screens all over the world. The bloodhounds (maybe 'bond vigilantes' is a better term) prowl the globe seeking those countries not pursuing investor-friendly policies. The agencies make ministries of finance tremble in their pinstripes by hinting at downgrades if their budget ratios are not more in line with international expectations.
- The Cold War divided us all into 'friends' and 'enemies'. The globalisation world tends to turn all friends and enemies into 'competitors'. (*That is, competitors for capital and investment, success in which depends to some extent on your rating.*)
- In coming years we will not talk about developed and underdeveloped countries but about transparent and non-transparent countries, not about the First World and the Third World, but about the Fast World and the Slow World. Investment will flow to those that are transparent to the financial markets. (*Transparency and good governance now have an elevated importance in agency analyses.*)
- No government can evade the consequences of rapid flows of money and information across borders. No country can hide from the collective judgment of the market regarding its economic policies. The financial markets are increasingly limiting national freedom of choice; international investors have growing power to dictate economic policies. Capital flees when the market determines that a country's policy fundamentals are out of line. (*The rating agencies are among those primary de-Terminators in judging if policy fundamentals are out of line.*)

Conclusions

- The flows of capital and real-time information make today's financial markets increasingly volatile. Institutional investors advance or withdraw funds from countries depending on their perception of a government's ability to pursue 'orthodox' macroeconomic policies, such as, those that will enhance an investor's return in the short run. As a result, sovereign issuers are being constrained by investors, international donors and the rating agencies to conform to 'sound and conservative' fiscal and monetary policies.

- Aside from sovereigns, the globalisation phenomenon affects banks and the corporates to which they lend. For example, globalisation has caused the demand for risk reporting to grow considerably. Banks and corporations are under more pressure to show their audiences that they recognise the risks they face in the daily context of doing business and that they are containing those risks. These audiences include investors, counterparties, shareholders, regulators and the rating agencies.

- It is the rating agencies' role, as self-appointed and government-protected proxies for investors, to evaluate an issuer's 'progress' along these lines and to reflect their evaluation in a simple letter rating.[3] The rating agencies are truly gatekeepers to the capital markets.

- Sovereigns, banks and corporates need to take anticipatory, cautionary steps to reduce the risk of creditor or investor panic. Issuers that value their ratings and their unfettered access to markets must themselves take a larger role in managing the rating process.

---

[1] Wolf, M, 'Globalisation', *Financial Times*, 13 June 2013.

[2] Friedman, T, *The Lexus and the Olive Tree*, 1999, Farrar, Straus and Giroux.

[3] A credit rating has been called the most concise financial editorial comment in the world.

7.2 Agency suppositions on sovereigns

Let us begin with the set of doctrines that guides the sovereign analysts at Moody's, S&P and Fitch. These doctrines are not based on anything the agencies will tell you. They are unspoken tenets or norms that underpin agency assessments on sovereign ratings. Remembering these will increase an issuer's understanding of how the agencies approach credit assessment and will give issuers leverage with the agencies.

These beliefs comprise a body of 'accepted wisdom' that influences the way the analysts approach their job and the way rating committees make decisions. These beliefs are part of standard economics orthodoxy, a set of regular 'establishment' views on the nature of group competition, open markets, capitalism, budgets, inflation, national savings, and public and private sector debt. As a whole, these assumptions are 'textbook mainstream'.

What follows are the beliefs that analysts subscribe to as they go about examining all the elements of a sovereign's creditworthiness, that is, politics, government policy, the economy, fiscal situation, external accounts and debt. These beliefs underpin their assessment. The rating agencies do not normally share their views on these topics and indeed are 'trained' to be poker-faced in their meetings with issuers. Thus, any exchange of information that can help reduce misunderstandings about the factors under consideration is to be desired. It is in that spirit of opening up the dialogue that the following material is presented.

It is useful for sovereigns at both the national and subnational levels to be familiar with these agency beliefs because they place themselves in a better position to achieve an upgrade and are better able to defend themselves against possible arbitrary action on the part of the agencies.

Major tenets

1 Sovereign debt ratings reflect the rating agency's view on a country's future debt servicing capacity. There are no quantitative formulas or formal checklists that generate credit ratings. Instead, ratings are based on a judicious weighing of economic and political factors. The methodology attempts to assess both political and economic risks as they are now and as they may evolve in the next few years.

2 *Economic risk* is concerned with the government's 'ability' to repay its obligations. This ability is a function of the external financial position, balance of payments flexibility, economic structure and growth, and the management of the economy. High marks in these areas result in a high rating. Countries almost always have *the ability* (that is, the resources) to repay their debts.

3 *Macroeconomic stability* is necessary for sustainable growth. Sound monetary and fiscal policies create a hospitable climate for private investment and thus promote productivity. Policies need to be sustainable so that consumers and businesses can base their decisions on reliable and credible signals and be spared disruption caused by changing policies. A stable macroeconomy promotes saving and investment, attracting foreign savings as well.

4 Economic growth is deemed sustainable if the economy can maintain its expansion without generating excessive inflation, external payments deficits, or foreign debt accumulation.

5 *Competitive markets* are the best way for efficiently organising the production and distribution of goods and services. Market-based policies will lead to a stronger economy. A stronger economy means greater wealth creation and thus greater capacity to service debt.

6 The *current economic policies* of a government provide the most valuable clues to its credit future. A rating depends to a large extent on the efficacy of current policies.

7 The economic future of a country depends largely on the structure and management of the economy. Particular emphasis is placed on the prospects for the *export sector* – the key source of foreign exchange earnings that are required to meet external debt service requirements.

8 Governments can best contribute to a stable macroeconomic environment by *increasing public savings* by means of reductions in government budget deficits. Excessive government spending results in over-expansion of the money supply, inflation, overvaluation of the currency and loss of export competitiveness.

9 The best way to increase *national saving* is faster growth (unless that growth is driven by fiscal dissaving). There is a strong correlation between growth rates and saving rates. For governments, faster growth brings higher tax revenues. The second best way to increase national saving is to reduce government deficits.

10 *Political risk* is concerned with the '*willingness*' of a sovereign to repay debt on time. The analysts assess the country's socio-political stability to determine if policy-makers can put needed policies into effect, if there are plans for orderly succession in political leadership,[1] and if there is a consensus on major economic issues. They ask, are there political developments, domestic or foreign, that foreshadow a major change in policy or a debt moratorium?

11 *Politics matters*. Ratings are high (or are raised) for countries where governments pursue consistent policies aimed at spurring economic growth while keeping fiscal deficits in check. Ratings are low (or lowered) for countries where governments pursue inconsistent or arbitrary policies that hamper wealth creation and generate large fiscal deficits. Governments may change frequently or suddenly but as long as a broad social consensus exists on regime legitimacy and on prudent fiscal policies, the agencies will assign less weight to political 'instability'.

12 The political framework can have public debt consequences. Countries with short-lived or minority governments (as opposed to those with regular changes of majority government) tend to accumulate public debt. Weak governments, unable to take necessary decisions to cut spending or raise taxes, fall back on borrowing instead (Italy in the 1990s, the US, Greece, Turkey and Spain currently).

13 *Credit distinctions among investment-grade sovereigns* are loosely correlated with their level of economic development. Income is generally taken as a proxy for payment capacity. Because developing countries typically have fewer financial resources than higher income economies, their creditworthiness is especially sensitive to shifts in policy. Therefore, the agencies have been inclined to rate emerging market countries lower than more industrialised countries. The more unstable a country is, the more qualitative the input to the rating decision.

14 An *independent central bank* is more able to implement restrictive monetary policies aimed at controlling inflation and is less prone to political interference. Central bank independence bolsters the credibility of a country's anti-inflationary policy. Countries with independent central banks (for example, US, Switzerland, Canada) have lower inflation than those with less independent central banks (for example, UK, India), plus a more stable exchange rate.

15 *Liberalised financial flows* around the world can destabilise a country's macroeconomic policy. A country's risk profile may be altered by the power of the financial markets. The agencies try to determine the extent to which governments lose the ability to manage the economy in these circumstances and how foreign exchange generation might be affected.

16 *Default* by a sovereign issuer on a foreign-currency debt (bond, note, bank deposit) ultimately depends on the willingness of the government to mobilise resources at its disposal to meet that obligation. There are both positive incentives (lower borrowing costs) and severe sanctions (denial of access to most markets) that encourage sovereign borrowers to repay in full and on time. The CRAs look with scepticism at the plans and promises of 'serial defaulters' like Argentina.

Beliefs about government policy and management

1 The *quality of a country's economic management* is the most important variable. The capabilities and capacities of officials affect a sovereign rating on two levels: (i) how much internal and external debt the nation assumes; and (ii) how the debt is managed over time.

2 Country ratings are changed depending on *how governments respond to fiscal challenges*, political instability, or market shocks. The CRAs watch government policy prescriptions and judge their appropriateness, adequacy and results. Expressed another way, the inability of government authorities to adjust quickly to external or internal shocks with appropriate fiscal and monetary policies may result in high inflation, an overvalued exchange rate and a balance of payments crisis. It is not external shocks so much as it is the domestic responses (or non-responses) that affect credit ratings.

3 All governments have options and face constraints. Ratings reflect how effective the authorities are in choosing their options and in managing around those constraints, given their economic structures.

4 The agencies have an implicit bias toward government fiscal, monetary and industrial policies that provide the environment for wealth creation and savings generation. The two most important determinants of creditworthiness are *wealth generation and debt reduction*.

5 Countries almost always have the means (that is, ability) to pay their debts; it is *the willingness* to pay that is crucial in an analysis. And here the key question is, does the national leadership have the stability, cohesiveness, resources, talent and political will to form a policy consensus and deal with unexpected events?

6 Wilful reneging on a country's debt is relatively rare, occurring principally in times of war and revolution, and primarily in countries with lower ratings to begin with.

187

7   Markets work better where *the private sector* has the leading role in the economy. Markets are not as robust or as efficient where governments are 'interventionist', that is, where they attempt to pick winners, subsidise industry, raise tariffs and so on. Heavy burdens of taxation and regulation lower an economy's growth potential.

8   Therefore, the *best role for government* is to adopt tax and regulatory policies that enable enterprise to flourish, that increase productivity and that generate wealth, because these policies support the repayment and servicing of debt. The agencies do not favour policies directed primarily at reducing unemployment or income inequalities, such as raising social welfare transfer payments or adding to the public sector workforce. Governments can successfully spur economic growth by curbing public borrowing and increasing public investment in education, in infrastructure and in research and development (R&D) (areas where the US is currently failing).

9   Improvements in *productivity* have to be achieved by the private sector. All government can do is to remove the elements under its control that inhibit growth in productivity.

10 The *global financial markets* act as a discipline on countries and strongly encourage rational economic policies. Capital will not flow in where the threat exists of either depreciation of the local currency or wide currency swings under floating exchange rates. High expropriation risk and legal uncertainties also deter foreign direct investment.

11 There is no 'right' exchange rate, but policy can aim for growth towards a sustainable balance of payments at an adequate level of employment. *Exchange rate* overvaluation retards growth and contributes to the decline of the agricultural sector and the deterioration of the external position. It contributes to capital flight.

12 *Capital flight* is a symptom of macroeconomic mismanagement, often compounded by political instability. If investors have little faith in the government to adopt credible and sustainable policies, they will send their funds abroad. 'Vulnerability to capital flight' has been given more weight in recent years in sovereign assessments. Capital flight reduces a country's financial flexibility as the markets become less willing to refinance debt. The potential for capital flight rises in those nations that have strict capital and currency controls. In these cases, the risk of non-payment by the debtor rises for the fixed-income investor.

13 *Structural reform* is the key to improving economic performance, because it brings a more rational allocation of resources (labour and capital). The agencies like to see:
    • privatisation of state-owned companies which results in higher investment, managerial innovation, better pricing of the company's services, and more efficient, cost-conscious operations;
    • removal of assistance to privileged industries in the form of protection from imports, subsidies and regulations that prevent competition;
    • reform of key public sector enterprises (transportation, communication, power generation) that add to the costs for other industries;
    • improvements to the working of labour markets, including work practices; and
    • improvement of education and training to raise the quality and flexibility of the workforce.

14 There is no consensus within or without the CRAs on the pace and sequencing of structural reform policies. Almost more important is the political will to persist once started

down the difficult path. Structural reforms are unlikely to succeed unless they are preceded or accompanied by fiscal and monetary stabilisation policies. Where countries undergo such reforms, the agencies study the society's *'tolerance for austerity'* by looking at living standards, labour market conditions, institutional rigidities and past efforts at adjustment.

Fiscal policy

1 Fiscal policy is the best *leading indicator* of credit quality. Shifts and trends in budget balances signal the seriousness of governments regarding their willingness to meet debt obligations. Fiscal policy provides a better gauge of future credit developments than does the stock of debt.

2 Fiscal policy influences a country's economic structure and performance as well as its balance of payments and external position.

3 The effectiveness of fiscal policy generally depends on the degree to which monetary, exchange rate and other economic policies are consistent with fiscal goals.

4 *'Fiscal flexibility'* is a key concept for the agencies. An issuer with fiscal flexibility has the ability to manage future shocks and fiscal deterioration. Fiscal flexibility means having revenue potential, substantial reserves or liquid assets, financing alternatives in the market, available taxation capacity and the political will to use it, plus a number of options to call upon in a stress case, such as the ability to delay capital expenditures. Financial flexibility gives an issuer room to manoeuvre and provides extra protection to bondholders.

5 A key indicator of fiscal probity is the *general government budget balance as a percent of GDP*. The trend in the primary budget balance (that is, ex-interest payments) also indicates relative repayment risk.

6 There is a clear link between domestic public finances and the level of external debt. The higher the fiscal deficit, the more probable it will be financed at least partially abroad. A rising external debt burden in the general government sector will be the result. A key question in the analysis is, does the government keep its policy promises? The two most important indicators of the answer are five or more years of data showing the general government sector balance/GDP and the ratio of net public external debt to exports. When these ratios are high and rising, red flags emerge.

7 Governments that run large chronic budget deficits usually find themselves forced to borrow abroad to finance spending. One need only look at a government's recurring fiscal deficits to see if their attempts at reform and restructuring are being successful.

8 *Ongoing budget deficits* and a high level of public debt have a number of pernicious effects. By exerting upward pressure on interest rates, they raise debt servicing costs. If this is combined with high unemployment and high tax rates, deficit reduction becomes extremely difficult.

9 Persistent budget deficits affect the real economy by reducing national saving. By definition, this reduces the amount of money available to lend to private borrowers and pushes up interest rates. This is turn has two effects: (i) it deters investment by making it more expensive to finance the purchase of capital equipment; and (ii) it makes domestic assets more attractive than overseas ones, so foreigners buy domestic currency, raising the exchange rate and thereby worsening the trade deficit.

10 At the same time, budget deficits are not 'bad' per se. Their appropriateness depends on economic conditions and on the consequences of deficit financing. That is, where savings rates are high and inflation is low and the foundation for future export earnings is being created, deficits can be financed domestically or abroad without high costs. On the other hand, budget deficits become a problem if the spending is not invested in physical or human capital but instead is used as subsidies or salaries.

11 Governments have privileged access to financial resources through three routes: taxation, borrowing and printing money. When these routes are abused, the consequences are severe. For example, excessive taxation promotes capital flight and the growth of an underground economy. Excessive borrowing (high and rising public sector borrowing requirements) tends to be covered by monetary expansion which eventually undermines the value of the currency and leads to a run on the currency, resulting in punitively high interest rates and a liquidity crisis when the government cannot sell new debt.

12 Moreover, with the build-up of debt, a government loses its ability to deploy an activist fiscal policy to combat recession. Monetary policy is left as the sole, usually imprecise, instrument for promoting a business recovery.

13 An appropriate fiscal policy is best achieved through disciplined spending cuts and revenue mobilisation. Higher taxes should be imposed only if necessary.

14 A key element of fiscal reform is *tax reform*. Governments need to rationalise the following areas: exemptions, inefficient tax collection, narrow bases and low compliance.

15 High tax rates, the widespread underreporting of assets and income, a flourishing cash economy, corruption and a loophole-ridden tax regime usually result in tax evasion with attendant losses to a country's treasury and ultimately to society as a whole. The consequences for society are a culture of cynicism and civic disobedience. Injustice in the tax system can breed loss of confidence in the state and resentment in the social order.

16 Tax evasion makes it difficult for governments not only to balance the budget but also to pay their civil servants a proper wage, one that keeps them honest. Countries with large civil servant payrolls and too many stifling regulations are most prone to corrupt activities, that is, those that reduce the economic efficiency of government. The existence of corruption is a deterrent to investment, which ultimately hampers economic growth. In an effort to raise revenues and balance their budgets, governments are often forced to raise tax rates, which has the counterproductive effect of stifling enterprise and encouraging more evasion.

17 Proceeds from *privatisations* are treated by the CRAs as one-off events, not recurring revenue gains.

18 Unlike income taxes, consumption taxes do not discourage savings, thereby helping to facilitate investment as well as the financing of fiscal deficits.

The external accounts

1 The key question in examining the balance of payments is the *reliability of access to foreign exchange* through trade transactions and capital flows.

2 External payments risks usually derive from *merchandise trade inflexibilities*, such as a heavy import or export concentration in certain products or geographic markets. This lack of diversity limits a country's ability to avoid adverse price and demand developments.

3 Other factors that heighten balance of payments risk are high interest payments on external debt and the possibility of capital flight that can drain foreign exchange reserves. These risks are magnified when debt carries short maturities and variable interest rates. Smaller, more open economies are particularly vulnerable to external shocks and international trends such as sharply higher oil prices, especially if they have a fixed exchange rate which cannot act as a shock absorber as well as a flexible exchange rate can.

4 A *current account deficit* is not an indication that a nation has low productivity or low-quality products. It means the domestic investment rate is high relative to the rate of saving, that aggregate domestic savings are not sufficient to fund current investment in a new productive capacity, and thus there is borrowing overseas to finance the shortfall.

5 A current account deficit covered by capital inflows can indicate strong investor willingness to finance that investment. Developing countries, for example, the Asian 'tigers', have typically run current account deficits reflecting heavy expenditure on capital goods imports.

6 Conversely, current account deficits do signal deteriorating credit quality when capital inflows prove insufficient to maintain adequate reserves or when the deficits result in excessive accumulations of foreign debt.

7 The most important question is: what is the *capacity for repaying and servicing the debt*?

8 The agencies tend to make the conservative assumption that all of a country's current account deficit will be financed by borrowing (that is, new debt) and not covered by foreign direct investment, equity portfolio flows or foreign exchange (FX) reserves. This assumption makes all the debt ratios look worse during the forecast period. Countries need to show the agencies the historical record of how much of the deficit was financed by various means and then convince the agencies to assume that only a small portion is debt-financed. Of course, debt financing is not always a negative factor, as long as it contributes to a more dynamic export sector and does not go toward consumption.

9 Weak external payments positions have been key factors in sovereign downgrades. Debt service tends to be disrupted in conjunction with external payments difficulties that prevent the sovereign from accessing the foreign exchange it needs to service foreign currency obligations.

10 An important judgment call by the agencies is whether a country has balance of payments (BOP) 'flexibility' – that is, the *ability to withstand external shocks* and maintain timely payment without adding to the relative burden of debt (measured by debt, GDP, debt or exports).

11 'Flexibility' in the BOP depends on two interrelated factors: (i) The responsiveness of a country's external payments position to changes in domestic and world economic activity; and (ii) the ability of the authorities to make policy adjustments designed to prevent or reduce internal and external imbalances.

12 Stocks of official *foreign exchange* are theoretically the first line of defence against an interruption in debt service. However, these reserves are: (i) always limited; (ii) subject to depletion due to speculative capital outflows; and (iii) not necessarily or usually drawn

down by authorities for the purpose of servicing debt. Thus, FX reserves are a cushion at best, not a fund for automatic debt servicing.

13 The adequacy of a country's international reserves depends on the vulnerability to sudden swings in export receipts and import payments and on the volatility of capital flows. The stock of official foreign exchange reserves is discounted in the CRAs' analysis if there are concerns about the flexibility of the country's exchange rate or the country's access to foreign credit.

Debt policy

1 Meeting one's obligations *fully and on time* depends on: (i) the *willingness* of the borrower to repay; and (ii) his *ability* (that is, economic capacity) to repay. Willingness and ability are closely intertwined.

2 Given the *severe penalties*[2] that today befall a government that defaults, sovereigns are increasingly deterred from missing a payment or from reneging altogether on their obligations. The harshest consequence is the inability of a government to issue debt since the capital markets boycott defaulters. At the end of the day, it comes down to a political decision whether or not to make those payments, that is, willingness.[3]

3 Borrowing represents a commitment to future servicing and repayment of the debt incurred. These payments must come out of future production. Policies that encourage savings and productive activity enhance creditworthiness, while those that encourage current consumption can impair the capacity to repay debt and thus invite a future downgrade. *Ratings are policy driven.*

4 When external borrowings are used primarily to fund domestic social programs, serious external imbalances are likely to result. *Borrowing for consumption* is ultimately self-defeating.

5 The key question for foreign borrowings is whether current and future export earnings can easily service such debt. The *capacity to service debt* is a function of the rate of growth of debt and the rate of growth of a nation's wealth or income generation capacity that can be devoted to repayment.

6 *Sound fiscal policy* at home obviates the need to borrow heavily abroad.

7 The analytical focus is on *total country debt*, not just public sector debt. The long-term debt raised by the private sector, while not 'sovereign', is an important component of the overall country risk picture. The ability of the private sector to repay its overseas debt is ultimately dependent on the kind of economic, fiscal and monetary policies the government pursues. The sovereign sets the rules, regulates business and controls the country's foreign exchange. Thus, the sovereign rating usually acts as a cap or ceiling over the ratings of other domestic borrowers.

8 *Short-term debt* is usually the result of financing external needs through the banking system. The debt-servicing capacity of a country with a large volume of short-term debt is more vulnerable to destabilising capital flows than countries with a smaller volume of short-term debt, because banks can cut their exposures quickly. The *maturity profile* of a country's external obligations is an important indicator of likely future payments stresses.

9   A growing stock of debt is not inherently bad if the means for repaying obligations in the future are being created by investing the savings of other countries. The agencies are worried when total overseas borrowings and accumulated indebtedness become large relative to the size of the economy (the ratio of total external debt to GDP) and to exports.

10 The *sustainability* of a country's debt is defined as the flexibility of the government to deal with adverse economic events while continuing to service its external obligations in a timely fashion.

11 A large debt overhang discourages *investment* because it implies that eventually some combination of higher taxes, currency depreciation and lower domestic demand will be required to achieve the required external transfer.

12 High levels of domestic and external debt strongly affect a country's fiscal stance. As policy-makers try to turn current account deficits into surpluses to service external debt, they may restrain domestic demand which, in turn, leads to a smaller tax base. The result is a shrinking ratio of tax revenues to GDP and higher fiscal deficits and, therefore, higher domestic debt. If nominal domestic debt rises too fast, investors bail out or demand premiums. In addition, governments are tempted to tolerate inflation to lower the real value of the debt. Fiscal rectitude will prevent this situation from arising in the first place.

13 High indebtedness restricts a government's *fiscal flexibility*. The preferred solution is for the government to create an optimal balance between reducing expenditures and augmenting revenues. Raising taxes alone can have a perverse effect on compliance and hence on revenues. Without fiscal austerity, the government will reach an unsustainable position in the long run.

14 High levels of public sector debt can lead to a vicious circle where rising debt increases interest payments, which in turn cause extra borrowing to cover the growing deficit. In the worst case, a country can fall into a *debt trap* where higher debt pushes up interest rates. The general guideline is: if real interest rates are higher than a country's real growth rate, debt will rise indefinitely unless a government is running a large enough primary budget surplus (that is, excluding interest payments).

15 Even when foreign borrowings are denominated in *local currency*, there is a potential claim on the country's foreign exchange, since non-resident investors holding these obligations can present the proceeds of local currency debt for conversion to foreign currency.

16 A heavy burden of debt service has consequences on the real economy and on finances. It is the impact of this burden that the rating agencies attempt to estimate. For example:
  • a heavy debt servicing burden limits the state's ability to absorb internal or external shocks, because the interest burden on the debt must be met regardless of reductions in revenue;
  • high debt servicing costs pre-empt resources that could otherwise be used for domestic investment;
  • worthwhile capital projects (traditionally debt financed) may have to be delayed or foregone altogether due to limitations of available debt capital in the market;
  • new sources of revenue, such as taxes, must be found to meet escalating debt costs;

- debt servicing obligations reduce the capacity to fund services such as health and education; and
- there is a danger of capital flight, high interest rates, and disrupted macroeconomic policy.

Inflation and unemployment

1 *High inflation is inimical to wealth generation.* It tends to reduce economic growth by creating an unstable climate, causing distortions in relative prices and absorbing scarce resources. The attention of the private sector is diverted from production and investment decisions to short-term financial matters.

2 High inflation usually leads to the following responses that reduce a government's financial flexibility and hence its debt servicing capacity.
   - Tight monetary policy that discourages borrowing and investment.
   - Capital flight due to perception of policy disarray and depreciating currency.
   - Currency depreciation that raises the cost of debt servicing in local currency terms.

3 *High inflation increases the risk of default* in a two-step process.
   - First, the higher the inflation rate and the faster it rises, the less control monetary authorities have over it. The result is capital flight, loss of confidence, high interest rates and a shortening of debt maturities.
   - Second, this critical situation prompts the need for an economic stabilisation program, which in extremis may involve a forced debt exchange – making investors take long-term, low-interest debt in place of their short-term, high interest rate paper. This constitutes a default on the terms of the contractual promise.

4 *Inflation is ultimately home-grown.* That is, high and persisting inflation is usually the result of weak or failing fiscal, monetary and wages policies. In a globalising economy with more integrated product and financial markets, inflation can also be imported, which raises the challenge to policy-makers.

5 A central bank's anti-inflation credentials are essential for lower inflation. If a zero target is believed, then wage settlements will be based on that, but if the target is not seen as achievable, then wage settlements will assume non-zero inflation and build that into their pricing.

6 High and persisting *unemployment* brings a variety of risks: political backlash, higher budgetary expenditure on social welfare, low consumer confidence due to fear of job loss, deterioration in human capital and exacerbated social problems. All these conditions sidetrack a government from pursuing orthodox fiscal policy.

7 As unemployment becomes a more structural phenomenon, not fluctuating with the business cycle, governments should shift away from standard prescriptions, such as providing income support, and concentrate more on active labour market policies that focus on increasing the incentives for the unemployed to seek jobs or improving training.

8 Attempting to fine tune the business cycle by timing fiscal and monetary moves is virtually impossible. Trying to do so will have perverse effects on inflation, unemployment and output.

The fundamental variable

The sovereign ratings groups at the various agencies operate their businesses somewhat differently, but in terms of sovereign risk analysis, it is fair to say they all agree that the key variable that affects a sovereign rating is the *quality of a country's economic managers – the skills of its leadership*. Ratings depend on the effectiveness of policy settings and that depends on a country's leaders. When a leader dies, the agencies ask, are there qualified replacements? How strong are the country's institutions? How well will they handle a leadership transition, and how will policy settings change?

A country can be resource-rich but have its endowments squandered by poor leadership. A country can be relatively resource-poor but be led by wise stewards of the country's given store of wealth. Evaluating a country's leaders is at the heart of a sovereign credit assessment, for it is these economic and political managers who either do or do not provide the right environment for wealth creation and who either do or do not manage the nation's liabilities skilfully.

Given the CRAs' standard beliefs and major tenets and their focus on the management skills of a country's leadership, it should come as no surprise that both Moody's and S&P downgraded by several notches Venezuela's debt ratings in mid-December 2013. The agencies cited declining international reserves, sky rocketing inflation and unsustainable macroeconomic policies caused by the 'radicalisation' of economic policy, raising 'the risk of an economic and financial collapse'. As we will further emphasise in 'Ratings as report cards' and 'Policy, policy, policy', *policy counts*.

- *Since ratings are ordinal rankings, a country cannot be too far out of line with those with similar ratings*. If the country's peers are improving their ratios and you are not, ministry of finance (MOF) officials may have to start worrying about a downgrade. On the other hand, if you can build a case showing your differential performance relative to peers, then by all means show it to the agencies. And then show it again.
- *Ratings are based on past performance and on the medium-term outlook, not so much on current conditions*. If past performance shows an improving trend and the agencies have confidence in your projections, then the issuer has taken a major step.
- *Management 'performance' is judged by the competence, openness and determination that officials show*. What counts is issuer performance in the meetings, the positive attitude of co-operation, issuer honesty and persistence, and the track record of keeping promises.
- *Past economic performance and skills in liability management are evidence of a country's future capabilities*. The agencies need to extrapolate based on the historical record. You have everything to gain by pointing out your successes in liability management and your unblemished debt servicing record.
- *A rating decision is based half on the numbers and half on agency confidence in management*. Your macroeconomic and financial ratios place your rating in a narrow range of two to three notches on the scale. Where the rating eventually ends up depends on the agency's perceptions of management's capabilities.

- *An upgrade occurs when the rating agency: (i) has confidence in future policy; (ii) acknowledges past performance data relative to peers; and (iii) overcomes inherent psychological and institutional barriers to upgrades.* The issuer is the agent that can instil that assurance.
- A *downgrade* occurs when the rating agency perceives that political or economic conditions have made debt servicing and repayment less likely – a subjective judgment. Analysts can be persuaded on these conditions.

This section can be summed up by stating that in sovereign credit risk assessments, there are no set formulae. Political and economic relationships are too subtle and variable to admit precise quantification. Yet over the past decade, partially under regulatory pressure, the CRAs have elaborated upon their traditional approach to credit risk analysis with the inclusion of metrics, mapping and matrices, and a more quantitative approach. The complexity of these scorecards with their sub-factors, sub-factor weightings and sub-factor indicators is evident on their websites.[4] Their ability to satisfy market participants and maintain the consistency of historical default rates over time is yet to be determined.

---

[1] 'Orderly succession' in leadership is more likely under a democracy than under an authoritarian or military coup-based government. Depth of leadership is the key to continuity. Sudden changes of leadership via coup or revolution can bring repudiation of past debt obligations. For sovereigns, this means a built-in bias by CRAs in favour of democracy because it provides a planned and peaceful transfer of authority.

[2] Sanctions include, but are not limited to, trade disruption, a decline in foreign direct investment and freezing of overseas assets.

[3] In the 19th century, governments defaulted because of war, revolution or economic depression. More recent causes of defaults are weak fiscal discipline, poor debt management and contingent liabilities arising from weak banking systems.

[4] For Moody's score cards on sovereigns and banks, see the 12 September 2013 report and the 31 May 2013 report respectively; www.Moody's.com/ratingmethodologies.

7.3 An ideological bias in sovereign ratings

Given the types of tenets used for sovereigns shown above and given the inherent subjectivity of credit ratings, can we identify an ideological bias at the agencies? The answer is that agency analysts cannot be easily categorised as Keynesians or monetarists, socialists or Adam Smithians. Nor are they firmly inclined toward 'efficient' private enterprise or a more 'humanitarian' socialism. These are inappropriate classifications. At the country level, they do not favour one standard developmental approach, economic structure or political system over another.

They believe there is no magic mix of fiscal and monetary policies that guarantees a government's willingness or ability to repay debt. Indeed, countries with socio-economic systems and political orders as diverse as Australia and Norway have triple A ratings, China and Saudi Arabia have double A ratings, Botswana and Malaysia have single A ratings, and Latvia and Brazil have BBB ratings (as of December 2013).

The agencies do recognise that unfettered capitalism can lead to abuses, corruption, and income inequalities, which may result in social unrest. Social unrest, in turn, can upset pragmatic macroeconomic policy settings and have unintended political consequences.

Generating wealth

What then is the analytical bias of the sovereign analysts? To be concise, they favour economic structures and government policies that help generate wealth. When the economy grows, political stability is fostered, financial flexibility is enhanced and country risk is reduced. These conditions also make it more likely that debt securities will be repaid on a full and timely basis.

Thus, the analysts lean more favourably toward any system that encourages entrepreneurism rather than toward one based on *dirigisme*, because they believe that the former provides a more favourable climate for wealth generation than does the latter.

The analysts believe the private sector creates wealth. Governments do not. Competitive markets are the best way for efficiently organising the production and distribution of goods and services. The result is that they believe governments should adopt tax and regulatory policies that: (i) facilitate and enable enterprise to flourish; and (ii) create a suitable climate for investors.

The rule of law

The CRAs hold as an article of faith that the rule of law is crucial because it fosters an environment in which business can flourish. As the engine of sustainable economic growth, the private sector requires that property rights and contracts be respected and that these rights be upheld by an independent judiciary. Only when this legal climate prevails will the private sector be confident enough to undertake investments. Domestic and foreign bond investors also seek evidence that the legal system provides effective redress against arbitrary acts by individuals, businesses and the state.

To foster competition, productivity and efficiency, the agencies look favourably on governments that remove subsidies to privileged industries, privatise public sector enterprises and liberalise labour markets. The higher the percentage of government expenditure to GDP and the larger the internal and external imbalances, the more the agencies feel the economy has the potential for sclerosis – a hardening of the financial arteries. Politics does matter as explained below in 'Does politics matter?'

However, the agency analysts still allow room for government intervention in pursuit of social goals. Ask them to define how much program spending or social expenditure is 'allowable', and they will hedge with the caveat that what works in one society may not work in another, so there is no single golden rule.

So is there a bias in ratings determination? If we agree that the analysts are orthodox Western economists, then yes, that is their bias or strong inclination.

7.4 Does politics matter?

How much weight do rating agency analysts place on a country's political system? How do internal politics factor into a rating?

A country's politics means a great deal to the agencies. But it is less the nature of the regime than *the way politics shapes policy*. It does not matter so much whether the regime is socialist, democratic or authoritarian. What does matter is whether conservative and conventional economic and fiscal policies are pursued consistently on the basis of a general social consensus. If a government follows a course that results in economic growth and debt reduction, then bondholder protections are enhanced. When this occurs, the stripes or ribbons the leaders wear are irrelevant.

Evaluating a country's leaders is at the heart of a sovereign credit assessment. The leadership either does or does not provide the right environment for economic growth, and they either do or do not manage the nation's liabilities skilfully. Governments can come and go rapidly, but if there is societal accord across the political spectrum on the need to adhere to fiscal conservatism and to facilitate wealth creation, then a change of government will not set off alarms at agency HQ. Political stability is important because it provides the context for the other rating factors (economic growth and sound debt management) to show progress.

Political risk is inherent in sovereign risk assessments. The analysts recognise that a government's structural weaknesses can limit or reduce a rating. For example, any of the following politically-based conditions will create an adverse environment for investment and growth, create a shock in the financial markets, and thereby perhaps trigger a downgrade.

- Pervasive official corruption and influence peddling.
- An internal revolution, as most recently in Libya, Egypt and Syria.
- Ineffective judicial, law enforcement agencies.
- Non-credible or non-existent electoral processes.
- Internal security threats that sap scarce resources.

Domestic unrest may follow that will complicate access to funding. When this financial flexibility is lost or compromised, then the rating will be precarious.

The US position

The US does not exhibit the five factors mentioned above but is not immune to other political risks that have rating consequences. In August 2011, S&P became the first and only rating agency to downgrade the AAA rating of the USA to AA+. In explaining the downgrade, S&P's John Chambers, Chairman of the Sovereign Ratings Committee, cited publicly two factors behind the decision to lower the rating – politics and the fiscal position (a rising debt burden). With regard to politics, he compared the US position with its peers, illustrating the relative ranking of issuers that is central to the ordinal ratings.

> Political settings in the US are still strong, but they're not as strong as some of our most highly rated governments… More profoundly we think that elected officials across the political spectrum are unable to proactively take measures to put US public finances on a sustainable footing in the same sort of manner as some of our most highly rated governments.[1]

Two years later political rigidities between the executive and legislative branches of government in the US still prevented headway in containing the rising debt burden and undertaking further financial reform. The US's two major parties have intractable differences over the role of government relating to public spending, the tax system and entitlements programs. Since most economists agree that the rising path of government spending and interest payments on the public debt is unsustainable, the stage could be set for further downgrades of the US debt rating in a few years.

Lesson for issuers

Remember that sovereign analysts at the agencies are predominantly economists or former bankers and are not always astute observers of politics. They may not be good judges of the *willingness* of a government to mobilise resources at its disposal to meet debt obligations. Uninformed perceptions of a country can influence a rating by a notch or more and ultimately affect the borrowing costs of the government and all resident banks and corporations under the sovereign ceiling.

To avoid an agency's misunderstanding your political situation, your ministry of finance and central bank must make an extra effort. If these officials do not take the lead on this topic, then this reluctance will permit the agencies to draw their own conclusions – a situation you want to avoid.

---

[1] Teleconference, 8 August 2011.

7.5 Ratings as report cards

Whenever sovereign issuers ask Moody's or S&P – 'are credit ratings a measure of government performance?' – the agencies reply ambiguously to such a direct query.

S&P writes in its *Corporate Finance Criteria*, 'A rating is not a general purpose evaluation of an issuer'. And Moody's, in its manual *Global Credit Analysis*, argues that a sovereign risk rating is 'not a judgment about the creditworthiness of individual debtors, or of the government as a separate borrower. It is rather a statement about the ability of the country as a whole to function in a co-ordinated way, to assure a viable allocation of resources, and to provide a framework conducive to timely payment of the contracts of any of its residents to foreign creditors.'

A rating is a symbol of default risk on a specific bond issue and is not a measure of the quality of policy or the orientation of policy as such. They say a rating is not an endorsement, nor is it a criticism of any particular set of policies. (In contrast, short-term ratings attach to the borrower itself.)

But the matter is more complex than that and the CRA view has evolved over the last 20 years. Look at it this way. All issuers have options and face constraints. Ratings will reflect how effective the management is in choosing their options and in managing around the constraints, given their economic and competitive structures. For governments, the agencies like to see an appropriate and flexible use of monetary and fiscal policy to pursue the two aims they deem important for creditworthiness: wealth generation and debt reduction.

In other words, how sovereign borrowers have reacted in the past gives the agencies a good indicator of their behaviour during possible future challenges. If officials have coped well before under trying circumstances, then it is assumed they will also have the future capacity to manage stressful conditions and to repay their debt obligations in a full and timely fashion.

Policy settings are crucial

Therefore, the quality of a country's economic management is the *key variable* the sovereign analysts consider. The capabilities of officials will affect the level of external debt a nation assumes in the first place and will affect how it is managed in the second place. The agencies do watch government policy prescriptions and do judge their appropriateness, adequacy, and outcome. The ongoing financial crisis in Europe is a good example of how important policy settings are to ratings, as several European governments are on the verge of default while their authorities argue over the political fallout when austerity bites.

The agencies never recommend one set of macroeconomic policy settings as 'best' for a country. As one senior S&P officer explained it, 'We're not in the policy prescription business.' But the agencies do have an implicit preference for government fiscal, monetary and industrial policies that provide the environment for wealth creation and savings generation. You can detect this strong preference (or bias) if you read their country reports and rating rationales carefully. When they point out that certain policies have had unfavourable outcomes, they are implicitly supporting a different set of policies. For example, if tariffs hinder domestic industry's becoming more internationally competitive, then policies that maintain tariffs will be viewed by the agencies not only as anachronistic in an open world economy but also as a constraint on industry's ability to generate foreign exchange through exports.

As the late President of S&P, Leo O'Neill said, 'Ratings are based on the financial strength and flexibility of the issuer, on its management's expertise, and on the economic outlook for the country.' Note that each of these determinants of a rating has an inherent policy and economic management component.

Borrowing represents a commitment to future servicing and repayment of the debt incurred. These payments must come out of future production. Policies that encourage savings and productive activity enhance creditworthiness; those that encourage current consumption can impair the capacity to repay debt and thus invite a future downgrade.

Conclusion

Ratings do indeed amount to report cards on government policy – the content, realism and efficacy of policy settings and outcomes. Ratings are policy driven. The agencies do evaluate governments on their ability to manage debt and to resolve macroeconomic problems.

Investment grade ratings imply the ability to withstand the shocks of a future downside scenario and thus reflect the *responsiveness* of policy to potential pressures. Investment grade ratings imply a sound capacity of policy-makers to reduce imbalances, manage and control the expansion of external debt, and make the rapid adjustments necessary in the face of changing circumstances. Ratings reflect the availability and productive utilisation of a government's policy options.

Those governments that are politically or structurally constrained from confronting their problems or who perform poorly relative to their peers under the stress of internal and external challenges are rated lower by the agencies than those who cope successfully. Policy and performance count. *At the end of the day, it is very hard to separate cleanly a judgment on the bond issue from a judgment on the issuer.*

This conclusion regarding sovereign debtors applies as well to bank and corporate officers who make decisions that directly impact financial health and thus their ratings. S&P wrote the following on the critical role of management.[1]

> A critical factor in the rating process is that each rating entity, whether a municipality or a corporation, is a coalescence of various types of resources which are controlled or influenced by individuals. This coalescence does not function automatically. It requires an overall controlling mechanism known as management.

---

[1] Standard & Poor's Ratings Guide, p. xxii.

7.6 Policy, policy, policy

The Big Three rating agencies publish many reports on sovereign credit ratings. These reports go into a lot of detail about default rates, the number of positive and negative outlooks, emerging market rating changes versus those in developed markets, and upgrades and downgrades as a percent of total ratings.

What is really important for us here is not the global statistics but an explanation of what it takes to get a better rating. Our study of upgrades in sovereign ratings over the past 30 years has revealed two main preconditions for an upgrade:

1 improving the fiscal balance; and
2 making structural changes in the economy that encourage wealth creation.

Note that the reverse conditions hold true as well. For S&P, the reasons cited for assigning a negative outlook or in justifying a downgrade are overwhelmingly the following:

1 delays in implementing economic and structural reforms; and
2 deterioration in a country's fiscal accounts.

For Moody's, the reasons for downgrades or negative outlooks are only slightly different:

1 fiscal deterioration or fiscal imbalances; and
2 low or uncertain economic growth prospects.

Policy settings and successes

Fitch's record of rating changes would undoubtedly reveal the same reasons. The common denominator in sovereign rating changes is policy settings and policy successes. S&P said it concisely: Rating changes 'originate from factors within the country – any downgrade will be the result of failure of the policy response and any upgrade the success'.[1] Moody's was no less precise: 'The underlying issue is what the nation's socio-economic system is capable of and willing to undertake to control the growth of external debt.'[2]

With lessons learned from various debt crises and with new analysts, Moody's has updated its sovereign methodology in recent years. Rather than relying on simplistic and misleading ratios, such as debt to GDP and debt to exports, analysts step back and question first of all the institutional framework of a country. The assumption is that while statistics can be dubious and dated, the structural context of a country (the rule of law, the honouring of contracts, the level of economic development, the health of the banking system, the independence of the central bank, the level of transparency and good governance, the exchange rate regime) is more pertinent and less volatile and, therefore, the proper starting point for analysis. Moody's has continuously expanded the economic indicators to include more meaningful ones to reflect a country's integration in evolving international capital markets.

Removing structural impediments to economic growth will have a more positive impact on the credit rating than an improving trade balance or falling stock of debt. Issuers determined to improve their ratings should reread the Thomas Friedman book referred to earlier, as it points to policy frameworks and inclinations that the agencies would agree with.

Issuers need to have actual, measurable successes to point to as evidence that policy is on track and management knows what it is doing. They have to show concrete evidence that structural reform is underway, not just progress in the budgetary position or a reduction in non-performing loans in the banking system. A show of bravado with no substance behind it will not win the day and will only undermine the credibility you are trying to build. Focusing on the last quarter's improvement in the trade balance product by product will be much less persuasive than emphasising how the authorities are liberalising the trade regime.

Options and constraints

All governments have options and all governments face constraints. Ratings will reflect how effective the authorities are in choosing their options and in managing around those constraints, given their economic structures. The agencies like to see an appropriate and flexible use of monetary and fiscal policy to pursue the two aims they deem important for creditworthiness: wealth generation and debt reduction. At some point, the subjective decision is made by the agencies that countries either are or are not following such policies and a rating upgrade or downgrade occurs.

This was clearly the case in November 2013 when S&P downgraded France one notch to AA, citing the government's policies on taxes and labour reform that would not, in their opinion, suffice to consolidate public finances or raise the country's growth prospects. Ratings are report cards on government performance. Ratings are policy driven. It is usually politics that interferes with good policies.

To illustrate how sovereign credit ratings are influenced by all the political, fiscal, institutional, economic and debt factors discussed, we now list the characteristics that pertain to a sample of rated sovereigns.

Triple A rated sovereigns exhibit these qualities:

- stable, transparent and accountable political institutions;
- flexibility to respond to shifting economic circumstances;
- openness to international trade and finance;
- diverse and resilient economy, with high per capita income;
- efficient public sector with low budget deficits;
- independent central bank, low inflation;
- diversified well-regulated financial sector; and
- ample external liquidity and low external debt.

Single A sovereigns look like this:

- political institutions evolving toward more accountability and stability;
- openness to international trade and finance;
- less diversified economy with generally market-oriented policies;
- progress in economic restructuring;

- fairly efficient public sector with moderate budget deficits;
- fairly independent central bank, moderate inflation;
- well-regulated financial sector, developing capital markets; and
- moderate external debt.

Triple BBB rated sovereigns have these characteristics:

- less transparent political institutions, social stress;
- openness to international trade and finance;
- less prosperous economy, vulnerability to shocks;
- government revenue or expenditure flexibility limited; greater need to borrow;
- fairly independent central bank but fewer tools;
- evolving financial sector, government contingent liabilities; and
- moderate to high external debt.

Finally, single B rated sovereigns look like this:

- higher degree of political uncertainty; government changes lead to economic policy disarray;
- weak integration with global financial markets;
- wide income disparities, undiversified economy, structural impediments to growth, less developed private sector;
- fiscal imbalances and sometimes high inflation; and
- large external financing requirement; moderate to high external debt.

Bottom line: policy matters. It is the way macroeconomic and financial policies are determined and applied plus the results that are crucial determinants of rating assignments and rating changes. David Beers, then head of S&P's sovereign ratings group, summed it up in October 2004 in the *Financial Times*: 'What's been driving ratings are home-grown policy actions.' These are the key. Government issuers take note.

Sumptus censum ne superet.
(Let not your spending exceed your income)

---

[1] John Chambers, Managing Director, S&P Ratings Group, *CreditWeek*, 12 January 2000, p. 16.
[2] David H Levey, Managing Director, Sovereign Risk Unit, Moody's Investors Service, interview.

7.7 Corruption and ratings

> In credit, character is more important than collateral.
>
> *J P Morgan*

Corruption occurs in every country, some more than others. We have all seen examples of corruption, whether it is a bribe to a customs official or nepotism, cronyism, favouritism. Whatever its form, corruption sends the wrong signals to people – that you need connections to get something done. Or if you know the right person in government, you can get a favour.

The problem arises when such 'favours' result in a misallocation of resources, such as when any company but not the best one gets the contract to build a bridge. Or when vested interests pay off legislators and prevent important laws from being passed. Or when a court system prevents high-level corruption cases to be heard. Or when state-owned enterprises being privatised are sold to friends of various ministers in a secret way.

Corruption is a deterrent to investment, especially from abroad, and a destroyer of confidence in governmental institutions at home. It raises the costs of doing business, reduces profitability, and diminishes the incentive for people to work hard. To uncover corruption, the CRA analysts look for these indicators:

- extensive controls and regulations;
- vast public sector bureaucracies; or
- low paid civil servants.

Due to globalisation, countries are now more than ever subject to the discipline of the external markets, which swiftly punish corruption and mismanagement, and reward transparency and conservative policy settings. Donors, such as the British Government, are demanding an end to corruption or their aid will stop. Some African countries are beginning anti-corruption campaigns. As one example, President Kibaki of Kenya undertook a five-year program to root out the problem, which he blamed for the decline in Kenya's economy.

Corruption is not on the list of key analytical factors for CRAs. However, corruption does have indirect effects on ratings. When corruption is perceived to be endemic or systemic, the rating agencies examine the effect on public policy and on the economy. The agencies believe corrupt officials (those who misuse public power for private benefits) are a hindrance to an efficiently running economy, a deterrent to investment, and a destroyer of confidence in governmental institutions. So corruption is not a moral issue for the agencies – it is a pragmatic, credit-impacting issue. Payoffs are minor and happen everywhere; it is when they impinge on good economic performance that it can affect the rating.

Incentive killer

In corrupt economies, there is less incentive for people to work hard and efficiently. There is more incentive for government officials to block structural reforms and to divert resources from productive projects. At some point, corruption results in higher tax levels. Outsiders have less confidence in national statistics, resulting in reduced or foregone foreign direct investment.

The IMF has provided evidence that corruption discourages investment and limits economic growth. It also alters the composition of government spending, with likely detrimental effects on future economic growth.

The CRAs do not have the time or resources to try to uncover examples first-hand. They admittedly rely on experienced observers, such as foreign direct investors, and infer corruption from various indicators, such as those produced annually by Transparency International (TI). TI's 2012 survey showed that Scandinavian countries plus New Zealand, Singapore and Canada are the least corrupt. Countries such as Serbia, Jamaica, India, Greece and Senegal range in the middle of the rankings, while many sub-Saharan African nations and central Asian former Soviet countries are found at the lowest end of the scale.

One can define corruption in the public sector as 'illegal activities that reduce the economic efficiency of governments', but as the IMF wrote in 1997, 'determining just how efficient government institutions are is not what would be called an exact science'. Even if hard to measure, corruption can generate popular anger that might destabilise societies and exacerbate violent conflicts.

Corruption cannot be directly measured. No data are gathered on it and the authorities do not highlight it in their presentations to the rating agencies. It is very difficult to put a dollar sign on its economic effects, because so much corruption is clandestine. Hence, corruption must be inferred from: (i) its effects; and (ii) the presence of conditions that encourage corruption.

High levels of corruption correlate with lack of access to information in a country and the lack of strong legal provisions against conflict of interest. The reverse is also true, for example, the more information available, the lower the level of official corruption. One needs to be careful in inferring corruption, because substandard economic performance by itself does not argue for the presence of corruption nor is economic success a sure sign of lack of corruption.

The agency views

S&P defines corruption 'within the concept of vested interests and political pressures to pursue some economic policies (for example, non-transparent privatisation), which are not optimal from an economic point of view but have been influenced by political decisions'. Corruption results in a misallocation of resources and hence a diminished ability to manage finances in a way that promotes debt servicing and repayment.

The CRAs have not been able to quantify corruption's economic effects and have not published anything substantive on the topic. But they agree that corruption can show up most prominently in government fiscal operations, on both the revenue side (due to special tax exemptions and trade restrictions) and on the expenditure side (within capital investment projects). As to the latter, S&P has pointed to Indonesia where major public investments were politically motivated and economically irrational. This type of corruption happens everywhere that governments control the purse strings, including the US. *Bottom line:* corruption hinders growth and investment by raising the cost of doing business and by diverting public resources from their intended uses.

When assigning ratings, a former Moody's executive placed a great deal of emphasis on the 'character of management and the history and culture of the country'. The reason for this emphasis was simple: 'Credit assessment is ultimately an evaluation of character.' For this analyst, official corruption or poor attitudes toward work had at least a one-notch effect on the rating. He argued that the numbers are only as good as the managers of the country can generate through good management. Moody's also cites the lack of price competition and an anti-competitive environment, when 'regulatory means trump market means'.

Another former Moody's executive expressed it this way: 'Corruption is no different than having a few people control many, whether it is a corporate board room or a sovereign government. In every situation that I can think of, corruption has been fostered by a misaligned system of checks and balances and characterised by a legal system that has no teeth. Corruption fosters uncertainty. Whenever there is uncertainty there is unpredictability, and unpredictability should have a downward effect on ratings.'

While no country or subnational has ever been downgraded solely due to corruption (with Paraguay the possible exception), the matter makes a difference at the margin, preventing an upgrade that is otherwise merited or hastening a downgrade from negative outlook.

7.8 Culture and ratings

Can a country's culture affect its credit rating? Are the 'hard-working' Chinese more likely to see their country upgraded than certain African countries with attitudes perceived generally as 'fatalistic, progress-resistant and tribe-focused'? Do the rating agencies consider cultural factors such as these in their assessments? Here is what managing directors at both S&P and Moody's said in interviews.

S&P said, 'It's dangerous to generalise about culture; it's better to speak of institutions and policies. We don't have a culture category in our ratings criteria. The word 'culture' implies entrenched attitudes or behaviour that won't change, but we believe that attitudes and behaviour do change as governments and policies change. "Laziness" is not a cultural factor; it's the result of the absence of incentives, and that's a political issue.

'Fifty years of communism or colonialism can have a big impact on people and does affect current behaviour. People say that cronyism and corruption run rampant in Russia and Venezuela, but this is not a cultural matter; it's a question of entrenched power and underdeveloped political institutions. These matters are discussed in rating committees and do affect ratings. Political risk is the big issue, that is, the maturity of political institutions and their ability to deliver effectively what citizens want.'

Moody's said much the same: 'Culture is quite important, but you have to be very careful – it's a slippery term. If it implies permanent features of a country, we don't buy it. Certainly cultural conditions in countries do enter into discussions in rating committees, and they can affect ratings, but "culture" is hard to measure and is not a driving factor in ratings. We like to think more in terms of a country's socio-political structure, that is, what are the incentives for people to behave in certain ways? How are people motivated to improve their lives, to invest or to keep working? What behaviour pays off in society?' What is the pattern of relationships that drives an economy? If there is too much government regulation and it stifles enterprise, then people will find ways to survive in ways that we might call 'corrupt'.

It is more politically correct for the CRAs to cite incentives rather than cultural factors in their country assessments, but Moody's was quoted in the *Business Times* of Singapore on 24 June 1999 that Thai cultural factors slow bank reforms. The article was referring to the Moody's 15-page report on the Thai banking industry, dated May 1999, which pointed out that cosy relations between Thai commercial banks and their large borrowers and the culture of 'favours' made it difficult for the banks to take a tough stand against borrowers to recover their loans. Because of these 'deeper cultural' reasons, Moody's believes the restructuring of corporate debt would proceed slowly.

Bottom line: words like 'culture' and 'democracy' are avoided in rating rationales, but rating committees do discuss whether certain attitudes, institutions, or patterns of behaviour in a society affect an issuer's ability and willingness to pay its obligations. The outcome of the discussion will affect the sovereign rating first and consequently all other issuers in the country that are capped by the sovereign rating.

7.9 Governance at the government level

One hears the term 'good governance' primarily as it applies to corporate behaviour. But the principles apply just as equally to how governments organise and perform their activities. Governance issues have a direct impact on sovereign ratings because their presence or absence affects the ability and willingness of a government to pay its debts. Let us build on our earlier discussion of corporate governance and ratings.

The rating agencies have joined the trend in the global financial community by more explicitly using the word 'governance' in their analyses and reports. There is heightened awareness on the part of the agencies that governance issues really do affect creditworthiness.

Governance and ratings

Governance at the sovereign level is a 'strength of institutions' and 'quality of management' matter, which as we have seen is certainly a component in the subjective aspect of rating assignments for all issuers. Here the analysts ask, how do government officials use their authority? With their power to command resources, do they choose to improve economic and social conditions or not? The answer to that question depends on each country's institutions, leaders, decision-making processes and implementation capacity.

Governance for governments often shows up first with respect to information issues (for example, lack of transparency or the authorities' inability to explain data or produce timely data). When the analysts discover impervious explanations and opaque documents on the part of governments, banks or companies, the rating committee (RC) does not hesitate to assign a rating at least one notch lower than otherwise applicable. When they see poor accounting practices, insufficient or non-credible data, or cronyism replacing competence, they mark down the credit. If the lack of transparency is system-wide, the agencies see this as a warning signal directly for the economy and indirectly for the sovereign rating, which depends on healthy tax revenues and investment flows.

Governance is 'good' when public institutions are both efficient and responsive, that is, when decisions are taken rationally and citizens' needs and rights are met. Good governance enables economic growth by encouraging investment. Its absence corrodes social bounds and prevents sustainable and equitable economic growth.

For sovereigns and multilateral lending institutions, improving their governance practices is the prerequisite to many desirable outcomes: money flows (foreign direct investment, official aid), more local confidence and investment, and faster economic growth. Without such growth, the resources of a nation cannot be allocated for such purposes as debt servicing and repayment. It follows that without wealth creation and domestic stability, credit ratings are limited in their scope to rise.

World Bank definition

According to the World Bank, good governance for sovereigns has these characteristics:[1]

- political stability and the absence of violence;
- transparency of government actions and decisions according to known procedures;

- ability of the public to observe and critique the process;
- accountability of public officials with safeguards against corruption;
- the rule of law, including the sanctity of contracts, and an independent judiciary; and
- the capacity to extract and mobilise resources and to not be 'captured' by special interests.

Another slice of good governance is to try to measure the 'effectiveness' of government, that is, does it have the capacity to effectively formulate and implement sound policies. According to a World Bank study,[2] there are five key measures that judge the effectiveness of a government:

- the quality of the bureaucracy;
- the quality of public service provision;
- the competence of civil servants;
- the independence of the civil service from political pressures; and
- the credibility of the government's commitment to policies.

Some of these measures overlap but the sovereign analysts at the rating agencies intuitively and explicitly test for these characteristics in their research and in their onsite visits. The presence of good or effective governance practices underpins a rating, while their absence undermines it.

Three different managing directors and sovereign analysts at the agencies expressed it this way:

> We consider governance issues very much because they affect long-term economic growth. In considering governance we look at how developed a country's political institutions and legal systems are and how legitimate the political institutions are.

> You can infer good governance from how efficient public services are delivered, such as hospitals and roads, and from how transparent public administration is. You know you have good governance when social expenditure is effective.

> The more transparent a system, the less likely you will find corruption eroding public confidence and affecting the legitimacy of public institutions.

There is often resistance by governments in emerging markets (perhaps everywhere) to improving governance practices, because vested interests oppose greater transparency and the exposure of their connections and privileges. The agency analysts are able to sense inertia in this respect. But when they perceive the rule of law, an independent judiciary, an open budgetary process and responsive public institutions, they know there is a good structural or institutional foundation, one that will encourage investment and growth. Examples of good governance that come to mind are the Scandinavian countries, Singapore and New Zealand.

It is just as easy to uncover examples of bad governance, such as a lack of transparency in government documents and decisions, unclear rules on inter-governmental transactions, or an inordinate role for vested interests. One can infer corruption from the lack of accountability.

Bad governance corrodes social relations and prevents sustainable, equitable economic growth. As we mentioned above in 'Corruption and ratings', TI provides an annual guide and ranking of countries according to their level of good governance and corruption. That survey is one of the myriad documents the agencies study since they do not have enough time themselves to undertake that research. Examples of bad governance would include Afghanistan, Nigeria, Russia and Venezuela.

The rating agencies sometimes translate their perception of good or bad governance in a sovereign into a low rating to begin with or a change in outlook or even a downgrade in rating. It would be wise for sovereign issuers to address this factor with some self-assessment, deciding ahead of time how to answer the issues the agencies may raise about it. Or it could be one of those questions you will not be asked but which will be raised in the rating committee.

Better yet, sovereign issuers should recognise that good governance is in their best interest regardless of the rating impact. Exhibit 7.1 was produced by an advisory company, Financial Consulting (Fincon), and shows graphically that even 30 years ago better governance in a country correlated positively with higher growth in per capita income. If the data were updated, one could be confident that the correlation would still be valid, with perhaps an even steeper curve.

Exhibit 7.1

Governance and growth go together; per capita income growth, 1982–2002 (percentage, residual)

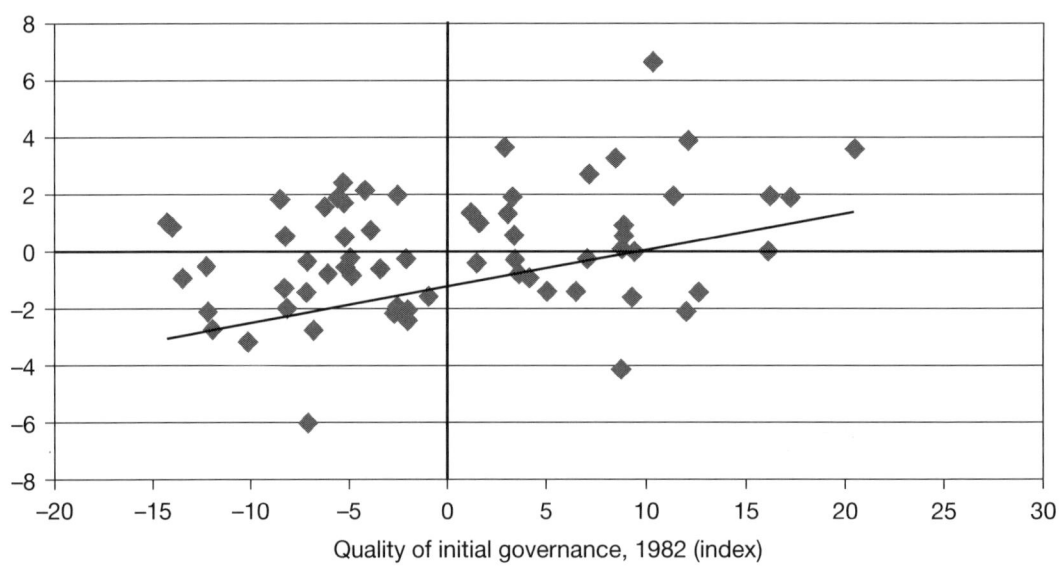

Source: Fincon

Governance and the private sector

Another aspect of governance is the manner in which the government facilitates or hampers good governance by the private sector. The agencies widely accept the view that private corporations are the 'engines' that drive national economies, because they raise capital, create jobs, and produce and trade goods and services. The value added is divided among stakeholders, including governments which tax profits.

Governments, therefore, have an interest in how corporations and banks are managed, because successful corporate performance is important to the country's economic general welfare. What should the role of government be in promoting good corporate governance practices? For one thing, the government needs to enact clear regulations reflecting international standards that encourage compliance and discourage non-compliance and then the government needs to enforce them.

As an example, governments could require that banks and companies exhibit certain core practices relating to accountability and transparency before they are granted permission to list on the local stock exchange. Finally, governments need to look more closely at their own practices since reform should start at the top. If governments choose not to, the agencies will not so gently remind them.

---

[1] http://info.worldbank.org/governance/wgi/index.aspx#home.

[2] See the paper by Kaufmann, D, Kraay, A and Mastruzzi, M, 'Government effectiveness' on the World Bank website; www.worldbank.org/wbi/governance/ pubs/govmatters3.html.

7.10 Sovereign upgrades and downgrades

No CRA has written anything publicly (or probably internally either) dealing specifically with the absolute causes of upgrades. The same holds for downgrades. Perhaps the reason why they have not addressed the topic publicly is that they do not want to commit themselves to a framework that would somehow give issuers the idea that an upgrade will automatically follow if only: (i) they would do three or four specific things; or (ii) their debt ratios dropped to a certain level. They do not want to be too prescriptive.

Clearly it is in the agencies' interest to maintain flexibility in the matter of rating changes, permitting them to examine each case on its own merits. Openly publishing criteria for an upgrade would encourage endless queries from issuers about their progress toward the goal ('are we there yet?') and even more speculation from investors and arbitrageurs on the timing of the next rating change. With continual meetings, trips and investor phone calls already, the analysts hardly have enough time now to write their reports.

When Moody's most respected sovereign analyst was asked what leads to upgrades and downgrades, he replied, 'An analyst will suddenly think the rating is not appropriate.' It could be that the other rating agency makes a move, forcing you to look more closely at a credit, or it could be that the country's peers have had recent rating changes, but in the end 'it's the analyst's own sense of appropriateness about a rating'. It is up to the analyst then to persuade one of the managing directors that the credit should be put on review for either upgrade or downgrade.

There is no single factor associated with upgrades or downgrades, he said, just evidence that things are or are not running smoothly. When the analyst perceives this, then he or she thinks through the dynamics of the situation and asks hypothetically how the situation might evolve. 'Where does this take us if there are certain stresses? Is issuer management capable of mitigating these stresses?'

If the dynamics and interrelationships of the key variables tell the analyst to worry, then the agency will place the issuer on review. 'It's like a mystery story where you look for things that are out of line and you ask what might happen.' You draw a coherent picture and see if a reasonable scenario can develop from that point on. Depending on that scenario, the analyst decides if the credit is currently rated correctly.

Reasons behind upgrades and downgrades

Since the mid-1980s the three agencies have upgraded dozens of sovereign ratings, several more than once, for example, Brazil, Czech Republic, Israel, Kazakhstan, Malaysia, Peru, Russia and Turkey. What were the underlying rationales for these upgrades? What factors were most common? An analysis revealed the following top reasons (in descending order) why S&P upgraded sovereigns.

1 Conservative economic management.
2 Rapid or steady economic growth.
3 Improving current account on the balance of payments.
4 A liberalising, structurally reforming economy.

5 An improving external debt position.
6 Improved monetary discipline.
7 Improved external competitiveness.
8 Rising foreign exchange reserves.
9 Low inflation.
10 Reduced potential for external conflict.

Moody's has a slightly different but basically corresponding list of top reasons for upgrades (in descending order of occurrence).

1 A liberalising economy.
2 Improving macroeconomic fundamentals.
3 Rapid, steady economic growth.
4 Fiscal consolidation.
5 An improving external debt position.
6 Reduced potential for external conflict.
7 High national savings rate.
8 Improved international competitiveness.
9 Reduced commodity dependence.
10 Improved monetary discipline, lower inflation.

Note an important inference one can make: upgrades (and downgrades too to some extent) occur *after* enough facts and data are on the books to warrant a judgment about trends. Among the sources viewed for sovereigns are the government's budget papers, the OECD publications, and the IMF's monthly statistics. These data always lag the present by six months or more and are subject to revision.

The point is that rating changes are made on the basis of historical information, just enough to provide a comfort factor to the analyst that the trends (good or bad) will continue. Issuers should not wait for the official data to be published but should keep the analyst apprised of trends, both positive and negative. Otherwise, a downgrade could happen without warning or an upgrade could be delayed.

Whether you choose the benign approach to managing your relationship with the rating agencies or the more proactive approach recommended here (see Exhibit 6.1), these upgrade reasons provide plenty of clues as to what levels of performance a sovereign government should aspire to.

Economic growth is clearly the *sine qua non* or indispensable condition among the variables for sovereigns. The reason is basic – faster growth is better because growth generates employment, higher incomes and higher tax revenues that make debt servicing and repayment more likely. To see if a country is using the right mix of tools and policies to generate economic growth, the agencies look at the potential constraints to policy and the obstacles to growth and examine their current status. Are the following investor-friendly and growth-encouraging policy steps being implemented by the government in question?

- Making the private sector the primary engine of economy growth.
- Maintaining price stability and a low rate of inflation.

- Shrinking the size of the state bureaucracy.
- Maintaining a balanced budget or close to it.
- Lowering tariffs on imported goods.
- Removing restrictions on foreign investment.
- Getting rid of domestic monopolies.
- Privatising state-owned industries and utilities.
- Deregulating capital markets.
- Making the currency convertible.
- Opening the country's industries or stock markets to foreign ownership and investment.
- Eliminating government corruption, subsidies and kickbacks as much as possible.

In the light of the 20 upgrade reasons for sovereign issuers shown earlier, we can infer what is needed to avoid a downgrade, that is, their converse. Sovereign issuers should ensure that the following six negative conditions are not in evidence.

1 Deteriorating public finances which feed through to the balance of payments through higher debt servicing costs.
2 A build-up of debt (domestic or foreign).
3 Deteriorating economic growth or export growth.
4 The inability to respond to an internal or external challenge with appropriate policy measures.
5 Delays in implementing economic or structural reforms.
6 An erosion in international competitiveness that could lead to a greater reliance on external funding.

The first thing an issuer can do is understand the reasons for the pressure on the rating and then come back to the agency with a reasonable explanation, some comparatives and some exceptions. As S&P sovereign officer Marie Cavanaugh stated,[1] 'It's rare that one factor will cause an upgrade, although one factor can cause a downgrade.'

At the end of 2013, it was evident that the US met many of these conditions here for a downgrade. The US government fell out of the range of policy behaviours that typify other triple A credits, so it was thought by some critics, including Fitch Ratings, that maybe the US no longer belonged in the same credit category as Australia, Canada, Germany and the Scandinavian countries. After all, a triple A security is supposed to be risk free, a safe harbour for investors and a model of certainty.

Will Moody's or Fitch take one notch off their current Aaa/AAA ratings of the US at some point in the future? Or will the agencies demur, perceiving perhaps that the US is a special case because: (i) it has enormous wealth-generating capacity; and (ii) it is the home of the world's reserve currency and can print as many dollars as needed to pay its debts. (About 85% of international transactions are done in dollars.) As always for sovereigns, it is a matter of politics and policies.

Practical steps for an optimal rating

Here are a number of internal, practical steps issuers should take to raise the odds for an optimal rating and to maintain it. The actions ought to be evident by now if you have chosen the proactive approach to managing the rating agencies. Let us summarise them.

1 Learn agency methodology, mind-sets and practices.
2 Emphasise goals and process; how successful strategies have played out.
3 Take charge of the agency relationship subtly; be constructive not adversarial.
4 Show that your corporate or fiscal policies are in place to maintain and/or improve creditworthiness.
5 Show consistent performance, not a 'yo-yo' effect with volatility of results.
6 Be willing to spend time with the analysts. Be open, frank and forthcoming with them. Take the analysts into your confidence; treat them as partners.
7 Disclose information in a timely way and trust the agencies to use it discreetly. Keeping the analyst informed makes him or her more confident in going to the rating committee with a positive recommendation.
8 Build some global or peer comparisons to support your case but do not force them on the agency.
9 Show consistent financial performance. For sovereigns show policy continuity with degrees of flexibility.
10 Do not abuse your taxing or pricing authority.
11 Improve the ratios that the agencies rely on; many are within your control and should be actively managed.

---

[1] Telephone interview, 27 March 2001.

Steps to take and questions to ask

Steps to take now:

1

2

3

4

5

Follow-up questions to ask:

1

2

3

4

5

Part 3

Appendices

The credit information bureau

If you do a search on Google for 'credit ratings', you will get 285 million hits! Most of the links refer to individual credit scores and credit information bureaus (CIBs), rather than credit ratings and credit rating agencies (CRAs). Given the use of the word 'credit' in both cases, confusion often arises about what each entity signifies. The main CRAs, of course, are Moody's, S&P and Fitch. The main CIBs are Experian, TransUnion and Equifax. Both types of intermediary began in the US and have been established in many countries with varying degrees of success.

Generally speaking, both CRAs and CIBs assess creditworthiness, the former on a macro level (sovereigns, banks and corporates), and the latter on a micro level (individuals). The assessment by both entities is based upon the history of borrowing and repayment, as well as the availability of assets and the extent of liabilities. In fact, it could be said the CRAs and CIBs are first cousins. Let us look closely at the similarities and differences between them.

The CIB

A credit information bureau is a public or private agency that researches and collects individual credit information and sells it for a fee to creditors so they can make a decision whether or not to extend a loan. CIBs are also commonly referred to as 'consumer reporting agencies'. Typical clients of CIBs include banks, mortgage lenders, car dealerships, credit card companies and other financing companies, all acting as creditors. A CIB does not decide whether an individual qualifies for credit. It only collects information that it considers relevant to a person's credit history and habits and passes it on to the lender for the lender's decision.

According to the World Bank Group, 85 countries reported having a credit registry in 2011, almost triple since 1990.[1] Many of these are government owned and operated, often situated in the country's central bank. Others are privately owned by entrepreneurs or banking associations.

CIB basics

The fundamentals of credit bureaus can be stated simply.

1 CIBs collect, verify, store and disseminate information and share it with creditors.
2 CIBs collect and process two types of data:
   • public information: the name, address, and ID number of the debtor; and
   • private information: the person's debt history and arrears profile, the outstanding debt, and court actions against the debtor.
3 CIBs provide two basic services: independent confirmation of data on individuals, and the provision of a credit history of individuals and companies.

The systemic benefits of CIBs

CIBs have major, positive 'spin-off' effects when they perform their function well.

- *Creditors* experience reduced loan losses because their debtor information base is better than pre-CIB; their operations are more efficient since they have saved time and money in the credit review process, and they are able to offer better customer service.
- *Consumers and small and medium enterprises (SMEs)* benefit because they can acquire financing more easily and more cheaply, assuming they maintain good credit scores.
- The real *economy improves* because easier financing stimulates lending, investment, employment, and GDP growth.
- A nation's *financial system* expands and deepens as more lending takes place and new credit products are developed, for example, credit cards.
- The *government* benefits since there is less systemic risk arising from personal, business and banking system insolvencies.

Similarities between CIBs and CRAs

There are a number of commonalities between credit bureaus and rating agencies. For one thing, they share the guiding assumption that *the best predictor of future behaviour is past behaviour*. Other similarities include:

1 both inform creditors about a borrower's payment record;
2 both facilitate financial transactions as intermediaries;
3 both need to maintain a reputation for impartiality, confidentiality and integrity in order to survive;
4 both are commercial companies that receive payment for an evaluation of the creditworthiness of their clients; and
5 neither one makes loans or loan decisions; creditors do.

Differences between CIBs and CRAs

Despite the similarities, major differences do separate the two.

1 CIB data come from creditors; CRA data come from a wider range of public information, audited reports, management interviews and government sources.
2 A CIB reports known debt and past payment experience (that is, *history*), while the CRA analyses public and private data, makes an independent judgment, and predicts *future* payment behaviour.
3 CIBs employ a simple formula and no qualitative input to calculate an individual's credit 'score', while a CRA uses more complex and varied quantitative tools plus a large dose of judgmental input to determine an entity's rating.
4 Credit ratings are the result of a more intricate process than individual credit scores, as ratings require more time to produce and they incorporate concepts of probability of default and the expected loss given default.

---

[1] International Finance Corporation, *Credit Reporting Knowledge Guide*, 2012, p. 5.

Agency analyst anecdotes

As they have continent-hopped seeking to expand their ratings market worldwide, the rating analysts have experienced a number of 'weird events', even threats, illustrating cultural and linguistic divergences and blunders. Here are some of the notable incidents the analysts lived through and were pleased to relate to the author.

- An S&P analyst walked into a meeting with an issuer to tell them they were going to be downgraded one notch. When the analyst left the meeting, he decided instead on two notches. The issuer had made his case worse by his responses to questions. Usually analysts leave a meeting more favourably impressed, not less so.
- In China, the Chinese officials brought in interpreters to do the rating meetings. It was partially a cultural move because they did not want to lose face if they spoke English poorly. But it turned out the officials knew better English than the interpreters. The officials got visibly frustrated and just threw out the interpreters and conducted the meetings on their own.
- In another incident, some Chinese officials had been advised by their investment bankers to show the agencies how far the country had progressed along the path to market economics. In the meetings that followed, the officials proceeded to mouth free-market platitudes. It shortly became clear they really did not understand what they were saying or how the concepts interrelated.
- During a review of a Chinese financial institution, the prospectus said clearly there was a sovereign support mechanism, specifically a window at the Central Bank that the institution could call on for debt servicing if necessary. Given this support, the Chinese wanted the rating to be the same as the sovereign. At a final meeting with the central bank, a high official stood up and said bluntly there was no such support mechanism, that the lawyers, advisers and prospectus were all wrong. When it turned out afterwards that the central bank official had just been wrong, not having been briefed by the lawyers, the government blamed both the advisers and the rating agency for even raising the question of support.
- A delegation of ministry of finance officials came to S&P to request a rating, not because they wanted to issue debt but because their country's largest state-owned enterprise wanted to do so. The question of the rating under the sovereign ceiling arose. The delegation was headed by the minister who spent 45 minutes explaining to the agency in no uncertain terms that his country did not want a rating, that the agencies were perfidious characters, and that ratings were usually wrong anyway. He so dominated the meeting that the other ministry officials brought along were left with nothing to say, so they got up and left for lunch.
- An investment bank had prepared a massive information memorandum for its issuer client that was presented to the visiting rating agency. When the meeting got underway,

the chairman of the company stood up and proceeded to point out all the errors in the document, mistakenly assuming it was the agency's prepared write-up on his company. The embarrassed investment bankers sat sheepishly by.

- A team of sovereign analysts from Moody's was asked to sign official papers when they arrived in a Latin American country, saying they were there without official permission.

- Central bankers in Brasília had apparently arranged to have their meeting with the CRA interrupted periodically by phone messages in order to impress upon the analysts how busy and important they were.

- A finance company was on the verge of a downgrade. The CEO of the company came to a rating meeting on crutches, having broken his leg in a skiing accident. He hobbled in like the walking wounded, symbolic actually of his company's fortunes. He made a speech and then ended by saying fervently, 'You're sucking the lifeblood out of *me*.' He had personalised the whole issue in a very wrenching and emotional way.

- After Moody's had downgraded Russia three times in 1998, irate Russian 'citizens' emailed the senior analyst for Russia and said, 'How dare you downgrade us? Don't forget that we have missiles pointed at New York City.' He also received a few death threats by email, saying 'your life is not worth anything if you keep this up'.

- The analysts were passing through security at the central bank of a Latin American country when someone dressed in jeans and a tee shirt pulled a long revolver out and waved it in the air. They thought their days as ratings analysts were over, but it turned out that the person was just showing it to security and was intending to hand it over.

- A water utility in Texas was downgraded. Officials there were furious, so they called the agency and asked what they could do. They offered to bring critical new information to the agency, and under those conditions the agency agreed. During the visit, it was clear the new data were not sufficient to alleviate agency concerns, so the agency told the utility that the downgrade remains. Again the utility were furious and sent 25 people to New York to protest about the rating. The agency could not find a conference room on the premises big enough to hold everyone. There were people standing around leaning against the walls. The utility went line by line through the credit report and tried to discredit each point. To no avail. The utility had certainly pulled out all the stops. This was one of the more vigorous rating appeals on record.

- A CRA analyst visited a new bank client in Kazakhstan shortly after the fall of the USSR and was taken to their headquarters, which was a beat-up building with run-down facilities and a dishevelled security guard at the entrance slouched in a chair with a shotgun on his knee. Most incongruous setting.

- Once a company laid out a red carpet for the analyst to walk as she boarded their helicopter. They were presumably trying to impress her – a nice gesture but not a factor she considered analytically.

The role of a ratings adviser

Issuers intending to acquire a credit rating or wishing to secure an upgrade in existing ratings should hire dedicated experts for the task, which is outside the mainstream of their own experience. To raise the odds for a good rating, management needs to know which factors and trends are the most important in the minds of the rating agency analysts, what rating committees really look for and what barriers need surmounting. Without such understanding, an issuer starts off at a disadvantage.

Rating agency intentions, methods and procedures are not always clear: how the agency analysts think, which ratios have more weight and how a rating committee functions. Understanding these key factors in the rating process and having a clear plan of action clearly improve the chances for the best rating possible.

Experience also indicates that the odds for an optimal rating increase when companies themselves: (i) take a proactive approach instead of relying on agency good will; and (ii) secure the advice of an independent ratings expert to assist in the preparations.

What services does a ratings adviser provide? The adviser will:

- identify the key issues influencing the rating outcome;
- develop a strategic plan for maximising the rating result;
- assist the client to prepare background and presentation materials that address the rating agency's concerns and likely questions;
- help organise and conduct the due diligence meetings;
- provide first-hand guidance during the meetings as well as any post-meeting follow-up; and
- help you stay 'ahead of the curve' of changing agency expectations, actions and trends.

Without such onsite advice, the eventual rating could be sub-optimal, that is, lower than the issuer merits given his economic and financial position. A sub-optimal rating will be costly in terms of a higher rate of interest paid on new and outstanding debt.

Issuers must manage the rating process, the information flows, and indeed the entire rating relationship better than ever in order to reduce the risk of an unexpected rating outcome or to raise the odds for a more desirable outcome. A professional ratings adviser can put you on the right track.

Related titles from Euromoney Books

Performing and Non-Performing Loan Transactions Across the World: A Practical Guide, 2nd edition

Edited by Simon Grieser and Jörg Wulfken with specialist contributors

Publication date: June 2014

Performing and Non-Performing Loan Transactions Across the World: A Practical Guide

Second edition

Fully updated for 2014, this second edition contains country reports for specific jurisdictions and describes local law requirements which need to be considered when implementing performing and non-performing loan transactions. Global loan markets and the sub-prime crises have experienced significant demand-supply distortions, soaring price volatility, as well as drastic and unexpected flow constraints or surpluses, particularly due to the more frequent and deeper financial crises affecting different regions or markets. As understood from the public discussions, loan trades are the appropriate measure for the time being. This comprehensive, authoritative and multidisciplinary practitioner's manual is structured in a way that the principles of arranging, servicing, financing and exit strategies of such transactions will be dealt with. It contains country reports for specific jurisdictions and describes local law requirements which need to be considered when implementing performing and non-performing loan transactions.

ISBN: 978-1-78137-197-8

Price: £175/$295/€230

Bank and Sovereign Risk Analysis, 2nd edition

Kenneth I'Anson and Liz Grossman

Publication date: December 2013

This book is a new edition and an update of the successful Bank and Country Risk Analysis. This book is a self-tuition course on Bank and Sovereign Risk with questions and exercises to check understanding. It uses many examples and case studies. The book provides specific elements of individual bank analysis (CAMELS approach: Capital, Asset quality and impairments, Management, Earning, Liquidity, Sensitivity to market risk).

It explains the differences in how the various rating agencies assign bank risk and what each agency offers understanding of. The book also focuses on the history and the explanation of the Basel rules, and evolution from Basel I to III with a detailed explanation of what each entails and how they are implemented. It details warning signals to look out for in predicting a potential bank failure, with illustrative examples. It explains sovereign and country risk and their differences and considers six broad dimensions of political stability, with further explanation through the case study country examples into the approaches and factors used.

ISBN: 978-1-78137-100-8

Price: £175/$327/€254

Credit Analysis of Financial Institutions, 3rd edition

Waymond A Grier

Publication date: November 2012

The book assists the credit analyst to assess the performance and financial condition of today's financial institutions and allow the analyst to weed out the good from the bad and justify a lending or counterparty relationship. This is done by providing the credit analyst with the background and tools necessary to assess the quality of financial institutions, notably retail banks, investment banks, insurance companies, finance companies, leasing companies, investment management companies and pension funds. This new edition assessed these financial institutions against the backdrop of a 'new normalcy' of the current Global economic climate, i.e. reduced profitability, greater regulatory surveillance, increased capital requirements.

ISBN: 978 1 78137 088 9

Price: £175/$327/€254

Valuing a Bank Under IFRS & Basel III, 2nd edition

Waymond A Grier

Publication date: December 2010

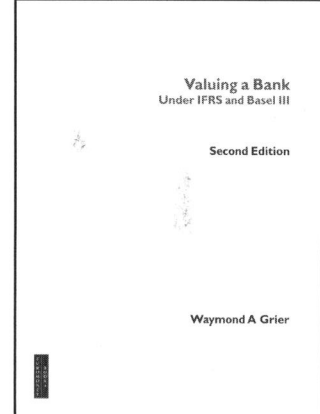

The 2nd edition is a complete self-study workbook, providing anyone involved in the valuation of a commercial bank for acquisitions or credit analysis with the essential tools and applications under the International Accounting Standards, International Financial Reporting Standards and within the new Basel III environment.
Valuing a Bank, second edition, has been fully updated and revised to:

● take into account Basel III and the new regulatory environment
● include and discuss new IFRS standards introduced since first edition and which are applicable to financial institutions
● include updated case studies in response to current market constraints
● broaden the scope of valuation models

ISBN: 978 1 84374 769 7

Price: £270/$450/€350